The Travels of a Happy Hooligan

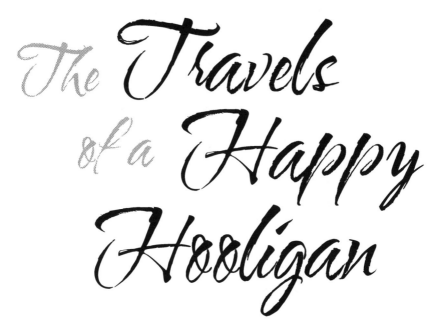

THE WORLD WAR II MEMORIES OF
FRANK A. SMITH, JR.

BY
FRANK A. SMITH, JR.
EDITED BY ELIZABETH SMITH DOERNING

authorHOUSE®

AuthorHouse™
1663 Liberty Drive
Bloomington, IN 47403
www.authorhouse.com
Phone: 1-800-839-8640

Published by AuthorHouse   03/18/2013

ISBN: 978-1-4817-2184-4 (sc)
ISBN: 978-1-4817-2182-0 (hc)
ISBN: 978-1-4817-2183-7 (e)

Library of Congress Control Number: 2013903669

DEDICATION

This story is dedicated to the men I served with, my own family, and my twin brother, Command Master Chief Gerald J. Smith, OSCM USN (Retired)

Command Master Chief Smith served honorably in the United States Navy for 23 years as a Radarman. He served as a Radarman soon after the development of Radar and served on ships of the line that depended on this electronic marvel for protection from enemy ships and aircraft, and for the navigation of vessels twenty-four hours a day, in all kinds of weather. He was in charge of the Combat Information Center on large aircraft carriers and other ships and was recognized as one of the finest U.S. Navy Radar experts.

Master Chief Smith served his country in World War II, Korean War, Vietnam War, and was entering the Panama Canal in a U.S. Marine Expeditionary Task Force in preparation for the Cuban Missile Crisis, before Russia removed their missiles from Cuba. He served as a Navy Ship Rider in the Cuban area and evaluated all the ships with Combat Information Centers that came into the Caribbean Sea for training. Gerry has so much "fruit salad" on his left uniform breast that it is hard to see the navy blue of his Command Master Chief uniform. He served with distinction aboard the following ships of the line during his sea duty days as well as being a Teaching Specialist at various Navy Command

Frank A. Smith, Jr.

Colleges and also served in several classified foreign locations during the Cold War:

USS Barnegat (AVP-10)
USS English (DD-696)
USS Manchester (CL-83)
USS Okanogan (APA-220)
USS Tarawa (CVA-40)
USS Ticonderoga (CVA-14)

FOREWORD

Born to Be a Sailor

Beginning in 2000, at age 74, I began to detail my military service during World War II. I thought it might be a good idea to record the types of activities that I was engaged in during World War II and give a thumb nail sketch of the people and the locales with which I was involved.

The main purpose is to leave a story for my wife, Lorraine Brodeur Smith, and daughters Patricia, Elizabeth, Catherine and their families, who know that I was a United States Coast Guard naval combat veteran, but did not have many details of events during that period. I have tried to recreate events, locales and conversations from my memories of them. In order to maintain their anonymity in some instances I have changed the names of some individuals.

My efforts are just a narrative of my comings and goings during almost four years of my wartime enlistment, from the anti-submarine warfare between the Allied Convoy Escorts and German Submarine Forces in the Atlantic and Mediterranean, referred to as "the longest sustained battle of World War II," and the Island Hopping campaigns in the Pacific Ocean areas against the Imperial Japanese Sea and Land Forces. My days in the Coast

Guard were filled with new experiences, the loneliness of a teen-age boy, and moments of sheer terror.

Family Background

The story has a natural beginning with the patriotic endeavors of my maternal grandfather, George Patrick Cullen. He spent countless hours during the pre- and post-World War I era instructing hundreds of immigrants on the United States Constitution so that they might pass their citizenship examinations. George was an immigrant himself. His parents left their beloved Ireland to find a new life in America. They traveled from Ireland to Liverpool, England, and struggled to earn the cost of passage to the United States. As immigrants, they progressed rapidly to full citizenship. In the days before radio, entertainers from the Old Country made the rounds of the small music halls in the American communities. One of Ireland's great professional tenors, John McCormick sang the story telling songs of the day and my grandfather was always on the program with him. My grandfather became the Superintendent of the Municipal Fire Alarm System. The day of his funeral, Fall River closed its municipal doors out of respect to his memory.

George Patrick Cullen, U.S. Army WWI

George Patrick Cullen was a First Sergeant in the U.S. Army. He fought in France during World War I and suffered from Shell Shock, in this day it is called Delayed Stress Syndrome. He kept a diary that was later destroyed when James Patrick Cullen, his only son and my mother's brother died in 1965. My grandfather was a friend of and had correspondence with poet Joyce Kilmer, the author of "Trees" who was killed in France during World War I. My uncle's wife disposed of the papers, without recognizing the historical value.

Frank A. Smith, U.S. Navy WWI

My father, Francis Anthony Smith, Sr., was a Fireman 2nd class in the U.S. Navy during World War I. When aboard his ship, he was down in the engine room operating the salt water evaporators that made the fresh water used in the boilers for steam and to provide the fresh water for the crew. His ship was engaged in Convoy duties and the anti-submarine warfare of the day. The disabilities he suffered during the war gave him a small pension and the opportunity to go to business school. His father, Henry Smith, was a seafaring man. He would take off for months at a time and come home and our grandmother, Mary Kelly Smith would usually become pregnant. She had 14 children. She supported herself as an attendant in a public ladies' Comfort Station. She was a City of Fall River, Mass., municipal employee and stayed to earn a pension. Henry Smith died in 1926 after being admitted to the Bridgewater State Hospital, with a diagnosis of dipsomania, which at that time was the term for alcoholism.

James Patrick Cullen, U.S. Army WWI

Uncle Jim, James Patrick Cullen, my mother's brother, enlisted in the Army Coast Artillery at 16, which is underage for the military. He went through the training and was in the Army for over 90 days. This qualified him for veteran status, but someone blew the whistle on him and he was sent home just as he was boarding a ship to travel to France in 1918.

My Early Days

Vision Appointment

When I was a boy, I learned that I had a cast (crossed) left eye. I was told that it was the result of Scarlet Fever. I was never told that it was actually a birth defect. The condition is called Amblyopia or Lazy Eye and it can be corrected to some degree, but usually the correction has to be done prior to age 14, in later years it was determined that the therapy had to be done before the age of four to have any chance of salvaging the sight in the affected eye. Surgery to lengthen or shorten the muscles in the affected eye was necessary, but was not a guarantee of long-term permanent success. My main complaint was double vision. The eye was somewhat crossed and instead of superimposing the image from each eye, I would look straight ahead and would have an image to the right and slightly below the image from my good right eye. The ophthalmologists said I had no fusion. I remember traveling to downtown Boston, to the high price medical professionals with my mother, (I must mention at this point, that my mother, Catherine Cullen Smith, was renamed Nannie in later years and it is interchangeable with Mother and Mom), and my aunt Peg with my twin brother Gerald to a recommended specialist. One must remember that the time was in the middle of the country's deep financial depression. People were lined up at soup kitchens, even digging into garbage cans for their next meal. Jobs were almost non-existent. My father, who had graduated from business school, had a job as a men's department

1

hat salesman in an upscale department store, named Jordan Marsh. In those days all men wore hats, summer and winter, and whole departments were dedicated to men's hats only. With salary and commission he was bringing home about $20.00 a week. He was working six days per week, and he had four children to support.

Medical insurance was unheard of in those days and when a woman had a child, the family went into debt to pay the bill or they could go to the Boston City Hospital with hat in hand. Medical emergencies were catastrophic. A family had a choice of several private hospitals, but you had to be able to pay the bills. When one went to a specialist, he knew what your financial status was, and his advice reflected your position. I remember him saying to Nannie when she inquired about the cost of my surgical correction, "Fixing the crossed-eye is strictly cosmetic." I recall Nannie being upset. The cost of any corrective surgery was beyond our financial circumstances. For better or worse, this one eye appointment would change my life forever.

My father, Frank Sr., received a 100% disability, from World War I. His injuries were not caused by enemy action, so no Purple Heart was awarded. A depth charge broke loose from its restraints during a storm at sea; he was on a Sub-Chaser, a four-stack destroyer, and the type of ship America gave to England prior to our entry into WWII. His ship was engaged in anti-submarine warfare in the North Atlantic. He suffered a crushed chest and spinal injuries. He had a large lump on his chest, where his sternum was wired to a metal plate. He contracted tuberculosis while in the Naval Hospital, was sent to a rehab-center somewhere in Montana. All this transpired long before he married. The resulting pension made our life really much better than most families we knew. As a matter of fact, on our street, which was five blocks long, there were four automobiles and we had one of them. When he bought the car, driving lessons came with it. The disability pension he had allowed him to go to business school, where he met another student, my mother, Catherine Mary Cullen of Fall River, Massachusetts.

My father's additional spinal condition was further diagnosed as Ankylosing Spondylitis and in addition to the other injuries, he was in pain all of his life and was very reclusive. He was a great salesman and worked most every day of his life. He had stomach ulcers from the stress, I suppose. I was also diagnosed with spondylitis. It usually appears at an earlier age, so maybe a genetic quirk held it in abeyance until after I retired from work. It would not bother me until I tried to sit or lie down. It started on the right side, and it made walking difficult for a few moments on arising.

Entering the Military

When World War II started in 1939 and prior to the U.S. entry into the war, my father had the habit of taking his vacation time and spending a week or two in a Trappist Monastery, to meditate. This didn't sit well with my mother. Although a devout Catholic, she felt that vacation time was for the whole family, especially one with four children. Well, my father thought otherwise. In 1941, when I was 15 years old, he took off again. She had told him that if he did it again, his belongings would be on the front porch when he returned. He did and she did.

When Gerald and I (16 years old at the time) became aware of the situation, we knew our mother had no independent income or savings of any kind and the skills she learned in business school were mostly lost from lack of use. We wondered how the house payment would be made, and we had no car to use for income possibilities. My older sister, Anne, was ready to get her driver's license, but when Dad got the word, he sold the car. He took such exceptional care of the vehicle it looked as if it had just arrived from the show room. He said, "No woman in my family is going to drive a car." Little did he know that Mother had been taking driving lessons from the neighbors. Nearby lived our aunt Margaret "Peg" Dennehy, whose husband, Mike, was a Boston policeman. Peg was like a sister to Mother and the closeness of their ages made it seem

3

like they were, even though she was Mom's mother's sister. Her maiden name was Margaret Byrne and she was a peach. I guess another bond between Mom and Peg was that her only daughter, Kathleen, was about the same age as our older sister, Anne. We had other relatives who might have helped out, but the depression had everyone hard pressed. Although none were in dire straits, it was nip and tuck in the days of the Great Depression.

The world was in turmoil and the military services were clamoring for enlistments. When Pearl Harbor was attacked by the Japanese, it was pandemonium and long lines were on the streets at all military recruiting stations. The three large Boston newspapers had headlines each day announcing the enlistment totals for each of the military services; the competition was fierce. We thought that if we could talk Mom into signing, we could relieve her of our burden and be able to make a monthly allotment to her after enlistment. Our younger sister, Barbara was very young and not aware of the financial situation. At the time my older sister, Anne, was dating Guy J. Panarello, who was in pilot training in the Army Air Force. Guy was afraid that someone else would scoop her up while he was away. They would be married in February 1942. Anne offered to help with altering the birth year on my birth certificate.

The Navy signed-up my brother, Gerald. The year was 1942. I tried all branches of the service and flunked the eye exam. I was legally blind in the left eye by this time. The amblyopia was now Amblyopia Exanopia. The brain was not able to compensate for the dual images, so it suppressed the one from the left eye and the vision would never return. I was devoid of depth perception although it never bothered me. The doctors said what I never had, I wouldn't miss. The only thing I was conscious of was the inability to catch a thrown object.

Everyone in the family by this time was aware of our family situation and knew what Gerald and I were about. I had changed my birth certificate to show I was old enough to enlist, and thought that if I was able to get into an exam line with examiner on my right side, I could move the paddle a bit on my right eye and read for my left eye to pass the exam. The eye exam was rudimentary; they didn't have the refractive apparatus as they do today. It all sounded plausible to any in the family I spoke to, but sympathy was not what I wanted. We had a friend, named Arnold Sebra who was married to our Uncle Bernard Byrne's daughter, Margaret; he was the superintendent of a large downtown Boston office building that housed the U.S. Coast Guard recruiting station. He called me one day and told me that the Navy had officially taken over, subsumed, the Coast Guard for the duration of the war. He said he had access to the examination rooms and scouted it out for me. He said the situation I had mentioned was in place and the room was swamped with enlistees. The examiners had all they could do to fill out the papers.

Joining the U.S. Coast Guard

My Enlistment, September 2, 1942

I hustled into downtown Boston and scouted the lines. What Arnold had said was an understatement. I got into line with my birth certificate, picked the busiest examiner, moved the eye paddle as planned, and received a Snelling 20/20 in both eyes. I was on my way!

My Train Trip from Boston to Newport, Rhode Island

We received confirmation of my enlistment, and I had to report for the swearing in the following week at the Boston Customs House. A hundred or more took the oath and marched down the streets to Boston's South Station, where we boarded a twelve-car train for the Naval Training Station, Newport, Rhode Island. I took off my glasses in summer of 1942 and never put them on again, until I was discharged in October 1945. I was very careful to never look anyone directly full-face and developed different mannerisms to cover my disability. The only thing I remember about the railway station was no one was there to say good-bye. Most of the other recruits had their mothers and fathers, with tears in their eyes, wondering if they would ever see their boys again. I was always looking over my shoulder for some military official to blow the whistle on me, and I was elated when the train pulled out of the station. The Naval travels of Francis A. Smith, Jr. "call me Frank," had begun.

The U.S. Naval Training Station, Newport, Rhode Island

The train took us to the Naval Training Station in Newport, Rhode Island. As with all recruits it was the entry into a new and strange environment. I knew that the Navy had taken over the Coast Guard for the duration, but to what degree, was the mystery. We were taken to the Navy Supply Depot and given the usual issue of clothing that all sailors wore. As we dragged the heavy canvas duffel bag that was now filled to overflowing, we came to a room with barber chairs. Each recruit was given a "to the bone" haircut and left the room to squat outside the depot to await final orders. Several of the men felt naked to be so shorn and draped towels around their heads. It was a revelation to some to see how much difference a head of hair made; my brother Gerry and I would learn this in later life when we would be bald, much to our chagrin. We waited until all the recruits were serviced and then we were all loaded on trucks for the journey to wherever we were going. The Naval Training Station was one of the largest in the country and we thought we would be included in their program. To our dismay we left the base and were headed to New Bedford, Massachusetts. I had relatives in Newport, my father's sister, Frances Kenney, who we called Aunt Francie. Her son, Danny Kenney, was the tennis coach for the Vanderbilt family. He lived on their palatial estate named "The Breakers" and all he did was teach the family tennis. The last time I had seen Aunt Francie was at Danny's funeral in 1936. He was a great athlete, but caught a strain of viral pneumonia and sadly died within a week.

New Bedford, Massachusetts

New Bedford wasn't far from Newport and I knew from visiting another aunt there that they had no naval training facilities. It was primarily a fishing fleet center and had a small wooden boat industry. It wasn't far from Fall River, Mass., where my grandparents and several aunts and uncles lived. Instead of leaving home, I was getting closer by the minute. We arrived after dark at a massive structure that looked like a large warehouse built on a huge dock that jutted out into New Bedford harbor. It was called The State Pier and was a Marine and Customs warehouse. The building looked fairly new and everything was in good repair. The only disconcerting thing was the fence topped with barbed wire that surrounded the landside and the shore entrance and was patrolled by side-armed uniformed men. We were the first to inhabit the new training facility. On entering the building, we saw that the living quarters were newly constructed with adjacent toilet facilities. It had a large modern commercial kitchen, large enough to feed several hundred and the sleeping quarters were new and divided into twenty-man rooms with double-decker bunks and large windows. The toilet facilities were a revelation. The booths had no doors, and were our first exposure to the absence of privacy in military life.

The non-living area of the warehouse was huge and reflected the effort that was made to make it a clean and open environment. It was newly painted and we would use it during inclement weather while we were learning close order drill and other military activities. This phase of the training was no problem for men from Boston. We had a mandatory program in all high schools and we were all called The School Boy Cadets; we wore uniforms, leggings, and a web belt and carried a sham rifle. We were trained in close order drill by retired Army officers and had participated in an annual parade in downtown Boston.

Moored to the pier were several cabin cruiser types of various sizes. We thought they might be part of our training, such as small boat handling. The training commenced the next day. The training staff was made up of mostly senior Coast Guard Chiefs and Warrant Officers with a handful of young officers, who were Chiefs or Warrants prior to being given commissions. The senior officer was a full lieutenant who was designated as the Acting Captain of the Port and his power was absolute, when it came to us and marine matters.

We would learn in later years that the flood of enlistments due to the war made the facility necessary. The Coast Guard had only a few small training facilities; the largest was at Sheepshead Bay, on New York Harbor, and was not equipped to handle the load. We also learned that the Navy was not about to share its training facilities with non-Navy personnel. It had separate operations for the Marine Corps that were a part of the Navy. The Navy called the Marines "Jar Heads" and nicknamed the Coast Guard sailors "Hooligans," after a popular newspaper cartoon featuring a fellow down on his luck. Prior to WWII, the main Coast Guard effort, with its motto of "*Semper Paratus*" meaning "Always Ready", was its Lighthouse Service, Lifesaving Stations, Buoy Tending services and small boat handling, as well as a large Revenue Cutter Service and the Iceberg Patrol as a direct result of the British ocean liner RMS Titanic disaster April 14, 1912. World War II would change the mission of the Coast Guard beyond any stretch of the imagination.

Our daily classes consisted of Seamanship and all things pertaining to life aboard a boat or a ship, identification of the parts of the rigging and the lines used and their purpose. Prior to enlisting, I had dreamt of going to sea and in particular the U.S. Navy. I bought a "Blue Jackets Manual", a sailor's bible. I read it from cover to cover many times and it proved to be an invaluable aid not only for my knowledge of things nautical, but my advancement to better career opportunities. We all had interviews, and our one-on-one sessions with the officers were meant to make them aware of our capabilities for future technical assignments, such as Fleet Service Schools. The first impression was the most important. If one came off as a dullard or a smart-ass, he was not going to transit into a preferred billet anywhere. The backgrounds of the enlistees and their education were diverse and encompassed every phase of civilian life. It was this testing and the interviews that would determine one's wartime career.

An older Chief Boatswains Mate, referred to as "Boats", interviewed me. He knew of the knowledge I had gained from the Blue Jackets Manual and asked if I could assist him with various duties before and after the classes. I thought it would be to my advantage to help, anyway I could. Whatever I did was in the framework of his lesson plans and consisted of making visual aid posters to be used during the classes. It made his class more informative and increased his students' knowledge, which he and the other officers appreciated.

When it appeared that the program was bearing fruit, it was evident to all that a new phase was about to begin. We began firearms training. We were taught to field strip all manner of pistols, rifles and several automatic weapons, how to maintain them and the safety aspect of it all. We had no firing range and as time went on we used the range at the Army's Fort Rodman, which was on the outskirts of New Bedford. Most of our firing was done out in the ocean off New Bedford in Buzzards Bay. While this was not a major part of the training program, it made us realize why we were there. Our part of the training was basically safety, familiarization and care of the weapons and more safety, safety and safety.

One day we were on the outside dock area. Directly across, about 75 yards or more, was another long dock where the fishing boats came in and tied up after they unloaded their catch. Tied up to our dock were several cabin cruiser types. The tide was low and one could just see the masts of the boats; our dock was primarily built for large ocean-going vessels and was much higher above the water level than the dock across the way for the fishing vessels. We heard a loud explosion and the area became engulfed in flames. A mechanic was working on the engine of one of the boats. He tried to start the engine and the fumes in the boat's bilges exploded from a spark. The sailors who were on fire duty manned the hoses and doused the fire. We all ran to the dock's edge and the mechanic was in the water floundering. Several jumped over the side and went to his aid; he was burnt badly and our ambulance took him to the New Bedford Hospital. I remember his name was Smitty; he was a Motor Machinist Mate and an older man. He was blown overboard by the explosion and that probably saved his life. The next day we had a long safety meeting and became acquainted with the procedure for starting an engine in any boat. Number one was to turn on a blower and vent the bilges and the engine compartment at least five minutes before starting the engine, more if some maintenance work had been done.

Our initial boot training period was coming to an end and we were all wondering what the next phase would be. It was autumn of 1942, the New England weather was beginning to cool down and we were all issued fingertip length, heavy canvas, and sheepskin-lined coats. We all had gone through a military security-training program. We had rotating duty stations and one of them was guard duty to keep the station secure. We were posted to patrol the various docks around the harbor on a 24-hour basis. We traveled in pairs and carried side arms consisting of a .38-caliber police special in a holster attached to a web belt. We would be issued the weapons each day at the time of our duty assignment. We would examine them and load them and turn them in unloaded when our duty tour was over. The patrols were four hours long that would continue on a 24-hour basis with a rotation scheme for the number of sailors available.

One of the large cabin cruisers, which had been a civilian boat, had been painted the usual Navy gray with military service emblems and numbers. It was used to distribute the guard pairs to the various locations around the harbor. It was difficult at night if the bay was choppy or we had inclement weather. We were all heavily clothed and a dip in the drink was not conducive to longevity, especially if you fell between the tossing boat and the dock. On one return trip, we pulled alongside a dock to relieve a guard pair and the boat was jumping up and down and the coxswain, "coxs'n", was having difficulty maintaining position alongside the dock. One of the pair jumped to the bow deck; I was in the cabin and looking out the windshield. The foredeck was flat and the place to land, except for a T-shaped bracket, a cleat, used to tie up a boat line. It was at night and our searchlight was very bright. I think the glare blinded the jumper and as he landed his foot landed on the cleat and his ankle bent to a 90-degree angle. I heard it snap from my position inside and about eye level. One of the crew was on the foredeck to assist, and caught the jumper as he went down and kept him from going overboard. He was fortunate to be on the last pickup dock and we sped across the harbor. The coxs'n had alerted the base with our onboard radio and the ambulance was waiting when we arrived.

The security detail was really a make-work program until assignments, if any, were forthcoming. There was no controlled access to any of the areas, even the boat building yards. The dock where the many commercial fishing schooners and trawlers were tied up always had some crew onboard or coming or going at all hours. The crewmen who came to the boats, after a night on the town and the bars closed, treated us as buddies and wanted to share a drink or two from a jug they all seemed to carry. They understood when we told them that we were on duty. I was surprised that so many people, even young girls, were about, even during the wee hours of the morning. We usually chased the kids off the docks. It seemed not only dangerous, it was foolhardy to expose themselves to a drinking environment with drinking older sailors. The girls were barely teenagers and the boys were looking for something to rob, knock over. The larger docks had small businesses, such as restaurant/coffee shops, seafood suppliers and ship-related suppliers scattered around. It wouldn't be difficult to break in and find something of value. When the weather turned cold, shelter was hard to come by, and a few of the business owners gave our officers the keys to some of the establishments that had to be heated; inside we could seek relief when we needed it. The best place was a 12-stool coffee shop/lunch room and the owner had a full coffee urn for the sailors. I think the base supplied the coffee, as it was a ration item at that time. When the autumn cold turned to winter rain and snow and sleet, those places were really welcome. The fishing boats went to sea in all kinds of weather and the crewmen really looked the worse for wear; most of the ones I met were two-fisted drinking men and ready to do battle at the drop of a hat. You took your life in your hands if you went into the local bars frequented by the rough and tumble fishermen. Most of the fishermen were Portuguese. New Bedford had a large Portuguese population, as well as the usual melting pot nationalities that inhabit the seaside towns of New England. After a few weeks of a fierce winter, I was ready for a new assignment.

The winter weather in 1942 was cold, windy and wet. Patrolling the docks all over the inner harbor was really meant to acquaint us with a typical onboard ship routine. When at sea the watch was set on a four hours on and eight hours off schedule; this was a normal at sea situation. In combat situations the watch would be four on and four off and under attack anything was possible. Most of the sailors had never been exposed to shift work or night duty; it took a bit of getting used to. Getting out in the weather at midnight or 0400 in the morning was a shock to most of the would-be sailors. Walking a patrol in foul weather made it worse. I caught the flu or a bad case of bronchitis and it got worse as each day went by. I was coughing to the point that I would up-chuck. I held on for about a week and finally turned myself in. We had a rudimentary sickbay, but no really qualified medical personnel. I was taken to the New Bedford Hospital and laid up for almost two weeks. The coughing slowed to a crawl and my breathing improved. I was returned to light duty for a week before I had to return to dock patrol. The rest of the time was mostly uneventful, except when the high tide became a flood tide and the water came over the docks. The flood tides were particularly frightening when they occurred during a storm. It seemed as if the fishing boats and the boats under construction at the Kelly Boat Yard would come up onto the docks. They never did. I have no idea what we would have done if they did; we would have run like hell, I guess! The real sailors knew what they were doing and monitored the storms very well.

World War II Arrives on the U.S. East Coast

In December of 1942, conditions were appalling along American shores. Oil Tankers and cargo freighters, all unescorted, were forced to hug the coastline at night, stopping at the closest port or behind improvised anchorages with submarine nets during daytime. The Nazi U-boats would lie in wait and launch torpedoes against ships silhouetted against the bright city lights along the coast. Later when the subs found the ships unescorted, they surfaced in the daylight hours, sinking the ships with their deck guns rather than firing a precious torpedo. The U.S. had only about 170 outdated Army patrol bombers to cover the coast from Maine to Florida. The subs along the eastern seaboard were in the 300-ton category and carried enough fuel for about 40 to 45 days, then had to load more fuel from submarine milch cows east of the Bahamas. The subs carried as many as 40 or more torpedoes and seldom wasted one. For the Germans it was like shooting fish in a barrel. The U.S. lend-leased to Britain 50 old WWI, four-stack Destroyers soon after the Japanese bombed Pearl Harbor since we were in a two-ocean war. Even though Britain desperately needed the ships, it left us with a critical shortage when it came to our efforts to protect the Atlantic vessels, and engage in anti-submarine warfare.

Massacre in the Atlantic

In the early days of 1942, the German submarines sank approximately a half million tons of shipping, most of it within Atlantic. The Germans had 60 to 65 submarines operating in the area from Ireland, the North Atlantic and into the Caribbean and the Gulf of Mexico. The U.S. efforts to overcome a loss of lives and vessels resulted in only 15 German submarines destroyed by U.S. forces in 1942.

Anti-submarine vessels were hard to find. What we had were mostly small, wooden sub chasers, or SC's, old WWI Destroyers and a few Patrol Craft, or PC's. The German U-boats came up off Cape Cod, Long Island, the Delaware and Virginia Capes, Hatteras, the coast of Florida, and even into the Gulf of Mexico to pick off freighters and tankers within miles of shore. Two tankers were sunk off of Virginia Beach, Virginia, in full sight of people along the shore. Nothing on the U.S. Atlantic coast was safe.

Washington politicians must have thought the American people couldn't take the Atlantic news along with news of Japanese victories in the Pacific. There was censorship of the news of the Atlantic sinkings. Years later, the government would release maps of the many documented Nazi sub sightings off the U.S. Atlantic coast.

In the month of March 1942, Nazi subs sank 76 Merchant ships within a radius of a few miles off the Atlantic Coast, and by July 1942 the figure had jumped to 519 vessels. The subs were sinking the ships faster than we could build them. And the Germans were building subs faster than we could sink them. Appeals to the British were without success. They only had enough escort ships to cover convoys within 400 miles of Ireland. Without armed escorts and adequate air cover, convoys were merely the easy targets for the German submarines.

In late spring of 1942, the first Atlantic Seaboard Convoy from Norfolk, Virginia, to Key West, Florida, consisted of 27 vessels, an American reverse Lend-Lease British Corvette, a WWI four-stack Destroyer, two Patrol Boats and two British Trawlers. The speed of the convoy was a pitiful six knots; a WWII Nazi submarine had a useful speed of seven to eight knots submerged. Escort ships did an efficient job. Each had a screening zone to sweep. Each maintained a distance of about 2000 yards from the convoy. Sonar was good for at least another 3000 yards. This way no sub could get within approximately 5000 yards, if the Radar and Sonar were working and the operators were alert.

The convoy runs to Florida and the Caribbean were called the Ping Run because there were so many submarine contacts, pings. In those areas, the German subs were hoping to cut off our major oil routes to the refineries in Aruba and Recife, Brazil.

It was shameful that so many men died in the Atlantic aboard small ships with only a brief press notice from the Navy Department in the newspapers. The Navy and the Coast Guard, undermanned in Escorts, were putting up a gallant fight, and the efforts deserved to be reported like the war in the Pacific.

The Corsair Fleet and the Beach Patrol

Most Americans were never aware that the submarines controlled the Atlantic coast and the Caribbean. I can remember sitting at night on a hill called Mother's Rest, not far from our home, and seeing the glow of ships on fire, after being torpedoed by the German submarines.

The Coast Guard undertook two important roles to protect the nation during this period. One role was to protect shipping off the east coast and another was to prevent enemy infiltration from the sea. On May 23, 1942, Admiral Ernest J. King, Chief of Naval

Operations and Commander in Chief, U.S. Fleet, authorized the Coast Guard to organize the Coastal Picket Patrol. Admiral King ordered all sea frontier commanders to expedite the selection of small craft for the picket patrol also called the Corsair Fleet. The orders stated that the vessels had to be "capable of going to sea in good weather for a period of 48 hours at cruising speeds."

The force was organized into six task groups: Northern, Narragansett, New York, Delaware, Chesapeake, and Southern. These small boats were to observe and report the actions of hostile forces and to attack enemy submarines when armament permitted. In the beginning, anyone who could man or steer a boat was welcome. With such a diversified group of people in one organization, the Corsair Fleet was often referred to as the "**Hooligan Navy**". Some uninformed Navy personnel also used the same term derisively and referred to anyone in the Coast Guard as a "**Hooligan**".

The vessels chosen were auxiliary sailing or motor yachts, fishing trawlers and other privately owned craft that were capable of being at sea for a minimum of 48 hours. The vessels were accepted as loans or were requisitioned. The crafts would be returned to the owners at war's end in first class condition. When the Coast Guard took possession of a civilian boat, it was painted Navy gray; it was quite a change for a beautiful white and varnished yacht. There is a story that one of the Corsair Fleet patrol vessels came out of a fog bank during the night and surprised a surfaced German submarine. The Nazi Commanding Officer of the sub, in perfect English, told the patrol boat to get the hell out of the area, before they got hurt. The U.S. patrol boat, which was overwhelmed and over matched, did just that.

Normal patrol areas were along the 50-fathom curve off the Atlantic and Gulf coasts. It was great duty in the summer time, but in the usual stormy winter weather, the crews had their seamanship tested and a strong stomach was needed.

The boats were also used for rescue and passive patrol duties, especially around the coastal islands.

Martha's Vineyard and Beyond

The Commander of our unit called me into his office one morning. He said several of the instructors had recommended me for assignment to one of the yachts being prepared for off-shore picket duty around the islands of Martha's Vineyard, Nantucket and Cuttyhunk, and within Buzzards Bay, which was like a funnel to the entrance of the Cape Cod Canal. We would be a crew of four consisting of a First Class Bos'n, a Second Class Motor Machinist Mate and two seamen. We were to have a week of familiarization before we were to be detached and assigned to the Coast Guard Station at Vineyard Haven, Mass., on Martha's Vineyard Island off the Massachusetts coast. Martha's Vineyard was a summer resort island. It had three small towns, consisting of small restaurants, dry cleaning, barbershops and small souvenir shops, and the usual boutiques for upscale tourists. The three main towns were Vineyard Haven, Oak Bluffs and Edgartown. The permanent residents lived in nice white cottages with white picket fences and the more affluent had somewhat larger homes with second floors. The towns all looked like the seafaring towns and whaling villages they evolved from. The people were all hard working and derived most of their income from the summer tourist trade that arrived on the car ferries from the mainland. It was a really beautiful place to be, especially in the off-season.

The yacht we were fortunate to serve on at that time was 60 feet long; it had a closed cockpit and was powered by two V12 Gray Marine engines. It had twin screws, propellers, and a top speed of 25 knots. It used high-test aviation gasoline, a greater expense, especially during this time of gasoline rationing. The owner was the Revere Copper Co., and the yacht was named the "Skunk." The origin of the name was unknown to us, and it certainly didn't reflect the name in any way. The interior was solid mahogany and chrome. The appointments below were first class as would be required by the CEO of the copper company and his guests. The stern compartments, below and behind the wheelhouse, could sleep six in two separate areas. The forward compartment below with access from the wheelhouse could sleep four and had a full galley with four-burner gas stove and a full gas oven with a broiler and a large refrigerator/freezer. It had food storage compartments and cabinets on three sides of the galley. No money was spared to make this a first class, custom-built yacht. The decks were teak and that included the deck over the bow and the walkways to the rear compartments plus a large open area at the stern for chairs, etc. The beautiful exterior had been mahogany and was painted over with Navy gray. The hull below the water line was covered with ¼-inch copper sheeting. All the deck fittings were heavy chrome plated and were now painted the same Navy gray. The rear of the cockpit had a partition and sleeping quarters for two; it was small but not cramped. The motor machinists mate latched on to it as his private quarters. The large marine engines were under the cockpit floor with access by way of large folding and removable deck panels, which were hinged in the center for immediate access to the most important parts of the engine, ignition and carburetion. The engine compartment had its own carbon dioxide fire extinguishing system actuated from the control panel that contained the throttles, and necessary control gauges.

We patrolled the islands in the area and the entrance to the Cape Cod Canal. The Canal was the main seaway from Maine to New York and anywhere to the south. It was built to give an inland seaway to the south and in my younger days was used by the coastal steamers and other seagoing commerce between Boston and New York. In the days of passenger railroads, a train would leave Boston every afternoon for Fall River, Mass., and was called the Boat Train. The train passengers, mostly affluent, were going to catch the New York Steamer for a trip to New York City. The ships used the inside passage down Long Island Sound, which was a lot smoother than the open ocean. We would be in Fall River on occasion to take my grandmother, Mary Kelly Smith, to the steamer so she could visit with my father's brother, Joseph, a coal and oil merchant, who lived in Lynbrook, Long Island, New York. It was a thrill to see the ship and be a part of the controlled chaos when it was leaving. I always dreamed of taking the steamer when I grew up, but it was discontinued for economic reasons. The steamers were owned by the New York, New Haven & Hartford Railway Company, which fell on hard times.

Our picket patrol came to be recognized by the inhabitants of the small villages around the islands as we patrolled. The islands had little inlets and small bays that some of the lobstermen and fishermen lived and worked out of. They had small cottages along the shore and a few children. Some were loners and liked it that way. They picked up extra money during the summer tourist season. We would patrol at night on an irregular timetable and tie-up to a channel buoy and swing with the tide. Two of the crew would be on duty during the night for a certain period, and would wake the others for relief. The regular watch hours were from dusk to dawn.

The Coast Guard Station for Vineyard Haven was just us. We had our own dock and a telephone, electrical power source and a fresh water hook-up. We did all that was demanded of us, but we were an independent unit and our Skipper, the Bos'n Mate, called the shots. It was great duty. We had an account at the market in town, about a five-minute walk from the shore. It was called Bain's Market and Mr. Bain had a contract to supply the groceries we needed for our crew. We rotated the cooking among ourselves and each took a week of that duty. No one was overloaded with kitchen duty. We would cook up a good substantial meal when we were in port and have a good breakfast on patrol and the endless, bottomless coffee pot was always ready, "joe" in Navy terminology. At sea we always had bread and most of the crew made their versions of Dagwood-style sandwiches; we had all the lunchmeats available from Bain's Market plus fresh beef, pork and chicken. We didn't have steaks or cuts of that type, but we had beef roasts and pork loin roasts, fresh eggs, bacon and sausage and all the produce we needed. Milk was a big item on the menu. We had all the necessities. The military was not required to have ration stamps for the foodstuffs on the list. When I looked back on this picket patrol duty, I can't believe it happened; to a kid it was a dream come true.

Emergency Call

One cold and blustery day we got a call to intercept a tug towing a large collier, coal ship, from a power plant in New Bedford, Mass., to another power plant in Fall River, Mass. The coal-fired power plants were located on the shoreline of most cities to avail themselves of the bulk products sea transport, which was cheaper than land transport. The coal could be seen near the plants and covered many acres and the piles rose many feet into the air. The collier had unloaded half of its cargo in New Bedford with the remainder destined for the power plant at Fall River. The mechanical apparatus that was used to unload the soft coal, bituminous, had difficulty because the coal was frozen. The crewmen on the collier had to try and keep the coal level to maintain the stability and seaworthiness of the ship. When the collier was under way on Buzzard's Bay, one of the men couldn't get the frozen soft coal to come off the sides in the hold. He climbed down into the hold to attack it from there; he had some success and continued from his position in the hold. He was taking his long rod with a wide blade-like end and poking the coal, when the wall of frozen soft-coal collapsed and buried him alive. The crew of the tug and the other crewmen of the collier tried to rescue him, but he died before they reached him. They called the Coast Guard to take his body to New Bedford; we received the distress call on our radio and relayed the message to the Captain of the Port, at New Bedford. We were ordered to assist as necessary. We took a basket litter from our dock and rendezvoused with the ship and tug. The collier crew put the victim's body in the litter and we placed it on our rear deck. He was covered with coal dust and

I noticed that his mouth, nose and eyes were full of the soft coal. What I could see of him, he looked middle-aged and I wondered if he had a family and what they would think when they found out how he had died. It was the first time I had ever seen a victim of a violent death. We proceeded to New Bedford and were met by the local coroner. We gave a report of the accident, the circumstances and the names of the crew members involved. We off-loaded the body and returned to our Vineyard Haven station. The trip took a couple of hours and not many words were spoken; we were all alone with our thoughts.

The off-season on Martha's Vineyard was really slow and in our area there was a small bowling alley; the pins were handset and were called duck-pins. The pins had a rubber bumper around the fat part of the pin and were smaller than the pins used in the alleys on the main land. The pins we had grown up with were called candle-pins; they were tall and slender as a candle and we rolled small balls as we did on the island. When we were off duty, the locals who had cars, and gasoline, would give us a ride to Oak Bluffs and Edgartown, the two other populated towns on the island. Most of the tourist accommodations were closed, with a limited availability of sleeping quarters. A car ferry from New Bedford and Woods Hole, Mass., serviced Oak Bluffs and Vineyard Haven and the island of Nantucket once a day in the off-season and twice a day during the summer. It was a beautiful place to be and the weather was usually wonderful, even during the winter because of its position close to the Gulf Stream. It was so serene during the off-season that as newlyweds, Lorraine and I, in September 1948, spent a week of our honeymoon there.

When I would go the Bain's market to order for the crew, the meat cutter behind the counter was a handsome man with a great personality. He had dark hair and I always felt that I knew him from somewhere. I learned his name but I never made a connection, until years later when I casually mentioned the meat cutter to my great-aunt, "Aggie." Leonora Agnes Byrne Finnegan lived with us off and on, and helped our Mom when she needed it. She was always ready to assist when the kids were sick. She was a friend to us all. She was quick with a joke and had a bubbly personality. She was my mother's aunt, and my maternal grandmother Annie Byrne Cullen's sister. My grandmother Cullen died in 1919 during our mother's high school years. During the depression, Aggie met and married a man from her hometown of Middleboro, Mass. She soon became pregnant and the gentleman deserted her and the unborn child. She tried to locate him, but his family was opposed to the marriage and concealed his whereabouts. The child of the marriage was a boy and he grew to be one of the brightest people I ever knew and a true friend, ready to help in any circumstance.

If he had been able to go the college, he surely would have been a lawyer, a doctor or anything requiring brainpower. He had to work to help support his mother; women didn't have much opportunity for employment during the 1930's and 1940's. Aggie never got a divorce because of religious constraints, just a legal separation. She worked as a waitress where and when she could, and with her son, managed to keep her head above water. She would have made a wonderful nurse or a teacher, she had so much ability. She was floored when I related the story of meeting the meat cutter at Bain's market in Vineyard Haven. He was the husband who deserted her and his soon-to-be son. Later, when she investigated my story she found out that the meat cutter had died and left behind a family. Aggie would later obtain his death certificate in September 1948 so she could remarry in the Catholic Church. Aggie met a widower soon after and married him. They were constant visitors at my mother's home. They had a home down by the seashore and, when the winters were severe, spent the winters at our house. It was always a pleasure to see them; her husband, Bill, cooked great corned beef ribs, and we all shared Aggie's love for New England lobster.

While serving on the picket patrol, occasionally a lobsterman would give us few of his catch, mostly lobsters with one claw. Lobsters had two large claws, one to hold their prey and the other to crush it or tear it. If it lost a claw in defense of itself, it would begin to grow a new one. We all remember the old vaudeville joke about the man who went to the fish market and saw a few lobsters with one claw. He asks the owner, "Why does the lobster have one claw?" The market owner answers, "He lost it in a fight." The customer says, "Bring me the winner." We were very appreciative of the treat whenever we were offered them. We were used to our usual fare, which was excellent by all the military standards we would get to know. We knew we were on the gravy train and the current emergency wouldn't last forever.

When we were doing security patrols in New Bedford, we saw the building of wooden 38-foot patrol boats, that would have a crew of three, and larger 83-footers that would have heavier armament and depth charge capability which would take the place of the commandeered yachts in the Corsair Fleet. The best part of our duty was the absence of a vast chain of command that was regulation bound. We all knew our jobs and did them well, with very little fanfare. The Bos'n got his orders and told us what they were and we adjusted our day to his command. Little did we know that our bubble would burst, sooner than we realized. The submarine menace continued and we were the proverbial finger in the dike. Our main job was to make our presence known to the islanders and make them aware that it was possible for the German submariners to be put ashore, get to the mainland and sabotage the war effort in some way. We were all aware that we could be smashed with very little effort. We had seen a fishing trawler that had returned to New Bedford from the fishing grounds at the Grand Banks. It had surprised a German submarine charging its batteries in a fog bank and the sub opened fire on them. The trawler had about 10 to15 holes stitched along one side from machine-gun fire. It escaped into the fog bank and got the hell out of the area. We saw the bullet holes in the trawler's thick planking; they were about the diameter of a 25-cent piece, probably a .50-caliber machine-gun. If it had been one of our little Corsair Fleet, it would have been a disaster.

Once in a great while we were ordered to take a VIP to Woods Hole to catch the train to Boston or New York. One of the celebrities I remember was Catherine Cornell, who at that time was called the First Lady of the American Theater. She was very friendly and was interested in our mission and our hometowns. Although I had never seen her in any theater production, my being raised in Boston, Mass., gave my family the opportunity to see Broadway productions prior to their opening in New York. Many of the shows were debuted in Boston, Mass., and Hartford, Conn., where changes were made in the hopes of making the productions more successful in the major venues.

The trip to Woods Hole was always a pleasure and a source of excitement. In some areas it was difficult to find the channel and the channel buoys, especially at night. On the shore were lighted markers in different locations or a series of lighted markers, usually one higher than the other, when it came time to make a turn, one light would appear above the other, then you would turn to port or starboard, whichever way the navigational chart required. The vessel would be in the main channel or in the process of acquiring more lighted markers. The Bos'n knew his way around. The navigation charts contained all the information a sailor would need and required real knowledge to avoid the many hazards that were presented.

Our New Corsair Fleet Cruise

We received orders to proceed to Osterville, Mass., to decommission our cruiser, the "Skunk." It was too expensive to operate and we were going to be assigned to a more economical vessel. Osterville was on the southwest part of Cape Cod and was a large small boat anchorage and an upscale summer colony. We went to the Captain of the Port and he took possession of the "Skunk." It was inspected in almost every way possible to assure that it was in the same condition as we had received it. It passed inspection and inventory and was decommissioned. We then took possession of a deluxe yacht that was used primarily for sword fishing. I'm sure that its career was really for fun and relaxation and not for commercial purposes. It had the same expensive appointments as our former boat, but it had the look of a real seagoing yacht. The berthing accommodations were four bunks forward and two bunks in the after compartment. It had a much longer mast and a long bowsprit with a platform and a railing, and one could imagine someone standing on the platform with a harpoon chasing a game fish. It was more ready for heavy weather than the "Skunk" and it was equipped with a powerful diesel engine which was a lot less expensive to operate and maintain. Even though civilian owners had a basic patriotic intent, when a boat was donated to the war effort, the owners paid no taxes or upkeep for the duration. The boat was guaranteed to be returned in the same condition it was received. If it were destroyed while in the government's possession, compensation would be paid at full fair market value.

We spent about three days outfitting the boat with food and supplies. It had the same type of galley as the "Skunk" and was a first class marine machine. We spent a day or two familiarizing ourselves with its gear and engine responses and the handling for docking and berthing. It had twin screws and dual throttles and had a top speed of about 20 knots. Whoever owned this nifty ocean cruiser kept it in showroom condition. In the evening, while in Osterville, we would go to a Howard Johnson Motel that had a restaurant and a piano bar. We usually had steamed clams, which were served in a large eight-inch porcelain pan, about four inches deep, with a bowl of drawn butter. As long as we ordered drinks, the clams kept coming for one dollar per bucket; it was a real treat, one I would enjoy throughout my adult life.

When we had all the supplies transferred from the "Skunk" and stored in their proper spaces; we topped off our fuel tanks and headed back to Martha's Vineyard Island and our base of operations at Vineyard Haven. The boat handled very well in the light chop we encountered; we weathered the sea without any problems. Little did we know our duty station was about to change. We continued our passive, see-and-be-seen patrols around the adjacent islands. Usually the bay would be crowded with yachts, but the rationing called a halt to that. We surmised that fuel was in short supply for the private boat owners and that the commercial boats were the only ones able to get rationed fuel. It was hard enough for anyone to get a sticker and ration stamps for a motor vehicle, if only just to get to work. Transporting the body of the collier worker was the only rescue effort we had.

We were in possession of our new craft for only two weeks when we were ordered to return to Osterville for decommissioning and transfer. The bubble had burst and the imagined life of the playboy sailor was coming to an end. We had seen several new small 38-foot patrol boats tied up at the dock in Osterville on our last visit; they were unmanned, but were ready for delivery. The 38-footers weren't meant for any kind of real sea duty, but they were Government Issue and would be used for close to shore patrol duty, not in heavy weather, and mostly during daylight hours. We didn't see any of the new 83-footers, which could be used 24-hours a day, at sea and in any kind of weather.

Farewell Martha's Vineyard, It Was a Great Experience

We had been in the process of going to Bain's Market to replenish our larder. We had milk, coffee, bread and lots of cold cuts; some fresh vegetables and a good supply of restaurant-size and smaller can goods. The Bos'n closed out all of our accounts; we topped off the fuel tanks and proceeded to Osterville. Not much was spoken on the way. We all wondered what the Coast Guard had in store for us. We docked in the same area at Osterville and went through the same procedure to decommission the boat. We off-loaded all that remained of our supplies, inventoried the boat and signed off to the Captain of the Port. We all had a 48-hour pass and I had filled a shoebox with bulk ground coffee and wrapped a 10-lb pork loin in my ditty bag. We went to Woods Hole and caught the train to Boston. Servicemen in uniform could buy a round trip ticket for the price of one way, which was a big help. My pay was $36.00 a month so it left very little to spend for anything else. I had the feeling on the train that everyone could smell that box of coffee, which was hard to come by, and the meat was another ration stamp item. I knew that anything turned in would disappear before we even left the dock. The extra food was appreciated by the family when I got home for the 48-hour pass weekend. I was ready to see what new duty station the powers that be had arranged for me.

Newport, Rhode Island, Again

When we returned to Osterville, a canvas covered military truck with long built-in benches, lengthwise along each side, was waiting for us. We loaded our sea bags and the rest of our personal gear aboard and we were told we were being transferred to the Coast Guard station, Newport, Rhode Island, for reassignment. Although the trip would take a couple of hours, we were given meal tickets for food along the way. Meal tickets were like traveler checks and were legal tender; they were treated like cash for specific maximum amounts printed on them. It seemed like a lot of trouble to truck us to Newport. We had all gone on pass to Boston and could have been sent to the Coast Guard Receiving Station at the Brunswick Hotel in downtown Boston. The ride in the back of the truck was windy and it was rainy at times and we all moved around for comfort, the bench seats had little comfort factor and we all earned stripes for our butts. We were on a two-lane highway and the truck was traveling at a pretty good clip. I was sitting alone on the driver's side; it began to rain a lot more and became windier. I moved over to the opposite side with the others, and about the time I sat down, something flew through the canvas and shattered on the wooden hoop-like affair that held up the canvas cover. The driver stopped and we all jumped out. A lumber truck from a local sawmill, loaded with pine boards going in the opposite direction lost part of his load. The board that flew through the canvas, right where I had been sitting, would have taken my head off. We all looked at each other, but I was the one with the dry mouth. The rest of the trip was uneventful and we were taken to the Coast Guard Barracks where we unloaded our personal gear and were shown our sleeping quarters, which was the usual military barracks type. We were given liberty cards and had no watch or other duties. We were slated for a further transfer within the week. I didn't go to see my Aunt Frances while I was in town; I really didn't know her that well and had not seen her since seven years before, at Danny Kenney's funeral. I kind of wandered around the town like a tourist, enjoying the sights. I wandered over to see the recruits from the Navy Training Station. After four weeks the recruits were allowed off base. They were not allowed in any of the bars and the Navy required them to be in "Undress Blues" and leggings. Undress Blues were similar to Dress Blues, except they didn't have the white stripes on the collar or the cuffs or button cuffs. This uniform marked them as recruits in training or "boots," and they could not be served any alcoholic beverages. Although I didn't drink anything but a beer now and then, I felt like an old salt and a superior being just for being able to strut by them. We received our orders in about four days; I was assigned to the Captain of the Port, Cape Cod, across the Cape Cod Canal, not far from where we had decommissioned the patrol boat. I couldn't believe we had wasted the time traveling to Newport, Rhode Island. Oh well, the military way was hurry-up and wait. The crush of enlistments had every one in a tizzy. It was going to be a long war and the country and the military weren't up to speed as yet.

Frank A. Smith, Jr.

Welcome to the Cape Cod Canal

As a boy, my family, when we had a family vacation, would usually share a cottage for a couple of weeks at Onset, Mass., in the immediate area. Sometimes it would be a nice day trip. We had a 1928 Ford two-door sedan, and would take a ride in the evening to see the ships all lighted up transiting the Cape Cod Canal. It was a thrill for us. My father was a World War I combat sailor and we were all born near the ocean and as children we enjoyed it for the swimming and seafood. Little did I know I would enlist to protect the area.

Two bridges crossed the canal, the Sagamore and the Bourne; they were the only routes that connected Cape Cod to the mainland other than the sea. The Coast Guard Barracks were at Bourne, adjacent to the canal. Our duty was to patrol the military and government buildings on the western side of the canal. It was easy duty and the tours were four hours long once a day with a rotation every two weeks. We were granted shore liberty every day that we didn't have the duty. The small base had a permanent mess staff and we didn't have any kitchen duties. I would usually go ashore after the evening meal, sometimes after the noon meal. The one bar in Bourne served steamed clams if you sat around and had a few beers. The area had little neck clams, usually smaller with a softer shell, steamed and dipped in butter, and as my twin brother, Gerald, would say, they were "Yummy, Yummy." We were told that the duty was temporary, and the information was correct. In two weeks, I would be reassigned and transferred back to Newport.

The patrol duties on the Cape Cod Canal consisted of guarding the government buildings along the canal and to show a presence. I think the main objective was to see-and-be-seen. The canal was a vital artery along the east coast and saved days of travel time by most of the ships using it. The duty in its self was boring but I enjoyed watching the ships going through. The most difficult was smiling when a U.S. Navy manned ship was making passage; the

Navy crew along the rail shouted smart-ass remarks and jeered at the hooligan doing his job. I gave them a big smile and a friendly wave; I was a Happy Hooligan. We were all in the military; I often wondered if they all survived the war as Gerry and I did.

Newport, Rhode Island, Part Two

My next trip to Newport was not on a G.I. truck; this time it was first class, by a 20-passenger bus. It was not as one would imagine in this era of air-conditioning and reclining seats with footrests. The seats were leather and well worn; the fresh air was from the open windows. The bus had a long hood that covered the engine compartment and had a large radiator cap on top. The radiator cap had a large disc with a thermometer in the middle that could be seen by the driver, and measured the water temperature. In those days it was called a motor meter. The luggage was in a compartment below the floor level; light freight was carried in a depressed section of the roof at the rear. It had large metal strap bumpers that protruded from the front and the rear. I can't recall if it was fueled by gasoline or diesel, but the interior reeked of a fuel smell; it was a pleasure to crack a window for fresh air. I had no second thoughts of this kind of travel, after the truck ride on the first trip; I thought this was first class. Servicemen had priority for travel on official orders and civilians had to give up their seats if requested by the bus lines. The bus driver had his hands full; power steering was unheard of and the driver got some real exercise shifting gears. He would give it the gas after climbing the hills in the rolling countryside to gain momentum for the next hill; in those days that was the way it was done. When I arrived at the bus depot in Newport, I asked a sailor on shore patrol duty if it was possible to get a ride to the base. I had my sea bag to haul around and didn't relish carrying it very far, everything I owned was in it, besides the ditty bag I carried with me. He directed me to a desk and they called the base for transport. About a dozen other Hooligans were going to the same base.

We were instructed in the ways of the station and made aware of mess hall hours and morning muster time. Having been here before, I knew all the procedures. Most of us were waiting for reassignment and had no other information, as was usual for anyone in the service. I had free-gangway, shore liberty, every afternoon at 1300 hours; I hung around the base until dinnertime and then went ashore and followed the crowd to see where the action was. Most towns with military bases nearby had bars and greasy spoon cafes all over the main part of a town. Newport had its share, but the Navy and Marine shore patrol kept everything under control. If a business had problems it was off limits and the military were forbidden to enter. The business owners knew they had to toe-the-mark or get shut down. These were the days before television and there was nothing to do if one stayed on base. Most large Navy bases had their own beer gardens and served 3.2% alcohol beer, although you could get snorkered if you drank enough of it. This small Coast Guard Base was not big enough and the Captain of the Port saved himself a lot of grief by not having a beer garden. Newport had one on the largest Naval Training Bases in the country. San Diego on the west coast was as big and got larger during the war because of the good weather. Any American sailor could get lost in the crowd at Newport.

My great uncle, Patrick Murray, my maternal grandfather's cousin, was an engineer at the Naval Torpedo Station in Newport. We never knew what area he worked in and it would have been a restricted area at any rate, so I did not see him. I toured around and looked again at all the mansions by the seashore. Whenever I saw the estates, I couldn't believe anyone could have so much wealth. I usually took the bus to sightsee and covered quite a bit of territory. It was quite expensive to live it up off the base and my wallet was thin. Coast Guardsmen had a white shield sewn on their right uniform sleeve, which identified them and their service, and we wore it with pride. Knowledgeable sailors especially one in his cups seemed to make a big deal of it and it would sometimes lead to a bad scene. I usually avoided the slop chutes where people were looking for trouble. My transfer orders came through, and about 20 of us were assigned to the Acting Captain of the Port, Sakonnet Point, Rhode Island, close to Fall River, Mass., and Horse Neck beach, which we visited as kids. The fun was about to begin. For the rest of the war I didn't see any of my mates from Martha's Vineyard or New Bedford.

Beach Patrol, the Sand Pounders

On the foggy night of June 13, 1942, a German submarine landed a four man team equipped with explosives and $90,000 in U.S. currency for bribes and expenses. They landed on the coast of Long Island, N.Y., near Amagansett, on the southeastern end of the island. They were paddled ashore by the sub's crewmembers. Another German submarine would land a team similarly equipped in Florida. The teams were to strike factories and railroads to promote panic and disrupt transportation. The Germans had the great misfortune to be seen by John Cullen, who was a Coast Guard Seaman 2nd Class making his six-mile patrol for the Amagansett Coast Guard Station. Cullen, armed only with a flare gun and a flashlight, was outnumbered. The Germans offered him a $300 dollar bribe and he took it. When he was out of sight, he ran like hell to his superiors. The Coast Guard notified the FBI who captured both sabotage teams within two weeks. Cullen was given the Legion of Merit, and promoted to Petty Officer 2nd Class.

The FBI had advised the military to establish beach patrols, but their warnings weren't taken seriously until the Cullen episode. On July 25, 1942, Coast Guard Headquarters authorized all Naval Districts that were adjacent to the coast to organize a well-armed and maintained beach patrol, with proper communication equipment to relay messages. Five days later, the Vice Chief of Staff for Naval Operations informed Commanders of the Sea Frontiers that the, "beaches and inlets of the Atlantic, Gulf and Pacific Coast would be patrolled by the Coast Guard whenever and wherever possible."

The patrol activities were meshed with the activities of the FBI, the Army and the Navy. The beach patrols were more in the nature of outposts to report activities along the coastline and were not to repel armed units; this function was left to the Army. The Army had a large base close to our patrol area, near Taunton, Mass., named Camp Miles Standish. The Army was equipped to resist any attempt by armed enemy forces or parties to penetrate the coastline by force.

Wartime beach patrols were primarily security forces. The patrols had three basic functions: to detect and observe enemy vessels operating in coastal waters and to relay this information to the appropriate Navy and Army commands; to report attempts of landings by the enemy and to assist in preventing landings; and to prevent communications between persons on shore and the enemy at sea. The patrol also functioned as a rescue agency and policed restricted areas of the coast.

Coast Guard Beach Patrol, Sakonnet Point, Rhode Island

I was now assigned to a beach patrol. The Coast Guard commandeered a Sakonnet Point private home for basing the personnel needed for a beach patrol in the area. Most of the homes on the seashore were for use during the summer, all were well constructed and equipped and some were suitable for habitation during winter months. The house we would call home had two stories with three large bedrooms on the top floor, with each bedroom having a dormer roof and windows. The large kitchen had been made over into a galley operation with a large commercial Wolf range/oven setup. Each second floor bedroom was equipped with three double-decker bunks and a couple of chairs and a small table, suitable for writing. A large bathroom was also on the second deck; I wondered if it would hold up under the wear and tear of the patrol members. The ground floor had a large living room, a large master bedroom, and a large dining room, which was set up with two banquet type tables with chairs. The master bedroom had four single level bunk beds and two tables and several wooden chairs. The master bedroom had its own large double sink bathroom with modern tub and separate shower. There was a lavatory and toilet in a room off the kitchen. The living room had several upholstered chairs and sofas of sturdy commercial construction. The walls in all the rooms had excellent wallpaper and were in a first class state of repair. The draperies and curtains remained, and from the outside the home appeared to be just another nice home by the ocean. The owners were to be commended for relinquishing this beautiful home for the duration of the war. The home was built with a view of the sea and was adjacent to the local country club fairways. It had a large gravel driveway, a parking area to the rear of the house and a large manicured lawn in the front facing the sea. The home couldn't have been more than five years old and was modern to that date in every respect. The owners were paid for a lease and it was to be returned to its original condition, when it was no longer needed. I would remember it as one of the most beautiful places I had ever seen.

Two large metal double-door steel cabinets were bolted to the wall in the living room and were locked at all times and contained rifles, pistols and machine guns along with all the ammunition to wage a small-scale war. Other cabinets contained hand crank field telephones in heavy leather weather-proof cases and round leather-bound clocks that had paper discs to record the time when a key was inserted. The clocks would be more familiar if seen being carried by a night watchman, to assure that he made his appointed rounds. The home was equipped with a radio transmitter/receiver for communication and was monitored 24-hours a day. We had three telephones; one was from a line that was strung along the beach patrol area where the cable could be connected to with clips on the portable telephones, if the base needed to be alerted when an emergency would exist.

Years later, we would learn that my mother's cousin, Mary Murray O'Donnell, had a summer home on the same golf course and the same area. I never thought to ask her where it was located. Her family was in love with the house and the area, and so was I; Nannie often spoke of it.

The Sand Pounders

The patrols were of four hours duration and consisted of a five-mile patrol. The sailor assigned would be driven to the starting point by jeep and he would be picked up at the end of the five miles. He carried the heavy crank operated field telephone, which could be connected to the telephone cable with two clips. There were five keys in small containers attached and sealed to five poles carrying the telephone wires. The clock was keyed at the first pole and at each mile pole. The keys would make a number impression on a revolving paper disc within the clock and indicate the time the patrol reached that point. The discs were removed after each tour and checked to make sure the patrol was doing its duty. Each of the keys had a different number that corresponded to the mile-post location. The walking was difficult because of the sand; there was no road or sidewalk and it took time for the legs to become accustomed to the effort. The uniform required was Undress Blues and white hat for the daylight hours, and dungarees and blue knit watch cap for after dark. The usual Navy foul weather gear was worn whenever necessary. It was often cold and damp, as one would imagine after dark, except in the summer months. All wore the standard canvas leggings, which were a great help keeping the sand out. The beach patrolled was at the end of a peninsula that faced the Atlantic Ocean, Rhode Island Sound and Buzzards Bay. The eastern end started at a tidal river; across this river was Horse Neck beach. The beautiful white sandy beach with bathhouse privileges was reserved for the property owners, and we had been extended the same privileges as the residents. As we traveled west we passed beautiful beach homes facing the ocean. One in particular was a mansion set back on a shallow bluff, with a long green lawn that came almost to the high water mark. The heir to the S. S. Kresge department store chain owned it. The owner would be out on the lawn practicing his putting or driving stroke sometimes when I was passing by. Past the bathing beach were homes on the bank above the high-water reaches. They were all beautiful and well furnished, as I could see when they were occupied and the drapes were open. The occupants all seemed friendly and would wave as I walked by. One older couple spent the summer in their beach home and always had friends visiting during the weekend. They came to recognize me whenever I was on patrol and always had a cold drink for me as I passed. One afternoon they offered me a wax paper-wrapped package of saltine crackers; the crackers were covered with thick peanut butter mixed with real bacon bits and they were delicious. To this day I can taste them. I thanked them and happily ate as I finished my patrol. After about a mile the beach was vacant of homes to the west and the end of the patrol. The patrol started in Acoaxet, Massachusetts, and ended in Sakonnet Point, Rhode Island.

One day when I was on patrol, I stopped at the fence of the Kresge heir's mansion and watched him practicing his golf shots. I noticed he played with left-handed clubs. He waved hello and walked down the long grassy slope, and he introduced himself; we talked for a few minutes. He asked me if I played golf and I said I had but didn't have any clubs and I played as a lefty. That made it difficult because all my friends played right-handed. He said he had an older set of clubs and he would leave them at the country club for my use. He said just mention his name and there would be no problem. I wouldn't have many chances to use the golf clubs, but they were appreciated.

The Beach Patrol wasn't bad duty; the small crew was compatible and the food was very good. The Coast Guard had provided us with two cooks who prepared everything including fresh bread and rolls with an occasional pie. We were able to get off base without any problem. It was operated on an honor system and there was really nowhere to go except the small town of Little Compton, Rhode Island. Being the summertime, it was great to hit the beach for a swim and for girl watching. The waters south of the cape were quite warm, compared to the ocean north of the cape, which were extremely cold even in the summertime; it was difficult if not impossible to enjoy a swim. I did get a weekend off and hitchhiked to Fall River, Mass., and visited my uncle Jim, my mother's brother, and his wife Margaret for an afternoon. They came down to Acoaxet the following Sunday and visited me. I showed them our weapons and they seemed impressed with the operation.

District Training Station, Provincetown, Massachusetts

My 25 days of duty at Sakonnet Point were uneventful. I was informed that I was on a list to report to the Coast Guard District Training Station at Provincetown, Mass., on the extreme end of the Cape Cod peninsula I was hoping that my next duty station would be sea duty of some kind. With all due respect to those who served on Light Ships or Buoy Tenders, my personal preference was on the ships that were headed for combat such as convoy duty in the North or South Atlantic Oceans, the Mediterranean or on the transports that were in the South Pacific. We heard that the Coast Guard was getting Destroyer Escorts and some Frigates. The Battle of the Atlantic was still raging and there was a steady stream of supplies to England and Russia. We would hear of the sinking of ships in the north by German submarine wolf packs and the loss of merchant vessels. All the news was mostly rumor and second hand, unless one would run into someone who had just returned from convoy duty. A common sign on billboards and posters was, "A slip of the lip could sink a ship", and public conversations that pertained to ship movements were strictly forbidden. Other areas had mounted horse patrols and dog patrols and the Coast Guard patrolmen would sometimes come upon the bodies of the victims of the submarine sinkings.

Provincetown, Massachusetts

Provincetown was a famed resort, artist colony, fishing port and tourist center, situated adjacent to the Cape Cod National Seashore. In my day the area could be reached by a steamer from Boston each day or by a long drive from the mainland over the Cape Cod Canal. The area was surrounded with beautiful white sandy beaches and clear and pristine temperate waters. The ship that brought the tourists to the town was the S.S. Steel Pier. I remember as a kid reading about the moonlight cruises to Provincetown in the newspapers and hearing the alluring ads on the radio. I never expected to be on the other end of the cruise. The sailors and others were always at the dock when the ship arrived, girl watching. It was a pleasant change from the Seamanship Training Program.

Our training was almost like another Boot Camp but not as intense. The emphasis was on seamanship; most of the students had previous sea duty and were members of the Corsair Fleet. The trainees at the school were not privy to the information that the Coast Guard was to man 30 Destroyer Escorts. They were to be formed into five escort divisions consisting of six destroyer escorts. Each destroyer escort was to be fully manned by Coast Guard crews of 222 enlisted men and officers, and the five divisions were to be under the command of a senior Coast Guard officer. After the crews were trained and their new warships put through their shakedown exercises, they would begin escorting convoys through submarine-patrolled seas to Great Britain, the Mediterranean and through the Caribbean to the Panama Canal. The training period was for a six-week period and covered every phase of working and living aboard a combat ship. We were still in the dark concerning future assignments. We all lived on rumors and listened to anyone who had the straight dope, or in nautical parlance, scuttlebutt.

The Training Station had its permanent complement of cooks and bakers and other enlisted ranks for the other duties around and on the base. We had escaped the usual disliked kitchen details again; we were leading a charmed life, so far. The station had a large complement of savvy instructors who were transferred to this station because of their knowledge and ability. They would rather have been at sea doing what they knew best. The Chiefs and the Warrant Officers were the backbone of the staff. My twin brother, Gerry, would later become such a person during a 23-year career in the Navy, instructing officers at the Navy War College in Newport, Rhode Island. It was difficult for an officer to take instruction from an enlisted man such as Gerry, but when he was able to answer all the loaded questions they threw at him, they became aware of his expertise. He served on and was in charge of the Combat Information Center (CIC) on several of the Navy's largest aircraft carriers and prior to that was the leading Radarman on other large ships of the line. So when shore duty beckoned he was always sent to a prestigious teaching position, and was well respected by his students. He had the opportunity to receive a commission but would have had to move out of his CIC field and take a pay cut. He retained his rate and retired as a Command Master Chief Radarman. Other friends in his situation accepted commissions and retired years later as Commanders.

Provincetown was one of the best liberty towns anywhere in the summer time. Provincetown was a sailor's paradise. The business section was composed of several bar lounges, first class restaurants to fit any budget and a host of tourist accommodations that catered to the visitors. Art galleries were everywhere. It was easy to get a date, if one had the funds to have a good time. One could go dancing every night and drink whatever one desired, all at a reasonable price. My favorite in any seaside community was lobster if I was flush and steamed clams or fish chowder any time. Most of the tourists arriving from Boston via the S.S. Steel Pier had jobs supporting the war effort. They would return to Boston, catch a train to their homes and have pleasant memories of their summer vacation. The first time I got a weekend leave, I was anxious to voyage to Boston on the S.S. Steel Pier. Having heard so much about it as a kid, I wanted the experience for myself; it was great, my first real cruise ship. The ship had all of the best. With all the rationing, I was surprised at the availability and the choice one had in the restaurants and lounges.

I would usually head for the beach for a swim in the afternoon. Most of the beaches close to town were crowded, especially on weekends. I would hitch a ride to an area off the beaten path. We had an area we used for physical fitness training. It wasn't reserved, but a few of the trainees liked the privacy and the beach was always clean. The beach was surrounded by grassy berms and waist high brush. The only access was through the weeds unless one took the long arduous trip up the sandy beach. I was in my swimming trunks and never gave the short waist-high brush a second thought. I walked right through them for swimming and lounging at the beach, returning a couple of hours later to the base. The next morning I woke up and felt warm all over, mostly from the waist down. I took a shower and felt worse. One of the men in my quarters came in as I got out of the shower. He said, "Smitty, what the hell is that rash all over your legs and arms?" I looked at my arms and legs; I was covered with an angry red rash. I went to the sickbay and they took me to a building off base that was being used as our hospital. The doctor on duty asked, "Where have you been?" I told him my story and he wrote on the report that I had the worst case of poison ivy he had ever seen! I remembered that Nannie would admonish us not to go near that bush with the shiny leaves and I know to this day what poison ivy looks like. I was admitted to the hospital and given a shot every four hours to relieve the pain. Three times a day I had to bathe in a tub with the water up to my neck, and they would add sodium permanganate, a purple solution. I turned purple from neck to toe and was a real sight! It began to work after the second day and I was more comfortable as each day passed. I was there for a week and my skin began to slough off after the treatment was concluded. I returned to duty and smiled at the stares and remarks about my purple-ness; I didn't have much choice but to be the Happy Hooligan. I was surprised when my hospital time didn't alter my training schedule. Our six weeks of training was coming to an end and the graduates were going to Boston for further assignment.

Boston, I Missed You

Our sea bags were being sent to the Coast Guard Receiving Station in Boston and we all had 48-hour passes on arriving at Boston. We were to report in at 0700 hours on the following Monday morning. We were still in the dark on what our next duty station would be. The trip to Boston was on the steamer S.S. Steel Pier and our liberty would commence after we reported in to the receiving station. The Navy receiving station was in what was called South Boston, in a remodeled multi-story warehouse. The Coast Guard took over an older, former hotel, in downtown Boston, close to the Public Library near Copley Plaza, one of the posh hotels of the day. It is still one of the premier hotels in the city, in the area where the famous Boston Marathon finish line is located.

The Brunswick Hotel, Boston Coast Guard Receiving Station

A receiving station is a place where military personnel are sent while in transit for duty to other stations. Usually it is a larger base to accommodate a large number of personnel who would make up the crew of a new ship or a few personnel who would increase the complement of a station or ship that had crew transferred to other billets or schools. The Brunswick Hotel on Boylston Street in Boston was described as ancient and was well past its prime. It had flush toilet water tanks mounted high on the wall behind the commode. To flush, one had to pull a chain that was connected to that lever that released the water to flush the toilet. Having been raised in a home with the same sort of conveniences, it was no mystery to me and the force of the water falling through a two-inch pipe from about eight feet was more than sufficient to clean the bowl. The hotel must have been state of the art for its day and one could see from the outside façade it had a prime position in the architecture of the day. The accommodations were good. We didn't expect the Ritz Carlton, but the Coast Guard did well with what was available. The food was good by my standards and any perceived inconvenience was going to be temporary.

Boston, being my hometown, had a lot to offer. As a boy we visited Paul Revere's home, the Old North Church, where the lanterns were hung to signal the coming of the British and gave the signal for Paul Revere to begin his famous ride. The Granary Burial Ground in the middle of Boston was down a short street from its famous capitol building and surrounded by the tall buildings of downtown, with its hustle and bustle of cars, trucks and people passing in almost endless streams. I often wondered as a boy if many who passed realized the debt they owed to the Revolutionary War fighters buried in Boston. To me, the Massachusetts State Capitol Building was the most beautiful building of Boston. With its red brick façade, its columns and its golden dome it reminded me of the era and the people who would not be pushed one more inch and bought our liberty and future with their blood. For me, it was always difficult to comprehend the forces that prevailed to bring so many great minds together to forge our Constitution and our Declaration of Independence. What amazing foresight of the people of Boston to preserve the historical places in the city: the Public Gardens; the Boston Common; the Old North Church; Faneuil Hall. Growing up, our family enjoyed the Swan Boats propelled by pedal power through the beautiful lake in the Boston Public Gardens. So much history to remember: the Midnight Ride; the Battle of Bunker Hill with its monument; Old Ironsides moored across the harbor in the Charlestown Navy Yard.

The city of Boston reflects it history in many and unique ways. As a boy I didn't think much about the hand laid brick sidewalks, the hand hewn granite curbs and the massive granite cobble stone streets lighted by cast iron lampposts and gas fired lamps. It was just a normal routine to see a man walk down our street each evening at twilight with a long slender pole. He would reach up and hook a ring and the lamp was lit, a continuous burning pilot light ignited the main burner. In the morning, after dawn, we would see him again; he would hook the ring and shut off the gas. On a regular schedule men would come by and remove the large glass covers and wash them and reinstall them. It was all so ordinary and it seemed as if no one paid any attention to his or her efforts; this happened all over the city.

The commerce of sailors was a way of life in Boston; it had a deep-water harbor and miles of docks and wharves. The Navy Yard had the largest dry dock in the country and the shipbuilding industry at the ForeRiver Bethlehem Steel Shipyard in Quincy, Mass., was building the largest of ships. A sailor's life revolved around his liberty, shore leave, and nothing was left out of the mix. Popular drinking places were Izzy Orts on Essex Street, the Silver Dollar Bar off of Tremont Street, or Jake Worths with draft beer from all over the world, in the downtown business section. Live entertainment ran the gamut from the Old Howard and Gaiety Burlesque theaters in Scollay Square to the several first-run movie houses, some that featured the live big bands of the era.

Fenway Park, the home of the Boston Red Sox, and Braves Field, the home of the Boston Braves, gave passes to all servicemen and women for the ball games. All one had to do was go to the Buddies Club located on Boston Common and get the tickets. The U.S.O. ran the club and had a list of parties and other functions where service people were welcome. Thousands of men and women from the metropolitan area were in the service and their friends and families treated the guests to their city as if they were their own. Boston was a great liberty town, even for one who grew up there. The Buddies Club had lounges and reading areas for quiet time with typewriters and stationery if one wanted to write home. The coffee and doughnuts were available at anytime, small sandwiches and various snacks were a welcome treat. I know the food was donated and the people and companies involved really never knew how much they were appreciated. The U.S.O. and its volunteers satisfied my hunger at a time when returning to base meant turning in my liberty pass and staying onboard. People would call the club and request one or several servicemen to come to dinner or just a party. Most lived in the suburbs of Boston and gave a telephone number to call for directions and the time they were expected. We always traveled by way of Boston's great public transportation systems; it only cost a dime and one could travel all over with free transfers to any of the various systems. With pay records always seeming to be in transit and with allotments to Nannie, being broke for me was a way of life. One could get an advance under emergency conditions; it was deducted from your pay and we were always paid off in cash. Five dollars was considered a sizable advance.

I had a key to our house in Dorchester, but Nannie and my younger sister Barbara were in Arizona with my older sister Anne and her husband Guy, near the Army Air Force Kingman Gunnery Training Base. Aunt Aggie was taking care of the house and working as a waitress at a place called The Little Brown Jug. I would leave her a note and a light on so she wouldn't be alarmed when she got home. She worked hard and was dog-tired, so I didn't see her but for a few minutes as I was preparing to leave to return to the receiving station at the Brunswick Hotel. She always asked me if I needed any money and usually slipped me a fiver. She had a large coffee can stashed in her closet, with her tip money and wanted me to use it if I needed any. I never did, but her generosity was appreciated. My downtown activities consisted of a few beers with some of my roommates and scooping up free tickets to prime events around town. We were told we would be shipping out to Virginia in a couple of days. My two-week visit to Bean Town was coming to an end. I didn't have much money, but I was 17 years old, a sailor, and having a good time. We were still in the dark concerning our assignments.

Farewell Boston, See You When I Get Back!

About 200 of us from the Brunswick Hotel receiving station were told to pack our sea bags and be ready to travel at 0700 the following Monday morning. Buses took us to Boston's South Station and we were loaded on Pullman sleeper cars for our trip to Norfolk, Virginia. We were going to the Naval Operating Base for further training and would be assigned to new Destroyer Escorts in the final phases of construction. The New York, New Haven and Hartford Railroad steam engines hooked up to our Pullman sleeping cars for the long journey south. I was really excited to be on my way, this was my second ride on a steam train and I was finally getting my wishes fulfilled. Never having been on a Pullman sleeping car, I felt I was in the lap of luxury; it was exactly like the movies I had seen. We had upper and lower berths on both sides of the car; the white-coated porters were able to put a table between the facing seats. Few played cards, most were like me, leaving familiar territory and venturing into the unknown as we traveled through Massachusetts, Rhode Island, Connecticut, New York, New Jersey, Pennsylvania and the Delaware/Maryland/Virginia peninsula. The countryside was much like Massachusetts and to me it was beautiful. We passed by hundreds of lakes and ponds, but my favorite views were when the tracks paralleled the ocean. The homes and the cottages along the shoreline were stunning. When we were kids around Fall River, Mass., and the rolling hills of Rhode Island, indeed the whole New England states, it seemed as if America went on forever and the green view was without end. The scene would deteriorate when we would approach a large city. The main railway depots were usually in an industrial area and the approaches went through run down areas that bordered the tracks.

The sound of the crossing bells as we sped through the towns called our attention to the windows to catch a glimpse of a town or a name. The steam whistle warned all to get out of the way as we approached each crossing. When we slowed to stop at a town to change train crews, sailors would crowd onto the platforms at each end of the cars to wave or whistle at the girls waiting for the train to go by. We were thrilled when the drivers of automobiles stopped for the train, blew their horns and waved us good luck. They saw our uniforms and all knew we were heading to help fight in the war.

We took our meals in diners connected to the train. The tables were all covered with white linen with heavy table service. There was no menu and the waiters brought our meals as soon as the whole car was seated. Milk, coffee and tea were the choices for drinks, and the meal was usually roast beef or fried chicken, mashed potatoes, gravy and mixed vegetables. With four sailors at each table, the food soon disappeared. The dining car stewards treated us just as any member of the traveling public and most of us left tips. When darkness dimmed our view out the windows, the car porter came along and lowered the upper bed and made them up with clean white sheets. For a city boy not used to this kind of treatment, it was another thrill upon thrills. We were all awakened at 0500, and all had to be shaved and dressed for breakfast in the diner. We had another great meal with a choice of eggs or French toast, with sausage or bacon and hash brown potatoes, or grits as we neared the south. The meals were more than adequate and the railroad was well prepared to serve the hungry hoards of sailors. Most like me were first time dining car customers. I must say that the coffee served on the diners was always the best tasting, and I found this to be true, when in later years I was able to travel by train in civilian life.

Cape Charles, Virginia

I don't recall the time of day that we arrived at Cape Charles, where we were to disembark from the train. We were almost at the end of the Delmarva Peninsula that juts into the sea, bordered by the Atlantic Ocean on the east and Chesapeake Bay on the west. The railroad tracks ended at Cape Charles, Virginia, adjacent to docks where a large ferry steamer was waiting, along with huge barges and tugboats. The steamer and the barges were capable of loading rail freight cars and automobiles for the trip across Chesapeake Bay to continue on to the south. Many of the barges were full of box cars waiting for the tugboats so they could continue their travels. I was told this ferry system was more direct and economical than to make a long journey over land. The locomotives changed from steam to electric in Connecticut for the trip to and through New York City. The dining cars, engines and crews became the Pennsylvania Railroad for the rest of our journey, as did the steamer at Cape Charles. The 18-mile steamer trip from Cape Charles to Norfolk has now been replaced with construction begun in 1964 for a series of two bridges and two undersea tunnels that pass under the shipping channels at the entrance of Chesapeake Bay.

The steamer trip across the entrance of Chesapeake Bay was a welcome change from the train, although my first long railway journey, first experiences with a Pullman sleeper and "Dinner in a Diner" were sensational. The steamer was fully loaded and the sea was calm. Many naval vessels were out in the water. The destroyers looked menacing and I spotted several classes, the newer ones, the Fletcher Class with five five-inch .38-caliber guns in turrets forward and aft. They were well armed with anti-aircraft weapons consisting of 20mm and twin 40mm, and ten 21-inch torpedo tubes. Looking north into Chesapeake Bay, we saw many merchant ships that appeared loaded, as they were low in the water. I supposed they were making up a convoy to somewhere. My main interest was to see what Norfolk looked like. I heard the derogatory name that the city was tagged with, and all sailors who had been here knew what you were talking about when they heard it. I had heard the City of Norfolk's economic life depended largely on the Navy, but its people, for some unaccountable reason loathed the sailors, and over the years the feeling became mutual. We never called it Norfolk, always referring to it as Sh-t City. Rumor was that some citizens of Norfolk put signs on their lawns that read, "SAILORS AND DOGS KEEP OFF THE GRASS." The city had a few large buildings and didn't seem out of the ordinary. The Navy was the center of this world; it seemed as if the entire Navy was visiting Norfolk. A string of gray Navy buses met us at the dock. By now we were several hundred Swabbies, some had joined us along the route, and we were soon on our way to the Naval Operating Base.

Welcome to Naval Operating Base, Norfolk, Virginia

The buses took us to a typical military housing area of long, two-story, white buildings with outside stairways to the second floor. We were all mustered in front of the area and were directed to specific buildings as our names were called. Our travel uniform was Dress Blues and we were to change to our work uniform of a light blue chambray shirt, blue dungaree pants, black shoes and the typical white sailors cap; we all blended with the other enlisted men on the base. We were told to stow our gear in lockers between double-decker bunks. Our barrack building was under the direction of a First Class Boatswains Mate, his name shortened to Bos'n. All the enlisted men and officers were Coast Guard and about 25% wore ratings insignias on their sleeves. A full Coast Guard Lieutenant gave us a short indoctrination speech. He told us about the type of ship we were being trained to man and he mentioned that our being Coast Guard sailors on a large Navy Base would be a tremendous opportunity to show how good we really were. It would be taken as a serious affront to the Coast Guard leadership if we sailors failed to make the grade or became involved with any type of friction between the Coast Guard and Navy services on the base. We were told to make ourselves familiar with our present surroundings and our barrack numbers and get everything squared away for our first inspection and barrack duty rosters. We made our quarters shipshape and waited for chow call. The base was enormous and consisted of hundreds of barrack buildings and three-story office buildings and many monster warehouses down toward the docks and berthing areas. The office-like buildings were schools for everything imaginable as well as the usual military administration types.

At 1600 hours we all mustered in front of our barracks and marched about half-a-mile to our designated chow hall. I have no idea how many sailors were on the base; I could only guess several thousand and left it at that. I know that servicemen were prone to complain about the food but I thought it was great and there was plenty of it. The servers on the chow line were permanent duty base personnel and future cooks in training. The old service axiom of "hurry up and wait" was evident but not bad. A sailor would enter the chow hall, grab a compartmented stainless steel food tray and walk by the servers. He could take it or leave it while walking down the line. It was announced that everyone would eat what they took and waste was not allowed or the penalty was extra duty. Fresh milk and coffee were in large aluminum pitchers at each table. After exiting the chow line you hunted for a spot to sit and eat. When finished, we took our trays to a G.I. can and scraped the remnants into it, under the watchful eye of a white-uniformed mess cook. He didn't have much to say unless he saw someone wasting food. A half-hour was the usual length of time allowed to eat, followed by another march to the barracks. We had no shore liberty scheduled, but we would be on a port and starboard duty schedule the following week, meaning half of us on base and half of us on liberty each day.

When I was off duty in the evenings, I walked the whole base. It had its own airbase and I would go and sit along the chain link fence and watch the planes take off and land. The runways were always busy and I could get the feeling that an aircraft carrier was in the vicinity. The airbase was an important anti-submarine patrol center, and I could see depth charges being loaded on some planes. With all the ships coming and going, it would be a natural for German submarines to track ships leaving the harbor and to try to ambush anything. The sea and air patrols were continuous. Larger aircraft such as PBY's and PBM's (Patrol Bombers) were used for long-range patrols of the shipping lanes and were armed for submarine attack. The airbase had a Chiefs Club on the perimeter of the base, but was restricted to Chiefs and their guests. I passed by it many times and it was close to the tower used by the air controllers.

We all became acquainted with the Navy slop chute, or recreation area. Beer with 3.2% alcohol flowed like water at 10 cents a bottle. A sailor could guzzle enough to get a buzz, but it would flow out of every orifice if he did. A movie theater was in this area and first run movies were run twice a night, a ticket was 10 cents. The Ship's Service Store was like a mini-department store selling most anything. I found a collection of pen and ink sketches of Destroyer Escorts in action to show the folks back home and remind myself of what I had gotten myself into. Cigarettes were one dollar a carton and the beer garden smoke was so thick you had to cut your way through it. In those days it seemed as though everyone in the service smoked. I'm sure it's the reason most elderly veterans are suffering from emphysema and related ailments. We had an outdoor area attached and it contained an elevated boxing ring. Sometimes bouts were scheduled and other times it was challenge bouts, most times by the inept "I can beat that bum" types, who usually got flattened. All in all it wasn't hard to stay on the base; I knew it would cost a whole lot more if I went to the city. The streets close to the base entrance were full of bars. If a sailor went into a bar it wasn't long before a sweet young thing would appear at his elbow. At our indoctrination it was mentioned that if anyone contracted a venereal disease, the hospital time would be added to your enlistment time and it would trigger 30 days restriction to the base. Extra duty would be assigned, usually in the scullery, washing trays and pots and pans. It was nasty, smelly, hot duty and really hard-paced work, but there never seemed to be a shortage of sailors assigned that duty!

I would go into the city occasionally with a few guys I came to know. Most of them were single and on the prowl. My funds were limited and I usually ended up at the local U.S.O.; it had local bands and entertainment on the weekends and juke box music other times. The free lunch and the coffee and donuts were what attracted most of us. Most of the servicemen were of the lower ranks, without rates. The monthly pay scale started at 21 dollars a month and increased to 26, 28, 32, and 38 dollars when I first went in the service. It was paid in cash twice a month. Being paid in cash made for some fantastic payday crap games at a dollar a chance. Many lost it all before the sun went down. The losers stayed on the base until the next payday. It was a good thing they had a place to sleep and eat. Our Chief told us not to lend money to anyone because you would probably never see it again. I learned from experience in New Bedford; I lent five dollars to a fellow sailor and before the next payday he was transferred to another base. Most of the married men had allotments, as I did, and it was sent to their homes by government check each month. Several I knew took out War Savings Bonds. The saving bonds sold for $18.75 and if held to maturity each was worth $25.00. In those days, that was a lot of money, when 25 or 30 dollars a week was a good wage.

Destroyer Escort Training

The first phase of our training was a classroom familiarization with the activities of Destroyer Escort Anti-Submarine Warfare. Escorting convoys was a mission that required vast amounts of technical skills, many that were not heard of prior to World War II. Much of the electronic warfare, search and destroy equipment, was beyond the understanding of servicemen not involved with its operation. The Radar, which is an acronym for Radio Direction and Ranging, was a super secret weapon. The strange antennas on Navy ships really made one wonder what was their purpose. Sonar, Sound Navigation and Ranging was for the underwater detection and tracking of submarines. In the post-war era, both of these were improved immensely for other purposes, but in WWII their purpose was basic and our military added improvement after improvement during the war. All the combat ships were equipped with a large table that had a clear Plexiglas top and was approximately waist high, high enough that one could bend over it or lean on it. Under the clear top was a compass rose, which is the face of a compass, and when actuated it moved in any direction that the ship moved. It had a large roll of translucent paper that could be marked on and the compass rose was projected on to the paper. A mark was placed on the paper when a submarine was detected and more marks and lines were drawn when subsequent sonar contacts were made on the submarine. What was visually saved was the original contact and, if the sonar was able to stay in contact with the sub, its location served to plot our Depth Charge and Hedgehog patterns. The ship had two long racks on the stern, fantail, loaded with depth charges. The depth charges weighed about 200 lbs. and rolled along an inclined track, into the sea, when an attack was under way. Our charges for the stern racks were of a new type; the old type resembled ash cans. Our depth charges resembled bombs and rolled on large rings welded to each end. The theory was they sank faster and were more efficient. The charges were filled with TNT explosive, and a hollowed out section in one end had two smaller charges, which could be removed for safety reasons. One charge was about the size of an elongated large juice can, with a small opening in one end, the smaller charge was about as large as a man's little finger. The charges were threaded into each other; the juice can not only had an explosive of its own, it contained the triggering mechanism that could be set to actuate at a specific depth. The smallest charge was fulminate of mercury, and was so sensitive it was stored in containers welded to the side of the ship away from any explosives, so as not to have a chain reaction to any adjacent explosives. These red, finger-sized explosives were only placed in the depth charges at the last minute. In Hollywood movie versions of the interior of a submarine during an attack, the sub crew would be shown listening for "Click – Click – Boom." The first click was the red finger exploding and the second click was the tomato can exploding, starting a chain reaction to fire the large charge of TNT.

Along both sides of the ship, toward the stern, were devices called K-guns; they had replaceable cradles welded to long pistons. The pistons were dropped into each K-gun and a regular depth charge was strapped into the cradle. The K-guns had a small replaceable charge in the leg to blow the depth charge away from the ship. We had four K-guns on each side that were inclined outward. If we were able to pass over a sub and bracket it with our rolled off charges, the K-guns would throw side charges a distance from the ship. Whenever the attack took place, the underwater explosions that occurred were followed by a most spectacular sight of tremendous fountains of water that rose from the sea. All this occurred as the ship was traveling at top speed and the ship felt as if it would rise from the water itself.

On the bow of the ship was a new anti-submarine weapon called the Hedgehog. The ship was armed with three torpedo tubes (launchers) amidships, which were removed after our first convoy run. They were to be used as a defense if we would encounter a German Surface Raider. Additional anti-aircraft weapons utilized the space. Our main batteries could be used for a surface or air attack. Two 3-inch/50 Naval cannons were on the bow forward of the bridge and one 3-inch/50 on the stern, all with six-man crews. The Hedgehog firing/loading area was between the two forward guns with four-man crews. There were 20 20mm anti-aircraft weapons, with three-man crews, and one twin 40mm anti-aircraft or surface weapon with a six-man crew, that could be fired manually or by a remote operator located above and behind the emplacement. All anti-aircraft weapons were equipped with special electronic optical sights that would automatically lead the aircraft being fired upon, to compensate for its speed. The main batteries were remotely directed for the weapon operators while watching large dials and matching the moving arrows, one for distance (elevation) and another for direction; they could also be fired manually.

During our training period all members of the crew, regardless of rank or rating, were required to be familiar with the duties and the operation of the various attack weapons, in the event that any of the weapons crews were killed or wounded. The training was constant and tedious; the purpose was to make ones effort automatic, to ensure that it was a matter of life and death, our life and the enemy's death. The torpedoes and the torpedo tubes and all equipment related to this operation were manned by a separate Navy crew assigned to the ship, as the Coast Guard had no such facilities, equipment or ongoing experience on any of its ships prior to WWII. This changed when personnel were trained at Navy Weapon Schools.

At the Naval Operating Base, mock-ups of ship interiors were so authentic that, when I was inside, I would believe I was actually on the ship. The interior was equipped with actual hatches, furniture and any electronic devices we would encounter on the real ship.

One of the most fear-provoking of the mock-ups was the interior of the ship that would be allowed to be seen as a compartment that had been damaged and water was entering at alarming rates. The crewmembers assigned to each compartment had to stem the tide with anything at their disposal, such as metal plates, mattresses and wooden timbers of various lengths and sizes. When undergoing this event, we had to climb into the compartment to Save the Ship. We would take off our shoes in the training phase and scramble to Save the Ship. One of our primary concerns was to save our feet! When the water rose to waist-high, the activity became desperate. If our efforts were to no avail, the instructors observing behind glass panels from above would stop and explain what we should have done. After the second time it was amazing how the ingenuity of the crew showed itself and it became a game to excel. This part of the training was called Damage Control.

When we were training for Fire at Sea, it didn't require much imagination to see that we had no place to hide or retreat when this would occur. It was fight the fire or die. Fire caused by any action or accident had to be extinguished and in the fastest manner possible. All of the crew had to be familiar with the various options and fire fighting apparatus. We were all taken to an outdoor area and were shown the types of hoses and nozzles. Portable pumps, called Handibillies, were located in strategic areas of the ship. They could be connected to hose lines and a similar hose could be dropped over the side for seawater. They looked like lawn-mower engines in a pipe-framework which made them not only light weight but easy to handle and move to the location that required them. Being gasoline-fueled, they operated above deck. All compartments usually had escape hatches on the top deck and the discharge hoses could be dropped down these hatches if necessary. All fire fighting equipment had to be ready for instant action 24-hours of the day and every sailor had to be able to operate it.

One of the most exciting phases of the fire fighting training was the extinguishing of a fuel-generated fire. First a small tank of fuel was set on fire and the instructors explained the method of fighting the fire and the type of equipment one would use. All members of the crew had to take turns with each group and be familiar with the methods and all the various attachments to the hose line. After all of us had the opportunity to extinguish the small fire, a large tank, open at the top and about eight feet in diameter was set ablaze. The fire was huge, with heavy volumes of black smoke and raging flame. About six men with a fireman at the front handle a two-inch hose with a controllable nozzle and a long one-inch pipe with a special spray nozzle attached. This nozzle made a huge cloud-like spray. The fire was approached downwind and that looked really hazardous. With fire in our faces, the instructor fireman turned on the fog nozzle and we pushed forward to the fiery tank. The fog nozzle made it look easy; the fog spray cut off the fire's oxygen. We held our position for about a minute to cool the area. It was an amazing demonstration and each member had to take an active part, always with an instructor fireman at the front of the line. It was not only a fire-fighting lesson, it was a confidence builder.

We practiced Damage Control and Fire Fighting several times during the training programs. All the programs were in the accelerated mode. Enough time was spent to acquaint the crew with the seriousness of the training. Damage control and fire fighting were to be assigned duties aboard every ship and teams would be made up as needed.

A great deal of time was assigned to the offensive and defensive armament. The gun-sights were new to most of us. About half our group had prior combat duty, but the electronic sights were a recent innovation. The gun-sights were on all the 20mm guns, and were in remote directors for the 40mm guns because of their size and loading characteristics. As mentioned, all hands had to be absolutely familiar with the ship armaments in case of enemy action and ready to step in if a gun crew or some of its members were incapacitated during an attack. The anti-aircraft guns were easy to operate and load. The ammunition for the 40mm was in four-shell racks and dropped into loading slots at the rear of the weapon. The 20mm had circular magazines previously loaded and stored in ready boxes around the perimeter of the gun station. The operator of the 20mm had semi-circular shoulder pads attached to the framework of the weapon and he was strapped to the pads with a belt. As he moved, the gun would move. A circular ring was welded to the gun mount and the operator would move his feet to stay in position as he traversed the ring, to assist him in his angle of firing. For elevation, an assistant would operate a wheel that could control his ability to raise or lower his angle to extreme high or low, whichever the gun needed. Around these weapon emplacements, or Gun Tubs, was a tubing framework that outlined the safe firing limits for the weapon. When the barrel of the weapon reached the framework it alerted him that his position was at its maximum use and coverage limit. If these tubing frame works were not in place it would be obvious that in the frenzy and high state of emotion that the ship and its adjacent crew members would be in extreme jeopardy from friendly fire. The 40mm guns were so much larger and more complex that the safety limits of the weapon were able to be pre-set with electronic and mechanical automatic stops.

The 3-inch/50, called three-inch-fifty, was a heavy weapon; it was a smaller weapon than the 5-inch/38 caliber that was used on the larger destroyers. The Destroyer Escort was for a specific purpose and the Destroyer, while having similar duties, was required to be able to protect capital ships and engage the enemy in many direct situations. The Destroyer was usually a steam-powered vessel able to travel at much higher speed and the newer vessels had twin 5-inch/38 guns in turrets fore and aft. In dry-dock, side by side the Destroyer Escort, DE, and Destroyer, DD, had similar hull designs, but the DE was 306 feet long and 37 feet wide and the DD was about 346 feet long and 36 feet wide.

The crew practiced hour after hour on its major weapon. There was a lot of complaining, but the purpose was evident when it came to firing the weapon in a combat, life-threatening situation. Firing was almost automatic and that was the intention. Firing a gun required a lot of coordination among the crew members: the handling the long shells; setting the time it would take the shell to explode after it left the gun barrel; and controlling the hot expended casing as it was ejected after firing. It was a coordination that was familiar to anyone involved in the activity, and LOUD.

The accelerated training program was about to end and the crews of 220, made up of mixed ratings and officers were assigned to the various Destroyer Escorts in the final construction phase, and ready for commissioning. The situation in the North Atlantic was dire. The German submarine force had been expanded, and their Wolf

Pack operations were sinking and damaging the Merchant Marine and Naval vessels. There was tremendous loss of life. The Germans knew ship destinations and had established a line, from Iceland to England, as their priority attack picket line and had a "You shall not pass" plan. The Destroyer Escorts and other anti-submarine ships were desperately needed. Russia was in need of arms and supplies and the only practical route was through the North Atlantic over to Murmansk, the largest city in northwest Russia. Over 500 Destroyer Escorts were to be constructed, and the U.S. Coast Guard was to man 30 of them. It was considered a prime assignment.

A Shoe Changes My Life

On the final day of our training schedule, we were in a marching formation, in a column of two's. The kid behind me thought he would be funny, and he stepped on the heel of my shoe. My shoe came off and I had to jump out of line, retrieve the shoe, put it back on, and return to my place in the formation. A few steps after returning, the guy did it a second time, causing the same reaction. When I returned to the formation this time, I growled something to him. He could see I was mad and he had an amused look on his face. I hadn't taken two steps and he did it a third time. I spun around, grabbed the front of his shirt and as I was in the process of pulling him toward me, he was swung at me with his right hand; his fist hit me with a crunch under the left eye socket on the cheekbone. His fist continued on and hit my nose, and I hit the deck. As I was lying on the ground I could see my nose, almost in front of my right eye. Blood was everywhere. The formation had stopped by this time. It all happened so fast. The Petty Officer in charge and several of the others came over to look at my bloody face. Someone found a towel and I used it cover up the bleeding. I was taken to the emergency room at the nearby Naval Hospital.

Naval Hospital, Norfolk, Virginia

The bleeding had stopped by the time we got to the hospital. The doctor who treated me didn't seem any older than me. He asked me how it happened and I told him that I had tripped and fallen against some machinery at the gunnery training site. He took my nose between the knuckles of his thumbs and crunched the nose back into place. It began to bleed again, and the pain was worse than the first blow. He put a dressing on my messed up nose and gave me a couple of pills to ease the pain. He started to fill out the medical report for the records. He asked me again of the circumstances. I really was in a panic now. I realized that if I had to have an eye examination, any competent ophthalmologist would see my crossed left eye and suspect my amblyopia. If anyone would shine a light in my eyes, a spot of light would be in the center of the good eye and off center in the "Lazy eye." I would be discharged. All this time I was trying to avoid the doctor's direct view. As he was filling out the reports, I noticed he was looking in a large medical book. The chapter I saw had to do with the nose and the different ways it could be broken. My story must have fit with his book, because he finally said I would be hospitalized for a few days to be observed for concussion and other symptoms resulting from a fall or blow to the head. I was real nervous and happy to get out of the ER. A Pharmacist Mate took me to a ward and I was admitted for observation. Most of the beds were full with swabbies with a variety of ailments, though none seemed to be life threatening. The nurses were all very busy and I didn't require any special treatment, so they didn't do anything except check the dressing and the tape on my nose. I avoided any direct eye contact, and I seemed to be out of the woods.

After the initial pain pill in the ER, the pain became more intense. I asked the nurse for help. She called the doctor and he wanted to wait until the next day for any medication. He was concerned with the concussion and didn't want anything to mask the symptoms. They gave me an ice bag that really helped. I didn't realize until later that I wasn't given an X-ray of the facial bones. Although my nose was broken, the usual black eyes did not appear. Being ambulatory and not requiring close-up personal treatment was a big help to me and my hopes for continued military service. The nurses were harried and when they asked me to run errands in the hospital for them, I was more than willing. I avoided the Ophthalmology area completely.

No restrictions other than not leaving the hospital were placed on me. I took all my meals in the ward and the nurses looked at my nose three times a day, and asked me if I was having any dizzy spells or had any vision changes. They entered the information on my chart and went on to other patients. I was still hoping to return to my unit before they shipped out. On the third day, the kid who started the whole chain of events by walking on the back of my shoe, came to visit me and apologized; he thanked me for not reporting the true event and his responsibility. He said he didn't need a Summary Court Martial or Brig time. He came to tell me that our unit was shipping out to Port Arthur, Texas, to crew the USS Leopold DE-319. He also said I was being reassigned to another DE crew that was shipping out in two weeks. I was shocked; my unit was leaving without me!

Explosion at the Naval Airbase

On the fourth day, September 17, 1943, close to the afternoon mealtime, we heard the thunder of a huge explosion on the base, and the buildings shook. All hell broke loose at the hospital! Doctors and nurses were all asked to report to the emergency area. The 500-lb. depth charges loaded on trolleys being hauled to aircraft at the Naval Air Base had exploded and practically leveled that base. I went to the stair well and the landing, which was over the main entrance to the ER. I looked out the window on the landing and saw ambulances and pickup trucks pulling up and backing up to unload at the ER. The trucks had one or two terribly injured men in them, and blood was all over the place, pooling in the trucks and draining onto the ground. The vehicles came for what seemed forever. The injured or the dead all seemed to be very young men. I had no count of the casualties, but it was a lot. The next day, I was informed that I was returning to the training unit to free up some beds for the casualties. My nose swelling had all but disappeared. The nurse said if I had any problems to go on sick call in the outpatient unit. I was really surprised that I didn't have a black eye or any other obvious signs of the punch to my face. When I returned to the training unit, I was reassigned to another draft. The unit hadn't received its orders and the destination yet. The technical part of the training was over and the only requisite was to report for muster at 0700 for stand-by duties. Those duties were the menial type; police the area to pick up papers and cigarette butts, and general clean up. The groups were mixed and the person in charge was not familiar with all the personnel. We were all released for midday chow and were to return to the same area after lunch to continue the exercise. While I was familiarizing myself with the base, I went by the ship landing area at the back of the base. I saw large groups of sailors waiting around. I went up to one group and asked a swabbie the reason. He told me that they had finished their training and they were being ferried to a couple of Destroyer Escorts out in Hampton Bay. He told me they were a mixed group and were told to get in one of the launches for the trip to the DE's. I slipped away from my clean up group the next afternoon, went down to the dock and melded with one of the groups. There was no way they could differentiate between the Navy and the Coast Guard and nobody challenged me. When I came aboard the DE, I just followed the crowd. I happened to get in a group that went to the bridge and the Radar room, which was at the rear of the bridge. A Radarman demonstrated the two radar sets; one you could just turn on and it was ready. Another which was used for greater distances, required more technical work before it was ready to operate. I was mesmerized with the equipment and hung around with each group that came through. I tried to stay in the background so I wouldn't be noticed. I watched the Radarman like a hawk.

I slipped away from the cigarette clean up detail and followed the sailors every afternoon after lunch. A couple of days there was no activity so I just toured the base. I wandered down to the Air Base and saw the effects of the massive depth charge explosion. The Control Tower was a wreck with all the windows smashed; some small buildings were flattened. One in particular, was the Chiefs Club. It had been a small two-story building. The second floor had a poured concrete floor; the explosion had collapsed the building and the second floor had crushed everything on the ground floor. I felt that anyone on the first floor at the time would have bought the farm. The damage to the whole area was tremendous.

I met a Chief who was looking over the collapsed Chiefs Club and he told me that a cart was towing several wheeled dollies in tandem loaded with depth charges. The depth charge main explosive was Torpex and it was cast inside the cans of the depth charge. One of the depth charges had shifted from the top of the stack and was dragging under the next cart. It was sparking and smoking from the friction. A sentry spotted it and told the driver to stop. An assistant fire chief ran up with a fire extinguisher to fight with, but he was killed when the first charge blew; then all the other charges went off almost at once. So many died or were injured; the area at the time was busy with civilian and military personnel. The damage I saw was devastating.

The USS Ramsden, DE-382

Assigned to a New Destroyer Escort

Before the two weeks were up we received word that the draft I was in now was to crew a new Destroyer Escort. The 220 officers and men were going to Houston, Texas. The ship was the USS Ramsden, DE-382, constructed by the Brown Shipbuilding Company in Houston. The DE building program was being accelerated and the ships were being constructed at several yards on the Gulf Coast, the west and east coasts. Some sections were being pre-fabricated at inland yards, even in Colorado, and shipped to be assembled at coastal yards.

Riding the Rails to Houston, Texas

We packed our sea bags for the journey. All of a sailor's worldly possessions were rolled, tied and neatly packed in a white canvas sea bag. I learned if I did it correctly, none of my clothes would be wrinkled when it came time to wear them. We all had ditty bags, small bags for personal articles used on a daily basis. The sea bags would be stowed in a baggage car and not accessible until we reached our destination. When we boarded our sleeping car, the whole train was just for our crew. The train was split in the middle and was connected to two dining cars. We ate from a limited menu that was designed for fast service, but the food was great and served in the usual manner with white linen tablecloths and heavy silver service. The coffee was always exceptional, and a favorite. We stopped many times along the way to change crews and to service the steam engines. The only major town we stopped for any length was Birmingham, Alabama. We were there for about two hours. We were allowed to leave the train and we were given a reporting time. Dozens of the sailors headed for the nearest bar and chugged beer. Many bought souvenirs and others tried to smuggle booze on to the train. Shore Patrol was all over the station, and they knew that sailors would try any way to circumvent the rules. When a sailor was carrying a package into the train concourse, it was inspected. If a sailor was carrying a small travel bag by his side, the shore patrolman would whack it with his billy club with enough force to break any bottle, even if it was shaving lotion. The Birmingham station was crowded with men and women of all services, outnumbering any civilians.

Houston, Texas

I can't recall how many days it took us to reach our destination; it couldn't have been more than a couple of days. The trip went smoothly and was uneventful. I spent the days looking at the scenery fly by and becoming acquainted with my soon-to-be shipmates. Being with a different group than the sailors I had trained with had its good side. No one knew of my stay in the hospital and I didn't volunteer the information. All signs of the broken nose were gone, but I began to have nagging headaches of varying severity. The last evening meal on the train was fried chicken and plenty of it. We arrived in Houston after midnight and we slept on the train. We would be met the next morning by buses at the station and transported to a large motel near the shipyard. We had toilets in each sleeper car and, because of the delay on disembarking from the train, the toilets had to remain accessible to the passengers. Large steel containers were placed under the toilet outlets, outside the train, at trackside. That night, the worst possible situation arose. During the evening about 100 or more sailors who ate the fried chicken came down with diarrhea. People were in panic and rushed to find an empty toilet compartment. The containers outside the train were soon filled to overflowing; it was a mess. I went into one of the large compartments where several passengers could wash and shave; it was equipped with large and small sinks. All of the regular sinks and the small sinks were filled with excrement. For some reason, the fried chicken didn't affect me or some of the others. When we left the station, it was apparent that the train cars and the platform would need emergency treatment as well as the interior of the train's restrooms.

At about 0700 we loaded up on the buses and were on our way to Houston. We arrived not far from downtown Houston at a large one-story motel with a two-story unit in the middle. Our motel was on a busy main street. The first strange thing I noticed was the lack of any security devices or even a chain-link fence around the compound. We were 220 officers and enlisted men and the motel had three or four double-decker beds in each room; we were easily accommodated. After dropping our sea bags in our rooms, we gathered on the large parking area and our officers informed us that patrols manned by the crew would be on a 24-hour basis and a duty roster had been established. We were to check the duty roster each morning after muster and before breakfast; missing duty time would be met with a restriction to the base, until the ship was commissioned. We were to be in Houston for a week and the crew would be taken to the shipyard by duty sections to familiarize each with their working area. All crewmembers not on the duty roster were granted shore leave at 1500 and must muster out on the parking lot at 0700, the next morning.

I went with a group to downtown Houston, where most sailors headed to the nearest bar. Not having a lot of money, I toured the main line of the city. The first place I visited was the Rice Hotel. It was a large modern hotel; the lobby was beautifully appointed. Off the lobby was a well appointed bar, near several large banquet rooms. It was fully equipped for a major convention on the main floor as well as the second floor, which had similar accommodations. I went into the main floor bar with a couple of sailors; there were about 20 or 30 older well-dressed businessmen having their afternoon drinks. We sat at a table and a waitress came over to take our order; our ages were never questioned. We all ordered the local beer. In a few minutes the waitress returned with our order. Usually when I went out with a group, each sailor would put a couple of dollars onto a pile on the table; when it was used up, more dollars would pile up again. It was the best way and no one got hurt when it was time to pay the tab. When we asked the waitress what the total was, she told us a couple of businessmen paid our bill, and our drinks were on them. It was the same situation in every one of the nicer places in town. They all knew who we were, what we were doing in town, and where we were heading. There was an Army Base outside of town but no Naval Base, hence using the motel for our headquarters. I usually stayed close to the motel or walked around the perimeter for exercise. Every day several Houstonians would pull up at the curb and ask if I could visit for dinner. If I could, I would tell them the time they would pick me up. I went a couple of times with other sailors and they treated us as if we were one of the family. The wars affected everyone in the nation, and most families we met had sons in the service. The families realized that their own kids were far from home and that a good home cooked meal would be appreciated by us. They asked about our parents, our hometowns, what we intended to do after the war. After dinner they took us back to the motel and we usually got a firm handshake from Dad and a hug from Mother; a great town and real fine people genuinely interested in the sailors' welfare. Many of the other sailors enjoyed this wonderful treatment.

Houston had its fair share of sketchier areas of town. I came out of a place called the American Bar where the curb was almost as high as the roof of the automobiles parked alongside. It was evidently a high water/flood drainage area. The curb had posts every four feet or so and chains fastened to the posts, every 10 to 20 feet were stairs to get down to the cars. We hadn't walked more than half a block when two women, about 25 or 30 years old, flew out of a bar. They were really doing battle; one hit the other and she fell over the chains onto the top of a car. The other one followed her and was punching the hell out of her. A patrol car pulled up and broke it up. We asked the guys that ran out of the bar what happened; they told us the women were fighting over a young sailor in the bar.

Boarding the USS Ramsden, DE-382

The keel for the USS Ramsden DE-382 was laid down March 26, 1942, and was launched May 24, 1943; it was sponsored by Mrs. James L. Ramsden, mother of Coxswain Marvin Lee Ramsden, USN, who was born January 2, 1919, at Pleasant Lake, North Dakota. He enlisted in the Navy on May 21, 1936, and reported for duty on the Aircraft Carrier, USS Lexington CV-2 on October 8, 1936. During the Battle of the Coral Sea, May 8, 1942, Coxswain Ramsden, a member of the Lexington's crew throughout his career, remained at his exposed station, continuing to operate a range finder in the face of enemy strafing and dive-bombing attacks until he died. For his gallant conduct, he was posthumously awarded the Silver Star as well as the Purple Heart for his unselfish dedication to duty during the battle.

Our visit to Houston was fast coming to an end. We were taken to the Ramsden and the crew was given duty and location assignments and our sleeping compartments. The cooks and bakers were familiarizing themselves with the galley and its equipment, as was the engineering staff. The deck force, under the control of the Chief Boatswains mate, Bos'n, were instructed in the operation of all the deck equipment which in part consisted of the life rafts, and a motor whaleboat, which had to be lowered from the davits that it hung on. Dry runs were made with the depth charge launchers and all the above deck devices that were exposed to the weather and the sea. This included dropping the anchor, hoisting it and stowing the anchor chain into its below deck locker. The signalmen were making sure that their signal flags were in their specified places and ready for instant use. The colored signal lights on the mast were tested as well as the large and small high powered blinker lights, used for Morse code communication. We were all involved with the Builder Trials of this new ship to ensure that all the equipment the Navy had ordered and specified was installed and in working order. It was a hectic time for all the crew, from the Captain and all the Officers, to all the enlisted men. Anyone who had prior sea duty was given an instructor's assignment. The 220-crew members were mixed in their experience, being made up of men new to the service with no experience, older sailors with a little experience and others who had a lot to offer. It was easy to recognize that in a combat or emergency situation, experience was going to save a sailor's life or limb. The secret was practice, practice and more practice. The repetition was a tremendous amount of hard, tiring work that went on hour after hour, day after day, until the job became second nature. Every function in every department had its unique duties, but all onboard had to be able to pick up other duties not in their specialty. For example, cooks and bakers had General Quarters Stations, such as firing anti-aircraft weapons, Damage Control and Fire Control Stations. Everyone "doubled in brass" as it were, and had to serve in more than one capacity. Most of all, the crew had multiple duties for specific situations. Seamen assigned to the Deck Force, led by the Bos'n mates for the proper stowing of the ship's above and below deck gear, were also responsible to the Gunnery mates for the proper safety and firing of all the ship's defensive and offensive weapons. This included the thousands upon thousands of rounds of ammunition and the tons of depth charges stored in the magazine compartments below. The Engineering Department made up of rated men and "strikers" (sailors in training for a specific rating assignments), were in control of all mechanical equipment above and below decks, such as the engine rooms and portable gasoline engines for the fire pumps and the engine in the motor whaleboat, the fresh water distilling equipment, all the electrical generating equipment. We had a former Chief Warrant Officer, the highest enlisted rank, as our Engineering Officer; he was a Lieutenant Senior Grade. He knew all the equipment related to his job and whipped his department into shape with a hand that had been there, done that. He was a big tough, red-faced outdoorsman, with the salt of the sea in his face. His group, the Black Gang (from coal dust clinging to everyone's skin), learned from his experience; they were the best of any in the service.

When the Officers were satisfied that the crew was fully familiar with the operation of all phases of the ship's complex running gear, we packed up our belongings and left the Houston motel barracks and went to the ship to locate our sleeping and locker areas. The different compartments were able to be isolated from each other, in case of fire or damage at sea. The sailor complement in each compartment was a mixture of all the departments that worked the ship. This was made necessary, so that the ship, if damaged in any way and in any specific berthing area, would not wipe out a whole section of trained personnel necessary to run the ship. We were about to begin the accelerated hands on phase of a new anti-submarine Destroyer Escort, the USS Ramsden, DE-382.

We departed our Houston dock at the head of the Houston ship channel and slowly headed south to Galveston. The ship channel was a narrow waterway and the topography was very flat. The builder's representatives were aboard to inspect every phase of the ship operations. These men were all civilian construction experts and were part of the instruction force who would participate in the Navy's acceptance trials on this new vessel.

As we made our way south toward the Gulf of Mexico, we came upon a wide plain, and in the middle of this plain was a high, obelisk monument. It seemed to be out in the middle of nowhere. It was a state park, near Pasadena, Texas. It marked the spot that Sam Houston and the Texans defeated the Mexican General, Santa Ana, at the Battle of San Jacinto, on April 21, 1836.

Galveston, Texas

The smell of petrochemicals was strong and the waterway was lined with refinery type installations. As we approached Galveston, we passed close to another refinery port named Texas City. The industrial smog was very heavy. Later, in 1947, two years after World War II would end, a freighter docked in Texas City with a huge cargo of the fertilizer ammonium phosphate, would explode, killing 500 people in the explosion and the raging fires that would ensue.

Late that afternoon we arrived in the Port of Galveston and the ship's company was given port and starboard liberty. I had never been in this part of Texas, and I was ready to see the sights. The war had all the industries working 24-hours a day and the Todd-Johnson Shipyard was one of the largest contractors. As we pulled alongside our dock, we saw three large ships; I believe they were oil tankers being repaired. One had a large hole in its bow; one of the others had a huge hole further back. The dock men told us the tankers had been hit by German torpedoes. The Nazis knew that America was importing huge amounts of oil from Mexico and South America and that the Gulf coast was full of refineries. Because of this critical supply for the U.S. military, the first large increase in anti-submarine patrols was in the Gulf of Mexico and the Caribbean Sea.

The most mysterious part of our preparation was the Degaussing of the ship. The process involved wrapping the ship with a large continuous cable. During its voyage the ship might pass over magnetic mines, and the ship hull could trigger the explosion. Another concern was the magnetic trigger torpedo. The ship, being a large mass of steel, was a real magnetic target. Basically the ship was de-magnetized by passing electric current through the cables wrapped around the outside of the ship. The interior of the ship had a cable network that did the same thing to augment the effect of the original Degaussing. A specific amount of electricity would be sent continuously through the ship's cables as the ship passed through known and different magnetic areas of the earth. Because of the magnetic differences on the earth's surface, the navigator had to compensate for this magnetism when plotting his course. A navigator knew the difference between True North and Magnetic North. All magnetic compasses and ship's clocks were removed from the ship while the Degaussing procedure was in process so that their accuracy would not be impaired.

Our ship was moored in Galveston for about three days. All the food and provisions were replenished and the freezers and refrigerated spaces were filled. Our ship was ready and we were champing at the bit. With our Captain on the bridge, we cast off all lines and slowly made our way through the harbor out to the Gulf of Mexico. Our day was spent with the officers maneuvering the ship at various speeds and headings. The officer on duty would call to the helmsman through a brass tube that had a large cone on each end. The helmsman, at the wheel, would answer and repeat the order that was received. His duty was to turn the ship to the compass heading or to signal the engine room via the Engine Room telegraph. The telegraph was received in the engine room and was matched by the person manning the throttle. The propeller shafts, driven by the engines, could be regulated by adjusting the number of turns, or revolutions, required to keep pace with another ship as in a convoy. Keeping pace with a ship was called Station Keeping.

There was the Radar to detect surface and air threats, the Sonar to detect undersea threats, and the radio to monitor assigned frequencies for incoming coded traffic to the ship. Many training problems were simulated and all required instant response. The General Alarm was ringing the crew to General Quarters dozen of times a day. The staccato piercing tone of the bell made us run like hell to our duty stations as if our lives depended on it. General Quarters drills were sometimes conducted in the dark with the lights turned off; I learned quickly where to go after the first collisions in the dark, followed with the usual sailor's cussing.

When the ship was underway, each crewmember had his duty area and his special duty to perform on a four hours on and eight hours off schedule. His combat station could be manning an offensive or defensive weapon, fire fighting station or damage control station. Each Division of the ship had duties peculiar to their ratings. When the General Quarters bell rang, it was controlled chaos. The accelerated training schedule was never ending, and the crew became more and more proficient as each day passed.

When the ship was undergoing its builder trials and acceptance, we did many high-speed runs and violent maneuvers, firing the weapons all with live ammunition, to test the vessel and to train on the weapons. Occasional depth charge patterns were laid down. The huge underwater explosions and the towering fountains of water were by far the most awesome display of power I had ever seen.

The Builder's Trials ended with a high-speed run and the firing of all weapons simultaneously, including continuous depth charge patterns, four charges from the K-guns on each side and the charges rolled off the stern. The ship shuddered and shook, the sound was deafening. Nuts and bolts left lying on overhead I-beams by the shipbuilding crews came flying down. The ship seemed as if the constant explosions would shake it apart. The engines were doing their maximum turns. We were cutting a path through the sea as if the devil himself was chasing us. All this was continuous for about 10 to 15 minutes. The exercise was curtailed and we slowed to a crawl. The whole ship was inspected for damage. The ship had many sealed compartments with removable plates. The sealed sections were opened to vouch for their integrity and resealed.

We returned to Galveston, delivered the ship builder's inspectors back on dry land, replenished our food and armaments and cast-off for our anti-submarine training and shakedown cruise at the islands of Bermuda. We cruised by Florida and passed within viewing distance of Miami Beach on our port side as we turned northeast by north and headed for Hamilton Island, Bermuda. Our real entry into the war was about to begin.

Anti-Submarine Warfare Training, Bermuda Islands

The cruise to Bermuda was uneventful, except for some squally weather, and rain showers. The ship tossed about a little, but no one seemed to be bothered. We had numerous proficiency drills during the trip, on all phases of our individual duty stations. My first General Quarters combat station was on an Oerlikon 20mm anti-aircraft and surface weapon. A three-man crew manned the weapon; one fired, another loaded the magazines and the other raised or lowered the mount with a large hand wheel that was turned quickly by a handle protruding from the wheel. The wheel and the whole gun mount moved as the gunner moved. The wheel was always in the same relationship alongside the moving weapon. Each member of the gun crew would substitute for any of the others. One of our first duties was to load the magazines with the shells to be fired. The magazines were heavily greased to protect them from the salt and damp air. As we placed the shells in the container, magazine, we had our hands covered with a special grease to protect the shell as well as being a lubrication source. Every sixth shell had a red tip; this was a tracer and was used as a visual aid for the person firing the weapon. It was seen as a bright bit of fire as the projectiles went through the air. When this effect was seen at night, between the lights were five fired shells also on the way. If the magazine had all tracers the heat would destroy the barrel of the weapon and eventually the rifling would burn out causing the shells to tumble through the air. It was possible during a combat situation to change the barrel, if needed. A spare barrel was in the gun position and a large five-foot long tube filled with water to cool the removed barrel, was welded to the outside of the gun tub. We had long padded asbestos gloves to protect our hands and arms if this barrel change had to be done.

The crews that were assigned to the 40mm guns had similar duties, but the shells and the projectiles were larger, more explosive and traveled a much greater distance. The 40mm gun was trained, pointed, two different ways. First, by a remote gunner some distance away from the heavy smoke. An electronic gun sight was mounted on a swiveling post equipped with handle bars like a motorcycle. As the gunner moved right or left and up and down, so did this huge, water-cooled, dual barreled weapon, driven by electric motors on the gun mount. Some of the ships had four-barreled guns. The 40mm gun could also be fired and trained manually at the gun site. It was an awesome weapon; it had a distinctive sound, "POM-POM-POM-POM."

All of the crewmen assigned above deck, had to be able to load and fire all of the weapons. The 3-inch/50, three-inch-fifty, was a true artillery weapon. The shell and its projectile were about three feet long. The projectile had rings on its nose that could be changed with a tool to change the time it was set to explode after leaving the 50-inch long barrel of the cannon. The shells were for different purposes and conditions: High Explosive, Armor Piercing, Star (for lighting the area), and the Anti-Aircraft (variable-timed explosive). The shell was rammed into a chamber on the back of the weapon, when it entered, a metal block slid up and the chamber was closed. When the gun fired, part of its recoil reset the gun to fire again and the large spent shell casing flew out the back of the weapon and was caught by the Hot Shell Man, who stood at the back of the gun while he was wearing large padded asbestos gloves that reached almost to his under arms. The hot shell man was supposed to catch the spent shell, not only to save the brass case for reloading at a shore facility, but also to protect the crew from harm. At times, the action during an air attack was so fast and intense that he slapped the shell casing out of the way to speed up the firing rate. Each person had a specific job to do; they were very coordinated and their actions were automatic. Their practice proved its worth. Brass was precious material during the war; the shell casings from all the onboard weapons were saved and stored in their original containers, to be off-loaded to be recycled.

The most dramatic of the armaments were the depth charges and the crewmen that manned the operation. It was hard work; the depth charges weighed about 200 to 300 lbs. Most of the charges were loaded in a long inclined steel rack on both sides of the stern. Usually when making a run on a German submarine, the charges were rolled off two at a time, one from each rack. The eight K-guns, four on each side, fired the charges a distance from the ship as the Skipper determined the pattern most likely to kill the sub. We all hoped that the Sonar had the sub in its grasp and we were as safe as the ships we were striving to protect.

In addition to the depth charges, we had a new series of anti-submarine weapon called the Hedgehog. It was on the bow of the ship, between the two forward gun tubs. A Hedgehog was a group of 24 mortar-type bombs, each three feet long with 25 lbs. of TNT, and the weapon was fired when a German submarine was detected in front of the ship. All the mortars were fired in rapid sequence to become an air-borne group, well forward of the ship's path, about 250 yards. The mortars detonated on contact with a sub, so if one mortar hit the sub and exploded, all would explode at the same time. When they were deployed, they sounded like an electric typewriter when a key was held down.

Three Navy torpedo men operated the three 21-inch-long torpedo tubes located amidships. Each torpedo ran underwater at a depth of about 10 feet when launched. I didn't think we were going to engage in any surface naval action, unless a damaged Nazi sub surfaced and was willing to fight it out. With all the artillery our ship had, such a naval battle would have all the aspects of a turkey shoot.

When we arrived at Bermuda, the Captain and some of the officers left the ship and visited the Senior Officer-in-Charge to set up our training schedule. While we were at anchor in the bay, I thought I would try my hand at fishing over the side. I didn't have any fishing gear except a string line with a hook and a sinker. I saw some barracuda looking the bait over, but never had a strike. We were in a large land locked bay and close to a seaplane landing area. I watched the take-off and landings of several Patrol Bombers to pass the time as night approached. Our landing ladder and stage was deployed so that anyone going ashore had access to our motor whaleboat, tied up alongside. We had a large light hanging over the side to light the way. I moved toward the light to see if the fishing was any better. One of the officers, an OD (Officer of the Deck), and an enlisted man standing Gangway Watch were close by, about 10 feet away and not paying much attention to my fishing efforts. Both the men were wearing a .45-caliber handgun. It was about time for them to be relieved by another pair. The officer drew his weapon and pulled the slide back, this caused a shell to be loaded into the firing chamber. I thought that was odd, but it passed through my thought processes without alarm. He ejected the magazine from the butt, pointed the weapon at the steel deck and pulled the trigger; he forgot that the hammer was back, the gun off safety and ready. The weapon fired, and the copper jacketed bullet hit the steel deck, disintegrating in all directions. I felt a sting on my right shin, pulled up my dungaree leg and saw a bit of blood dripping, not much, but enough that I knew that I was hit. The officer and the enlisted man had similar scratches, but the angle of impact caused the main part of the bullet to ricochet over the side. I thought the officer was going to faint! He finally composed himself and the accident had to be reported. He was a reservist, not like the other officers who had been Chiefs and Warrant Officers with lengthy service times. I became more aware of things going on around me and I did my fishing in a non-traffic area from that day forward.

The next morning we weighed anchor at an early hour, left the anchorage and proceeded to sea. There were several other destroyer escorts along with us in the exercise, including the USS Leopold

DE-319, the ship I was supposed to be assigned as a crew member. We had a submerged Navy submarine in the area, and we were to simulate a search and destroy mission. The main focus was our Sonar Gang; so much was expected of them. The Sonar equipment and the operator were in a small room off the flying bridge, close to where the officers spent their watch at the con (controlling the movements of the ship). My underway duty that day was as a lookout with binoculars and a Polaroid mask that could be changed by an adjustment knob between the lenses to block out the sun, even to be able to look directly into the sun. The lookout's duty was to scan the surface continually for anything unusual. The officer that fired his handgun onto the deck was on duty with the other officers, but he didn't have much to say, except when the Captain asked a question at him.

We spent the whole day at sea on the anti-submarine exercise. I don't recall if our team ferreted out the sub, but I knew the exercise was over when I spotted a smoke bomb in the water about a mile away. It was our submarine warning all to stay away, that it was going to surface. It communicated through its own sonar with the ships in the vicinity using Morse code. About ten minutes later the sub rose to the surface. It was quite a sight climbing out of the depths when it surfaced.

We went through these exercises every day. The whole ship was involved in every department and I thought the General Quarters alarm would wear out. We didn't fire our weapons, but went through the motions for stopwatch timing. We didn't make any points with the Skipper, but our time did improve as the days wore on.

With the duty roster being four hours on and eight hours off, we still had other activities during the daylight hours. The ship had to be maintained and other seamanship exercises took place. One of the things the deck force had to do was to lower the motor whaleboat, our version of the ship's launch. While docked or tied up to an anchor buoy, this was a snap. When the ship was underway, this was a challenge and it was a thrill to be involved. The whaleboat had to be lowered into the water, starting the engine a split second before hitting the water and casting off away from the ship. It was kind of scary the first time. Coming alongside and matching the whaleboat speed to the ship for hooking up was also tense the first few times. The Bos'n knew his business and showed us how.

Cleaning the ship was a never-ending job. Dirty quarters or habits were not allowed and any variance was soon corrected. Special attention was given to our sleeping quarters bedding such as mattresses, and mattress covers. The canvas bunk bottoms were tied to pipe frames with line, rope. Our mattresses had a fireproof cover and when we hit the deck for duty, the last thing we did was to spread the cover, then place straps across both ends to hold it to the frame and raise the three high bunks to the overhead, hooking them with a small chain. The only ones allowed to sleep-in were the sailors coming off the mid watch, (2400 to 0400 in the morning). A sailor would take his life in his hands if he woke up someone sleeping after coming off mid watch.

We were scheduled to go to Hamilton, the main Bermuda Island, on the following day. The Navy had a large anti-aircraft firing range located on the southeastern shore. We were to spend the day firing all the weapons installed on our vessel. The different gun crews were to have a full day of firing at targets towed behind planes at various altitudes. One of the firing platforms was rigged to roll and pitch to simulate a ship at sea. We were disappointed to learn that it wasn't on our schedule for that day.

Welcome to Hamilton Island, Bermuda

Our ship was ordered to leave our anchor buoy in Great Sound and proceed to the long dock at the Hamilton Island Government Station. The street that paralleled the dock was Front Street, a popular shopping area, and we were told this was where the cruise ships tied up in peacetime. After the ship was secure, it was announced that we were on a Port and Starboard watch, which meant that half the ship's crew would go ashore for the firing exercise, and the other half would maintain security and the operation of the ship. Several Navy trucks loaded the 110 Officers and Enlisted men and slowly drove through the town on our way to the firing range. There were no other cars on the road, only bicycles. The homes on the way were beautiful and very expensive looking. All were brick or stuccoed and painted in pastel colors. All of the buildings had areas that were paved and had rounded domes with a curb around its perimeter. The island did not have a large water supply and all were required to have cisterns to capture all the water that fell from the rainstorms on the island. I remember Bermuda had beautiful semi-tropical weather. I recalled my mother's stepsister, Lillian Goff and her husband, Edward Sullivan, spent their honeymoon in Bermuda prior to World War II. Ed had been the New England regional manager for the Lilly Drug Co. and was now a Naval Officer during the war.

We went to the island several times for anti-aircraft training. The rest of the time we were training on the anti-submarine phase. We chased our subs in the area and they pulled out all the stops to hide from us or attack us. The Sonar had a "PING" sound when we had a sub in our grasp. The early World War II Sonar screen was not very sophisticated. When a sonar man was pinging, he was searching and directing his ping from a rotating device under the ship. He could change its direction at will, but when part of a convoy, he would most likely have a quadrant he was responsible for; the Destroyer Escorts would provide a screen to protect the full 360-degrees around the convoy.

The First Class Bos'n Mate had a request from the Quartermaster to make available light canvas covers for some of the equipment on the bridge, such as signal lights, etc. I volunteered and he had several bolts of light canvas, waxed twine, sewing wax, a leather-sewing palm and heavy curved needles. I had a fair idea what to do with the assorted equipment and went to work. I made covers for all the signal lights on both sides of the bridge and other small items, exposed to the weather. When I was finished, I painted them Navy gray to waterproof the canvas and the seams. I installed brass grommets along the bottom for a draw cord, to secure them from the wind and the weather. The project was so successful it became almost a full-time job. It was tedious work, but I worked at my own pace and the Bos'n left me to my own devices. It was a lot better than "chipping and painting," a sailor's full time, daylight job when not on watch.

When I was taking a break, I would seek the shelter of the bridge and wheelhouse. To the rear of the wheelhouse was the Radar room, with the two Radars, one was a PPI type, (Planned Position Indicator) which could see 360-degrees out to the horizon and well beyond. The parabolic Radar antenna on top of the mast really determined the distance the Radar could see electronically. The second type of Radar was for greater distances, and its antenna looked like a coiled mattress spring, so naturally it was called a Bed Spring antenna, and was attached to the highest point on the main mast. The equipment was exactly like the Radar on the training ships I had visited when training at Norfolk Naval Base.

We were given shore liberty, close to the end of our training. We were transported to Hamilton Island and the City of Hamilton for a brief six-hour visit. We were ordered to be at the dock to catch the liberty boat back to the ship, which was no longer at the dock and had returned to its anchorage in the bay. Our Dress Blues uniform was the uniform of the day. I was walking down Front Street, checking the shops and having a good time, minding my own business, when a Navy gray jeep with two Marine Shore Patrolmen pulled up beside me and ordered me to halt. They said I was out of uniform, ordered me to get into the jeep and took me to the Navy Brig! The brig was a large room with cells around its four sides. The guards sat at desks in the center of the room. I was asked the usual name, rank, serial number, my ship's name and when my liberty was over. They put me in a large cell with some other swabbies who told me not to give the Marines any static, to my peril. My offense was walking down the street with my Dress Blues cuffs unbuttoned and folded back. I would be released a few minutes before my liberty boat was to return to the ship, with an order to properly wear my uniform. My only liberty in Bermuda and I spent it in jail! If the uniform of the day had been Summer Whites, without those button cuffs, I would have been home free. The Marine Guards smacked around several sailors who cussed about the Brig time. It seemed to me the guards got a perverse pleasure in this, as well as ruining our only liberty. When I returned to the ship, I reported my experience to our Executive Officer, XO. He said he had heard that the Marines were being heavy handed in Hamilton and not to worry, there would be no report made. I thanked him, and breathed a sigh of relief. It wasn't until further in my story that I changed my mind about Marines, and the guys I met in Bermuda were not good examples of their branch of service.

When aboard ship, any information concerning the ship's coming and going was at a minimum, and only the Officers were privy to our destinations. The Quartermasters, who served on the bridge and assisted the Captain, the Executive Officer and the Navigator, would prepare the maps for the areas our orders took us. A large cabinet with large full-length drawers and a full-size table-like top was fastened to the bulkhead on the bridge. This was a secure area that also contained the Radar equipment, the Dead Reckoning Tracer table, the Navigator's nautical clock, stopwatches, sextant and other small map related instruments. Usually the maps being in use at the moment by the Navigator were in the drawers. Most of the other Line officers were also required to know to how to navigate by the sun and the stars. The only time anyone not assigned to the area was permitted to enter was if the weather conditions required safe passage below, via the inside ladder, stairway. The Navigator would plot his course on a drafting parchment-type paper taped to the tabletop. It could not be disturbed, or else the Plotting and Pantograph instruments would not coincide and the Navigator's calculations would be off. The parchment paper could be drawn on and any errors could be erased. The Nautical Map for the area was for reference and probably one of a kind. Nautical maps from the Oceanographic Office were classified and secured in one of the several locked drawers. The Quartermaster kept the Ship's Log, a ledger-like book, which was a record of all the weather and course and speeds and all pertinent shipboard details. It was handwritten and later transcribed another day by the ship's office yeoman. The log was a fulltime record of the ship. All vessels that traveled the seas were required by international law to keep them, and any daily entries had to be witnessed and signed by the Officer of the Day and the Quartermaster at the end of their tours.

I was doing canvas work in and around the area. I knew all the Officers and the Quartermasters and the Radarmen and they knew me. I would sit with the Radarman while he was calibrating his long distance radar. I had seen it done many times in Norfolk and was completely familiar with both types on the ship. The seas weren't really rough at any time, but one of the Radarmen was struggling with seasickness. We had a few onboard who were chronic and it made it difficult to substitute for the sick person on a continuous basis since every member of the crew had a specific job. Usually sailors with chronic seasickness were reassigned to shore duty. I could empathize with that sailor, even though I had never been seasick on any occasion; Scared, yes, many times, but not seasick.

Our Skipper, Lt. Commander J. E. Madacey, USCG

Our Captain was Lt. Commander J. E. Madacey, a graduate of the Coast Guard Academy at New London, Connecticut. He is now buried in Arlington Cemetery after dying while on active duty in 1957. The first time I met him was not a very auspicious occasion. Before we departed Houston, I was standing gangway watch with an Officer and a Petty Officer; I was the messenger. A message came for the Captain and I carried it to the Officers' Mess. They were having a meeting; all the officers were seated at the wardroom table, having coffee with the Captain. I knocked on the doorframe, the curtain was drawn, a voice told me to enter, and I did. I was a bit nervous, because this was my first time in Officers Country. The voice I heard was at the head of the table, asking me to state my business. I said I had a message for Mister Madacey. The man rose to his feet and said to me loudly in no uncertain terms, "Sailor, as long as you're aboard this ship, you will address me as CAPTAIN MADACEY." I said, "Aye, Aye Captain," handed him the message and got the hell out of there. The next time we met was on the bridge, when we were underway. He asked me how I was doing, and I replied, "Very well, Captain." It was his way of letting me out of the doghouse, after teaching me a bit of naval etiquette.

After weeks of intensive training, our Shakedown Cruise was completed. This didn't mean that our training was completed. During the daylight hours, we never knew when we would be called to General Quarters. The Captain and the other experienced Officers knew that all our lives were at risk and seconds honed off an exercise were the difference between life and death. Launching the depth charges when a submarine was detected, might force them to take evasive action and delay the German torpedoes coming toward us or a convoy we were there to protect. When our Radar spotted German aircraft, manning our anti-aircraft weapons quickly would protect the ship. It might have seemed that the drudgery of the constant exercises was wearing thin, but the Skipper knew what was needed. He was a war veteran who had already seen duty in Guadalcanal. The call to General Quarters extended to all hours of the day and the night. The whole crew was working like a well-oiled machine, and began to show what the Skipper expected of us, even though we were extremely tired.

Destroyer's Atlantic Fleet

Our Shakedown completed, the Ramsden was assigned to Destroyer Force, Atlantic Fleet, to operate as an escort vessel. We were about to become intimately involved in the Battle of the Atlantic, the longest continuous battle of World War II. We sailed to New York City for a two-day visit. I saw the Statue of Liberty close-up for the first time. I felt the same thrill as my ancestors had, and knew they all would be proud of me and brother, Gerald, for our efforts. Our ship was assigned to CortDiv 23 (Escort Division 23) and would be engaged in anti-submarine escort duty with our first convoy, NY-47. We formed up the convoy outside of New York harbor. The convoy consisted of heavily laden, large troop transport ships headed to Panama for passage through the Panama Canal. Their first stop after transiting the Canal would be Hawaii and then to the war in the South Pacific. Our complete round trip would take about 21 days.

The Panama Canal, Convoy NY-47 (New York to the Panama Canal)

This was the first time most of us would get a glimpse of the Canal. When we approached the entrance, we had to wait for the submarine nets to be opened. Some of the ships entered through the breakwater and anchored inside a large bay, some had to wait outside until there was room for them. The traffic was steady and ships were already traversing the Canal. The Escort Ships formed a screen toward the sea, the whole area being observed by aircraft stationed in the Canal Zone. Several Navy destroyers were also active and constant vigilance was required. It would have been a disaster of major proportions if the Canal was damaged and blocked for any length of time.

Our duty station on the trip was at the front of the convoy; several ships were aligned across the front and down the sides, with others covering the rear. The Sonar gear would project overlapping fans with the sound gear to cover the whole area. If a ship had a submarine contact it would be in a Hunter-Killer mode and the others would close ranks to cover its position, all on the alert at General Quarters, ready to pounce if necessary. If a German submarine were to get inside the convoy ring, we would be easy kills for it. The sub could let loose with its bow and stern torpedo tubes, almost certainly hitting a ship and, in the ensuing search confusion, try to slip away. My regular duty station at this early date was as a lookout on the bridge; at night it was on one of the starboard 20mm Oerlikon anti-aircraft guns, which was quite effective as a short-range surface weapon. During the daylight hours using the high power binoculars, I was able to view the decks of the nearby troop transports; I saw many of the soldiers leaning over the rails and upchucking in steady streams. This would be standard for all the ground-based troops on the convoy runs I was to be involved in.

When a ship approaches a port, the Captain of the ship radios ahead and requests a man called a Pilot, who knows all the problems and all the nautical hazards to be encountered when entering or leaving a port, a harbor or any navigable waterway. A Pilot Boat, with several of these experts aboard, usually meets the ships near the harbor entrance and a Pilot is taken aboard and assumes control of the ship until it is anchored or tied up to a dock. The Pilots had served years of apprenticeship and knew all the buoys, the location of all the docks, and were paid quite well for their knowledge. They worked in all kinds of weather and with many kinds of ships. The Pilot Boat was not very large and if it was tossed around quite a bit in stormy weather, when it came alongside, the Pilot had to be physically able to climb the ladder we hung over the side. Several times I'd seen how dangerous their job was, with both our boats rising and falling, except our Destroyer Escort was bigger. The Pilot took our ship to the Navy docks at the Coco Solo Naval Submarine Base, a couple of miles inside the protective breakwater and the anti-submarine nets. We were to be at the canal for three days, before heading back to New York.

Liberty Ashore in the Canal Zone

The Captain set a Port and Starboard liberty schedule. As soon as it was announced and we were tied up to the dock, a swarm of white-suited Starboard sailors hit the bricks for town. I was on the Port liberty schedule and had to wait until the next day. It turned out to be a better deal as we would quiz the Starboard sailors when they returned. Liberty was from 1200 to 2400. The first crew members had a ball and a few came back tipsy. No problems occurred and we were regaled with stories of the terrific night clubs and dancing girls, the souvenir shops, the best deals, and what to buy for the girlfriends or wives. The Navy, Marine and Army Shore Patrol were everywhere. Servicemen crowded the Canal Zone shops. One of the guys I went ashore with headed for the nearest tattoo shop. I went in with him and he chose a small eagle, wrapped in an American flag to be tattooed onto his shoulder. The artist gave him a shot of rum, took about 20 minutes to create the work of art, and then charged ten dollars. I asked the artist how much it would cost to draw my initials on my right forearm; he charged a dollar and gave me a shot of rum. I changed my mind about the tattoo after the war, and I have regretted it ever since, usually concealing it with a long sleeved shirt. I think the reason I haven't had it removed is to remind me that some choices in life remain for the rest of their days, for good or ill.

I went to a barbershop in the better part of the zone; the people were very pleasant and friendly. There seemed to be no shortage of anything, and the servicemen were buying everything that wasn't nailed down. One popular item was the Parker 51 fountain pen because it was rarely seen in the states and could be sold for twice the price in the states. The famous Chanel No.5 parfum seemed to be in everyone's locker. We were told to beware of counterfeits. My friend and I walked down one of the main streets and saw that the buildings were similar to store fronts, but the doorways looked just like double-swinging garage doors that we had at home. Standing in front of each doorway was a young and attractive woman. When one beckoned to us, she opened one of the doors and we saw a full bedroom in the brightly lit interior. She smiled and said, "Come see me honey." You didn't have to hit us with a ton of bricks to let us know we had stumbled into the Red Light District. The street was crowded with servicemen from every service, foreign and domestic. The Shore Patrol kept the foot traffic moving. Further on was a three-story building, with service men by the dozens milling around. We asked them what was going on, they told us this was the busiest place in the Red Light District. We all had been informed that anyone catching an STD would suffer dire consequences from Naval Command, so we quickly headed back to the downtown area and toured the shops and hit a few bars.

The drinks were cheap and each drink came with a young lady who wanted to sit on your lap, only if you bought her a drink. Many years later I mentioned the Canal Zone to a fellow worker, and he asked me if I had ever visited The Black Cat Bar. I told him I remembered the El Gato Negro bar, and it turned out we were at the same place. He said all the ladies got paid by the drink and the drinks cost the sailors five dollars. In the other bars, a beer was 25 cents and a mixed drink cost 50 cents. My budget was so slim all I did was drink the local beer and I walked back to the sub base in time to check in with rest of the crew.

While we were enjoying the balmy weather, we were inclined to think of our first convoy duty as a boring milk run. Although it seemed that way, with the volume of traffic traversing the canal in both directions, defense had to stay alert at all times because of the German submarine threat. For a real feel for what was happening, an educational and detailed account of the World War II naval battles in the Atlantic is titled "Coast Guard-Manned Naval Vessels in World War II," written by Robert Erwin Johnson.

Convoy Escort Duty to Europe and the Mediterranean

During World War II many news reporters came to the top of their profession. None was any better than the man who came to be known as the friend of the enlisted man, journalist Ernie Pyle. Ernie wrote a description of his trip aboard a Destroyer Escort, the USS Conklin DE-439, at Ulithi Atoll in the Philippine Sea in 1945. His words could easily have been describing my ship, the USS Ramsden DE-382. Sadly, on April 18, 1945, while reporting a battle, Ernie Pyle was fatally hit by Japanese gun-fire on an island near Okinawa during the fiercest battle of the South Pacific:

> "Drenched from head to foot with salt water. Sleep with a leg crooked around my rack so I won't fall out. Put wet bread under my dinner tray to keep it from sliding.

> A DE, my friend, is a Destroyer Escort. It's a ship long and narrow and sleek, something like a destroyer but a bit smaller.

> They are rough and tumble little ships. Their decks are laden with depth charges. They can turn in half the space of a destroyer. They roll and they plunge. They buck and they twist. They shudder and they fall through space. They are in the air half the time, under water half the time, the sailors say they should have flight pay and submarine pay both."

(Written by Ernie Pyle, 1945)

Edward J. Toczylowski, Ed, a fellow plank owner (original commissioning crewmember), and I served on Destroyer Escort USS Ramsden. Ed was three years older than me. He was a Motor Machinist Mate, and after the war, in a public newsletter for veterans, responded to a letter from a USS Ramsden crewmember of a later period, when the ship was assigned as Plane Guard Duty on the air routes in the Pacific Ocean, between Hawaii and Japan:

> " . . . . but when you say that life aboard the USS Ramsden was boring, I must agree that it could get boring. When you were aboard, it was Peacetime and the crew had nothing to do but paint, etc. You mentioned seeing the same movies over and over again, yes, that could be true, but we were aboard a battleship gray warship. We had no time to lie around doing nothing. We were on alert 24-hours a day, pulling watches for four hours on and four hours off, and some days eight hours or more, constantly going to General Quarters to be perfect for the day we went into action.

> When we were at sea escorting a convoy and chasing German submarines, it was not a dull life. This was the reason that the Ramsden was the best trained ship in the Flotilla. We gained the knowledge and the experience from that. We were out in rough seas. When you looked up, all you could see was water and sky. When you looked down you were sitting on a tidal wave and seeing space and water. We did have a few days that were dull. What did we do to offset it? We sacked in to catch up on our sleep or shoot dice and maybe play cards. I personally would love to go back into time and relive my sea duty.

> We were in both theatres, the European and Pacific. We sailed through the Panama Canal through to the Pacific Ocean, and believe me, we saw a lot of water and had plenty to do just to take our minds off what was going

on, and wondered whether we would ever get home to see our loved ones. *Semper Paratus.*"

(Ed Toczylowski, USS Ramsden
newsletter, Winter 1994)

We departed Panama with other Destroyer Escorts for a fast trip to New York; DE's were scarce and the other ships that were overworked and nearing exhaustion needed help. The DE's were being built with several types of engines. The Ramsden had Fairbank-Morse geared-diesel engines, rated at 6,000 horsepower and capable of at least 20 knots. Other DE's had steam turbines, and were rated at 12,000 horsepower, capable of 29 knots. On the way back from Panama, Captain Madacey and a Captain of one of our other DE's traveling to New York decided to see what the engines were able to do. We were both steaming along at about 15-18 knots. Our Captain asked the other to "let it out" (flank speed). We both signaled our engine rooms for Full Speed Ahead. The other DE took off like a shot; it was no contest! It really was necessary to know our top speed if we were called upon to assist each other in any way.

My daytime duty station was on the flying bridge as a lookout. I overheard one of the officers speaking about a problem he had in his communication division. It seemed one of the qualified Radarmen had chronic seasickness, and was unable to perform his duties. The Radar and the Sonar were two of the most important pieces of equipment on the ship, and without them the anti-submarine capability of the ship was compromised. We were several days out of New York, the nearest point to obtain a replacement Radarman. As I was leaving the bridge after being relieved, the two officers were directly behind me discussing the problem. I thought, "Here goes!" stopped and addressed them directly. I said, "Sir, I can do that job, I know exactly how to calibrate the equipment and call the distances on all targets on the PPI scope and the A-scope on the long range

Radar." He had a look of disbelief on his face and in the tone of his voice. He said, "Okay, smart guy show me."

We went to the Radar room behind the main bridge and wheelhouse. The SA Long Range Radar was not being used at that time. The officer said, "Go to it." I powered up the equipment, it had to stabilize. In those days solid state electronics wasn't even in the lexicon. All electronics were vacuum tube sets, and they required a lot of electricity and needed to heat up. I went through the procedure to calibrate the system. The officers were standing there with their mouths open. I finished the necessary procedures and operated all the parts to obtain the range and the bearings on the ships we were traveling with. I picked out a contact and switched the antenna to follow and lock on, even as we changed our compass heading. I gave him the true compass heading and the other heading as it related to the relative location to the ship. I spent about 30 minutes and showed him that I knew what I was talking about, and I did it well.

The other Radar set onboard was called a PPI type set, or a Planned Position Indicator. It had a circular scope, about 12-14 inches in diameter, with concentric circles, equal-distances apart, meeting at a common center. From the center was a sweep, from the center to the edge, which turned with the antenna on the mast. A radio signal was transmitted by the set to a highly directional point. If that transmitted beam hit any object in the area it was pointed, it would bounce back and be indicated on the scope as a dot called a "Blip." With the location of the blip on the face of the scope and its relationship to the lines etched on the lens covering the scope face, it was easy to determine the object's distance and location. The sweep traveled 360-degrees clockwise around the scope at a set speed. The operator could make the sweep reverse and make what looked like a piece of pie if the operator found something in an area he needed to concentrate on.

The Communications Officer called the Deck Division Officer and had me reassigned to his gang. I spent the next two days with them as they checked ranging and distances with a Stadimeter. This was a hand held instrument that the operator would point at the top of the ship's mast above the water and line up the twin prisms. The Stadimeter then would indicate the distance from our ship to the other. I passed these tests with flying colors and was placed in the Radar crew's watch rotation.

The other Radarmen were happy to have a full crew again. They gave me all the help they could, a tip here, a tip there; it really speeded my progress and in no time I had the full confidence of the officers who had the ship under their control, especially at night. When my twin brother, Gerry, and I compared notes after the war, we realized our skills on radar helped us do the same magical thing of predicting rain. If we spotted a rain cloud, we would plot its course and speed and determine if the ship would in time intercept the cloud. If it would, we would call the bridge and inform the con that the above deck watch should don their foul weather gear; it was one of the many independent actions Gerald and I found out we shared as twins.

We were steaming on a northerly course to New York and the ship was slightly north of the Delmarva Peninsula, off the coast of New Jersey. The Sonar was sweeping the whole area as usual and the Radar was active as always. I had a Radar contact on my screen. Our ship turned toward the contact and the other DE's were alerted. The contact was about five miles away and the blip was beginning to fade. Sonar swept the area for about 30 minutes and the DE's in our group were pinging in their areas. No other contacts were made. We secured General Quarters and returned to our course to New York. If it was a submarine, we spooked it.

New York, Again

On January 9, 1944, as we approached New York, a Pilot met the ship at sea and boarded from a Pilot ship. We put a ladder over the side for him to climb aboard. After he introduced himself to the Captain and the other officers, he took complete control of the ship as it entered the harbor, and was the Boss until we were ready to unload our explosives to enter the inner harbor. One of the many complexities that confronted a naval vessel was the tremendous amount of high explosives that were aboard the vessel. One of the ways the public was protected was for the ship to unload its explosives prior to entering a harbor. The crew under extreme time constraints had to unload all the ship's supplies of ammunition, whatever they may be, to a barge, or a remote dock. The whole enlisted crew was engaged in this activity and all realized that these explosives and more had to be reloaded prior to our ship leaving the port. The work was exhausting, but necessary.

We were to be in New York for two days, enough time for all of the crew to go ashore on liberty. Most of the sailors headed for a restaurant to have a big steak dinner and lots of fresh milk. Some had family and friends and wanted a taste of home. I was 17 years old, and I wanted to walk around Times Square to see what downtown life was like. I visited the statue of Father Duffy, a hero of World War I. He had helped carry stretchers of the wounded, the dead and the dying and gave the Last Rites to hundreds while serving as a chaplain during many deadly battles in Europe. New York had something for anyone's tastes. I went to the Automat in the middle of Times Square. It was a popular self-service cafeteria with marble floors and stained glass windows. The walls were lined with rows and rows of compartments with little glass doors; each one had a change slot. Drop the correct coins in the slot and the door would open. Just reach in and pull the item out onto your tray. The compartments contained everything from full meals to sandwiches and desserts. The prices were right for me. I then took off to find a nice bar for a nice cold glass of Ballantine's Ale. Not having any relatives to visit, except my Uncle Joe and his wife Annie, way out in Lynbrook on Long Island, I headed back to the ship around midnight. The whole crew had a great time and all made it back to the ship on time and in one piece.

We took on another Pilot and went to a fairly remote anchorage area. We hooked up to an anchor buoy and in a short time a Navy ammunition barge, came alongside. The whole crew was in work uniforms and we loaded up with all we had off-loaded, plus topped off the ammunition magazines above and below deck. The work was hard and long, but no one complained. The loading of some Hedgehog mortars was handled gingerly, they were mostly unfamiliar armaments. The barge and its tug took off to a distant Naval Ammunition Depot. With all the naval activity, they were more than busy.

Convoy UGS-30, United States to the Mediterranean

On January 11, 1944, we formed up our Escort division and a large group of merchant ships and the first large-scale convoy of LST's, (Landing Ship Tanks). At that time the LST was the largest of the ocean going amphibious landing ships. Later, it was joined in service by the other large ocean going amphibious ship, the LCI-L (Landing Craft Infantry-Large). Our convoy was UGS-30 and we were headed across the Atlantic for the Mediterranean. Little did I know that the LST would be a significant part of my Hooligan Navy career.

We had eight Coast Guard-manned Destroyer Escorts and a Navy Destroyer that comprised the Sonar and Radar defense screen. The convoy Commander was aboard the somewhat larger Destroyer. Our Captain did not relax any of his vigilance; training was a full-time part of our routine and we all strived to shave seconds off our General Quarters and Ready for Action times. Walter Palmer, now deceased, was a Gunner's Mate, First Class, who wrote a letter to the Destroyer Escort Sailors Association 50 years after the war. Walter knew that the sailors aboard the USS Ramsden were a disappearing breed, by reason of our ages. Walter was a former Navy man who had enlisted in the Navy prior to World War II and took his discharge prior to the attack on Pearl Harbor at Pearl on May of 1941. When war broke out he wanted aboard another Destroyer. The only guarantee he got was to help crew one of the Destroyer Escorts to be allocated to the Coast Guard. The Coast Guard was fortunate to get so many qualified sailors of different rates to switch to its service, and Walter was a good one. Walter mentioned that the USS Ramsden had the best-drilled gun crews of any of the ships he had served on, and he had served on three. Captain Madacey would have been proud, after the long hard efforts the officers and crew had put forth. We all knew our lives depended on knowing and doing our assignments well.

Our convoy UGS-30 was a couple of days at sea when our Radar picked up an aircraft contact about 50 miles away. We were close to the range of planes that covered the convoy routes. The plane checked out when I activated the automatic Identification Friend or Foe, IFF, system. The commander of the plane knew enough not to fly over the convoy. By this time all the ships and the Navy Armed Guard crews aboard the merchant ships were at General Quarters. The plane was not German Luftwaffe; it was a Navy PBM-Patrol Bomber. It signaled with its blinker light to the lead convoy escort. The blinking Morse code message could be read by any of the escorts. The Navy plane had a failure of its navigation systems and was unable to find its way. If they tried to fly by dead reckoning, a degree or two of compass heading could put them off course to nowhere; they were on the way to the island of Bermuda. The commander plotted their course to Bermuda for them. The Navy bomber crew thanked all, took the new heading and flew off.

I had a Radar contact one evening, and we had a few Sonar contacts, but engaged no enemy. I can't recall if we dropped any depth charge patterns on this phase of the voyage, but it was almost automatic if we had a viable contact. Submarines usually ran on the surface at night and recharged their batteries for submerged service. Their surface speed gave them the ability to cover greater distances and search for convoys. We left the screening of the convoy to investigate one Radar contact, after the other Escorts were informed to cover our Sonar screening area. The contact was steady on the Radar screen and we headed toward it. As we closed on the target, it did not trigger an answer to our IFF recognition code. This area of the Atlantic near the European and African continents was a tremendous fishing ground. When we closed to about five miles, the contact began to fade and slowly disappeared with each sweep of the antenna. We finally arrived at the area and the ocean and the Radarscope were empty. I was told that the Germans were using a high frequency radio device that could detect our Radar emissions. Once they detected any U.S. naval vessel, the Germans could inflate a foil-covered balloon with a slow leak, submerge and get the hell out of the area. The leaking balloon would sink and the Radar contact would be seen as another false echo. Since it was night, any contact was considered a danger and the crew was at General Quarters. Nothing was left to chance and the Sonar searched the area thoroughly until we rejoined the convoy. Better to lose some sleep than consider the alternative. When the British were tipped that the German submarines were listening for our radar emissions to warn of our presence, their electronic scientists discovered that the radio-like instruments the Germans used would also give off emissions our side could detect. Checkmate.

The weather was blustery and rainy at times and the sea was in turmoil many days. We encountered a major storm that stove in the shield of the Number One 3-inch/50 on the bow. The storm was so bad I thought we would founder. The water that came over the bow bent that gun shield like it was a piece of paper. The storm lasted for about four days, and the crew ate only cold-cut sandwiches. Whenever the ship would change course and run across the waves, the ship would roll to such a degree I thought it would never come back, and then it would roll the other way. The ship seemed to stay in this position for what seemed an eternity and then shudder and start the opposite way. When I tried to sleep in my bunk, it was so bad I placed the straps that held the mattress to the bunk frame across my back; they were made of a heavy cotton canvas material and were adjustable with heavy metal clamp-like hooks. The hooks were supposed to hold onto the pipe frame of the triple tier bunks; during the storm, they kept me from being thrown out on to the deck.

During a storm, and there were many bad winter storms in the North Atlantic, life lines were installed to use if a sailor had to venture out on deck. No one I ever saw went out unless it was a mandatory emergency situation. Even though heavy cable and heavy netting was attached to stanchions was all around the ship, when the waves broke over the ship it would be death-defying being outside.

The guns were manned 24-hours a day, no matter the weather. The only gun crews that had to stand-by inside, at the ready, were the crews manning the weapons forward of the bridge. During heavy weather, tons of water broke over these positions continuously. All standing deck watches were dressed in this manner: long woolen underwear; dungarees and chambray shirt; heavy woolen socks, long sleeve turtle neck sweater; long weather proof and insulated bib type overalls; zippered and button jacket, with a hood attached. Finally a wool watch hat and a olive green rubberized canvas waterproof pants with a waist draw cord and the same type pull over jacket with another hood. All this outerwear had snap type buttons on the cuffs, legs and the neck. A facemask with eyeholes and a piece to snap across the mouth, storm boots and double-thick insulated leather gloves completed the outfit.

The duty watches were of four hours duration with eight hours off, unless attack was imminent and then it could be four and four. The threat of air attacks caused the crew to sleep and eat at their gun positions. The winter watches were the worst; it was easy to see that if the worst happened, anyone that had to leave the ship for any reason had a short life expectancy. No one dwelled on this subject, but it was there.

The gun crew members and the officers on the flying bridge exposed to the weather were relieved every hour or so to seek shelter and have a sandwich and a hot steaming cup of joe. I remember just holding the large white porcelain navy cup; the heat of the coffee cup felt as if it was lifesaving and it was almost punishment to return to the gun station. At night no white lights are allowed inside the ship; all the night-lights were red because exposure to the ordinary light destroyed our night vision. If we had to go into a regular lighted area we wore goggles with a red filter, covering the face tightly. One's night vision could be lifesaver when watching for the enemy. The goggles were required even for lighting a cigarette on break. Almost every sailor smoked; it seemed everyone owned a Zippo lighter.

The food was served below decks in the combination sleeping and mess deck. The food was prepared top side and served below. In stormy weather the chow line was by the galley and top side if the large quantities necessary to feed 200 or more couldn't be carried below. When the galley closed down due to a thrashing storm, sandwiches had to suffice. Quite a few lost some weight during stormy times; it was difficult to get past the odors of seasickness, even for the ones not afflicted.

It was during this period that I had the Radar duty alone. I had confidence in my ability, as did the duty officers I worked with. I detected a changing target inside the first two columns of ships. I would see it, and then it would fade, see it and fade. It seemed to keep pace with the convoy's speed. I called the bridge and we immediately went to General Quarters. The Communications Officer came running into the Radar room to verify my contact; he saw what I had reported. The problem was that we had to get into the middle of that column, and with the bad weather and the churning seas, it was a hazardous assignment. All the ships in the convoy and all the other escorts went to General Quarters.

The proper configuration of ships in a convoy, with all things being equal, was a spacing of 500 yards on all sides, fore and aft and starboard and port. For Radar purposes we considered 2000 yards to be a mile. I wasn't in a panic mode, but I was in an unfamiliar situation and the thought that I was to direct our ship between the other ships to enter the alley, as it were, was not a pleasant thought, especially in the dark of night and in a stormy environment. The Communications Officer relieved me of the responsibility and took over the Radar. It was to be some tense moments and I felt that he was unsure of my abilities. I had news for him, so was I! The Radar target continued its pace inside the convoy, bobbing and fading, and then the convoy's speed overcame its progress. It seemed to be the classic example of a submarine that had gotten into the convoy and was waiting for its opportunity. I'm sure that everyone in the convoy had a dry mouth. The convoy's speed was no more than 10 knots, at best. A submarine, submerged, had a top speed of about 8 knots. We fell behind the convoy and still had the target as the convoy continued on, all sleepless and wide-eyed at General Quarters. During the hours of darkness the convoy had moved away from us. When dawn broke, the Sonar crew could not establish a contact; it never did ping anything during the night. Our Radar still had the contact and the ship made a Hedgehog attack approach. Sonar still had no echoes. There was thought that it could be a floating mine. We were towing an anti-submarine device, code name Foxer; it made a noise in our wake, as defense against any acoustic torpedo the Germans could fire at us.

The sun rose and the object was spotted with binoculars. Our mystery Radar contact turned out to be a 55-gallon drum, probably part of the cargo of a sunken freighter. Most of it was underwater and it went up and down with the wake of passing ships and waves. Its progress through the sea was affected by its catching the wind when it rose in the sea, following the currents. The drum was photographed and one of the gunners mates fired at it as it slowly sank. Better a false alarm than being dead. The other Radarmen gave me a pat on the back and an "attaboy" from those men was all this 17-year-old needed.

The Strait of Gibraltar

The Strait divides Spain and Morocco and the continents of Europe and Africa. A channel about eight miles wide, with a depth of about 1000 feet traverses the center of the Strait. Entering the Strait was always a daytime procedure and the speed of the escorts and convoy vessels was adjusted to go through the channel. Prior to landfall, our Radar had a contact blip on the screen. With the Ramsden crew at General Quarters, we approached the target that was determined to be a fishing trawler. With all guns manned, we searched the area with our Sonar. The fishing trawler was suspiciously in a direct line with the channel entrance. The officers examined the boat visually and the Captain called for any of the crew who spoke Spanish or Portuguese to report to the bridge. One Ramsden crewmember, from New Bedford, Mass., spoke Portuguese fluently, and used the loud hailer to relay questions from our Captain. The whole crew of the fishing trawler was lined up along the rail for inspection. The questions were answered satisfactorily, and we continued our sweep, releasing the fishing trawler. The Ramsden, on full alert, returned to the convoy. With our convoy being a super prime target, the fishing boat was in the wrong place at the wrong time. The crew really looked nervous, and had a right to be; they came that close to being attacked by the Ramsden weapons.

We had Radar contact of the continent at about 60 miles and had a visual at about 25 miles. As we approached Spain, to port, we could see the green rolling hills that sloped to the ocean. Even though I could see the beauty of the Spanish countryside, I thought of the Germans sitting on those slopes, counting the ships and reporting on our UGS-30 convoy. The escorts circled the convoy vessels. We entered into the Mediterranean with other escorts to create a Sonar screen on all quarters. The merchant ships and the large LST contingent entered under our protection. We were met by a combined British contingent and saw a British Anti-Aircraft Cruiser bringing up the rear. The ships were now in range of the German Heinkle long-range bombers and sub forces in the Mediterranean, as well as the Atlantic. We turned the convoy over to the new group of protectors, and withdrew our escort force from the Mediterranean. With the Germans being able to view the comings and goings through the Strait from the nearby shores of Spain, it was expected the convoy would come under Luftwaffe air attack around sundown. We hoped for the best for our convoy and its crews.

Refueling at Sea

During our transatlantic trip we had the opportunity to refuel at sea. For me, it was one of the most amazing procedures to witness and be a part of, fraught with danger and high excitement. The original idea was conceived and developed by Admiral Chester Nimitz in his early days. The exercise was conducted by one of the hardest working sailors it was my pleasure to meet, Boatswains Mate First Class, Henry H. Winiarski. Henry was a regular Coast Guardsman as opposed to most of us being reservists. Under the direction of a Chief Bos'n Mate, Henry was in charge of everything above deck, including lowering and retrieving the motor whaleboat while the ship was underway. He freely taught his craft to the other sailors by his example. He and the other Deck Petty Officers knew their business. I remember his name because he really stood out from the crowd.

Refueling and Underway

A tanker and our ship to be refueled had to be sailing on parallel courses and not too far apart. Then a thin string line attached to a long brass bolt (rod) was shot from a rifle-like launcher, to the other ship and attached to subsequent larger lines until the final heavy one was attached to a large fuel hose. The fuel hose was suspended on pulleys at various intervals along the main line and hauled onto our ship, with crews on both ships maintaining enough slack on both ends for the hose to be connected to each other's fuel tanks. The distance between the ships had to be maintained, regardless of weather. It might sound simple, but it required absolutely perfect seamanship from both crews. The tanker crews were the most expert, having to do refueling so often. By the way, the safety railings were removed during this operation, making the operation more dangerous. The operation was carried on with the crew-handlers wearing their bulky life jackets. Sometimes 16mm movies would be swapped and mail passed over after refueling. Occasionally a person in a breeches buoy canvas seat would be transferred between ships.

Casablanca, French Morocco

Leaving the Strait of Gibraltar and steaming into the Atlantic, our group of escorts proceeded on a southern course to Casablanca for refueling and provisioning before our return trip to the United States. During World War II, Casablanca was one of the three major landing places in the invasion of North Africa by Allied Forces. As we entered the huge harbor, one of the largest in Africa, we saw the American, British and Free French flags being flown on the many ships tied up at piers and at anchor. When we tied up to our dock, we saw a sunken French battleship at its dock. It didn't appear to have sustained much damage, but our view was partially blocked by other ships. Its name was the Jean Bart and prior to that time it was a prime part of the Free French Navy surrendered to the Germans.

The USS Massachusetts BB-59 battleship had sunk it at the dock from 14 miles at sea, with its 16-inch guns, when the initial Allied Forces landings took place.

After our ship was secured and all duty assignments were staffed, shore parties were allowed and a limited number of the sailors from each section were granted liberty from 1000 hours until an early curfew time of 1700 hours. It was determined that it was still not safe for American military to be out and about after dark. Although most of the people living in the area were thought to be friendly, several sailors had been killed while ashore and the commanders required the liberty seekers to travel in groups. A stern lecture was given to all on the religious practices of the Muslim population and the serious attention they would give to anyone who showed disrespect to any of their women. It was forbidden to accost a woman wearing a veil and the long robes; a violation of this nature could be dangerous to one's future. A notice was given to all ships that a sailor's body had been found on the harbor breakwater, sexually mutilated as a warning.

Before the liberty parties went ashore in Casablanca, we were warned not to try to sell anything on the Black Market ashore. A 10-pack carton of American cigarettes that sold on the ship for one dollar could be sold for one dollar per pack ashore. American-made Parker 51 brand fountain pens worth about five dollars aboard ship were selling for fifty dollars or more ashore. Cotton bunk mattress covers could be sold for five dollars. Other items were mentioned as contraband, and the officers made it clear the penalty for dealing in the Black Market was a General Court Marshal offense, no if's, and's, or but's.

Military flatbed trucks with side racks took us to the downtown part of the city. The traffic was very heavy, jammed with the movement of war supplies and dockworkers. I was smoking, as were most of the others; I think that every man in the service smoked. We passed a low flatbed trailer taking local dockworkers to town. They were sitting with their feet dangling over the side of the trailer, just a few inches off the pavement. One of the sailors threw a cigarette butt away, and about four of the dockworkers jumped off and ran to get the butt, just missing being run over by the following vehicles. I had never seen someone put their life in jeopardy for a crummy cigarette butt. The dockworker scooping up the cigarette butt had a big smile on his face, and they all ran to catch up with their trailer. It was easy to see why a dollar per pack was the going Black Market rate.

We got to town and left the truck, meeting up with other groups of military personnel taking in the sights. We talked about going to the Casbah, a bazaar. A 1938 movie titled, "*Casbah*," starring Charles Boyer and Hedi Lamarr, was a love story and had been a big hit on the silver screen. The exotic Casbah became the buzzword for a tempting and mysterious place, with hidden pleasures. All the sailors were eager to enter. In this part of Morocco it was known as the Medina, but the Americans considered it the Casbah, and were curious to see it.

The older part of Casablanca was a walled city. A large archway opened to the bazaar; shops were on each side of a fairly wide brick street. The storefronts were all decorated with the products for sale. The shop owners were all yelling at us that they had the best merchandise and the best prices. Just after we entered, a local boy about ten years old approached us and offered his services as a guide for a couple of dollars. He would direct us to the better shops, and would tell us if the product was worth the price or not. This was my first exposure to bargaining. I didn't carry much cash, primarily because I didn't have much to spend. Our group of crewmen from the USS Ramsden went into one of the leather goods shops. We had been told that the leather industry was a home-type operation and excellent tanned leather at bargain prices was available. I think back and car dealers from the United States must have come here for their training! Several of the sailors were interested but the prices were too high. One sailor looked at a leather cover for a hassock. It was just a cover, and needed filling to become a hassock. He didn't buy it. After we left the shop, the boy we hired as a guide pulled the hassock cover from under his clothes and wanted to sell it for half the price the shopkeeper wanted. He did this in all the shops the sailors went in until we left the Medina. I watched him like a hawk and never saw how he was stealing. Amazing, and he was just a kid!

A few of our group purchased what the kid had shoplifted; each time the item was half the price of the bargaining price. We speculated that the kid picked up the merchandise from the owner after we left the shop and sold it to us at the real price that the shopkeeper would have charged. The kid came running up to me as we were returning to the Ramsden; he had something wrapped in soft tissue paper. He unwrapped it carefully, revealing an ornate carved men's gold ring. I asked him the price, and five dollars seemed like a real bargain. I bought it, rewrapped it, stuck it in my pocket and congratulated myself on my shrewd purchase. I put it on the next day and wore it until the sea air made my hand turn green; it was a great piece of brass. Pretty, but it was brass, not gold.

As we wandered through the Medina, I noticed that each shop had a stairway at the back for the living quarters above. The street was about twenty feet wide and there was a V-shaped sort of channel running down the middle of the street. I learned later that this was their sewer system; it had a constant flow of material in it. We passed several storefronts and several of the military, sailors included, seemed to be bargaining with the owner in front. I walked over and looked in; it had several single beds with curtains in between. Sitting on the beds were girls, probably no older than thirteen or fourteen, tops. They were prostitutes, just children.

A small group of us returned to modern downtown Casablanca; it had a French influence and several hotels with nice bars. We ordered beer and it turned out to be very good. We sat around enjoying the scenery and ogling the European ladies. They all were well-dressed, American style, and accompanied by French officers.

I left the party to go to the men's room. I was expecting the usual bathroom facilities. To my surprise it wasn't usual at all. It was a shared bathroom, with no separate compartments, just several white porcelain tiles about two feet square with two footprints cast in to them and a large hole at the rear to carry away the waste. As I was leaving, an Army Captain entered. He had a brown leather riding crop, or a swagger stick, that I had seen other British officers carrying. I mentioned that it looked real sharp. He said, "You really don't know how sharp it is." He grabbed it with both hands, and pulled it apart. One leather scabbard end came off and exposed an eight-inch sword. It was undetectable as a weapon. He said in warning, "Never travel alone." I got the message.

We all returned to the Ramsden before curfew and I was happy to be back onboard. Some of the crew had many souvenirs for wives and girlfriends. We stayed for about three days; the ship provisioned and refueled for our return trip to the United States. We had no idea what our next port of call was and where the next convoy would take us. The Captain and the Officers were the only personnel privy to that information. Being so close to the continent made the Radar and the Sonar operators stay on their toes and made everybody else nervous. Our Allied Air Force patrolled part of the return voyage. It wasn't until late 1943 that long range Radar-equipped planes could sneak up on a submarine that had surfaced out at sea. Many subs were surprised by British Radar-equipped long range Lancaster bombers. Air support for the convoys improved with the introduction of Escort Aircraft Carriers, nicknamed "jeep carriers." The jeep carriers were small converted merchant ships with space for about 10-15 planes. Anyone who saw them was amazed that a plane could take off or land on them, but the pilots did it with a lot of expertise. Their aerial surveillance contributed greatly to anti-submarine warfare, especially on the convoy runs from the area of Iceland to England. There was a hole in the air coverage until long range air protection was inaugurated late in the war. The joint efforts of the small jeep carriers, the larger Escort carriers, the long range patrols from Bermuda, the Azores and our bases in Africa gave us a certain amount of comfort, even though the German submarines tried to intercept our convoys on their way to the Mediterranean.

Chances for successful convoy transits improved as the Allies continued to crack the codes generated by the German Enigma cypher machine. The messages from Admiral Doenitz, the German submarine group commander, were intercepted when he communicated to his wolf packs. The Americans discovered they could accurately pinpoint the origin of submarine radio transmissions using High Frequency Direction Finder, HF/DF, and nicknamed "huff-duff," to obtain the sub's bearings. With the assistance of other HF/DF units to form a triangulation plot, our naval forces continued to locate the packs and even if depth charge runs didn't sink them, having to stay submerged destroyed their chances of communicating with each other to locate the convoys, deterring torpedo attacks.

On the return, long before the Ramsden made landfall, our Radar picked up Navy blimps far out to sea, patrolling the sea lanes. We were heading for Charleston, South Carolina, home of a large Navy blimp force. I had never been to this city, but it was supposed to be a beautiful city. Usually when I got off Radar watch during the day, I would exit to the bridge and call up the speaking tube to the officer at the con, requesting permission to relieve the man at the wheel. Having done this many times before, the helmsman got a break and a smoke. The ship handled easy and quick; I sometimes used the joystick, but it reacted faster than the wheel. It was easy to maintain a compass heading, and the con let me take her into the harbor. The helmsmen thought I was crazy, but I was one happy hooligan.

Welcome to Charleston, South Carolina

Charleston, South Carolina, was situated on a narrow, low-lying peninsula between the Ashley and Cooper rivers, at the head of a broad bay leading to the Atlantic Ocean. Usually the first thing we did on liberty was head for a nice low-priced restaurant, and if a steak was available, we got the biggest one on the menu. On the way to the restaurant, I felt waves of nausea coming over me, but they passed. I mentioned it to a couple of my mates and they said that after a long time on the ship, the inner ear had gotten used to the constant rolling and pitching of the ship. The ear's ability to do this controlled the primary cause of seasickness. We all had great steaks and shared a large pitcher of cold fresh milk. We had finished our meals and were trying to decide the next course of action, when I was overwhelmed by a nausea attack so strong I was in the throes of vomiting. I had my white sailor hat and turned it inside out quickly to deposit my regal meal in it. The hat saved my clothes and the surroundings. I made for the restroom on the run, dumped the hat and washed it in the sink. I was embarrassed, and my crewmates had some choice words for me. It was lucky that the restaurant's business was slow and we were hardly noticed. Fifty years later my wife, Lorraine, and I had a similar experience on returning from a two week cruise through the Panama Canal, although it was just waves of nausea, thank goodness, until our inner ears became accustomed to being back on land.

Charleston lived up to its billing. It was a beautiful city in every respect. The beautiful homes and buildings were preserved or restored. It was nice to see that the people recognized what they had, and spared no expense on their architecture. Walking down the street past the beautiful houses, I had the feeling I was in Antebellum Charleston. Most of the visiting sailors went looking for a watering hole and Charleston, like most seaports, had its share. All the bars in the preserved downtown area were nice, well appointed and reasonable. The residents put out the welcome mat for all who cared to behave. We met more of our crew as we traveled about and we had a good time. Although overseas local beer wasn't as cold and tended toward the flat side, I always felt I never had a bad glass of beer or ale on liberty; it was a chance to recharge ourselves after the tension of escorting the convoy.

We all ended up at a bistro with live music. On the ship we listened to Armed Forces Radio with the music of the day, Glenn Miller, Tommy and Jimmie Dorsey's orchestras. When at sea and off duty, I would use the Navigator's earphones to listen to the radio when he wasn't using them. The radio had several bands and it was interesting to be far at sea and be able to pickup and identify the regular stations by their call letters. We were able to pickup a World War II German propaganda personality, by the name of Axis Sally. She had all the latest American and British music but her programs were laced with talking designed to alarm anyone away from home. She spoke of the infidelity of wives whose husbands were away at war and the grand purpose of Hitler and his forces. Once in awhile she would shock the listeners and mention their military groups by name and speak of their coming annihilation. I can't think of anyone who heard her tripe express any anxiety. We just liked the music.

When we were leaving the Charleston Navy Yard for shore liberty, we passed a former U.S. Navy older destroyer, now flying the English Naval Ensign. Many of these four-stack ships were given to Britain prior to our entering the war under the Lend-Lease program. As we were passing the ship tied up to the dock, I saw a torpedo on its deck with the warhead removed. It wasn't unusual to see this. When we returned later that evening, the immediate area of that ship was roped off. A small group of naval officers were standing around the area. When we got aboard our ship, we were told that a British crewmember with a machinist hammer in his hand, walked by the torpedo, and struck the end of the propulsion tank. The tank was under great pressure and exploded, immediately killing the British sailor. We all wondered how his family would be notified of his accidental death, so far away from home.

We stayed in Charleston for about two days and departed with a group of escorts for New York. We headed for the Brooklyn Navy Yard for some storm damage repairs from the crossing to the Mediterranean. When the weather was sunny and the sea was smooth, I would watch the flying fish jumping and gliding for a short airborne flight. Occasionally, five or six dolphins in a pod would ride the pressure wave from the bow ahead of the ship. It seemed as if they were playing with us and sometimes, as they swam along-side the bow, you had the sense they could see you watching them. They were truly beautiful and I watched them for hours when I was off duty.

Brooklyn Navy Yard

We arrived at New York on February 23, 1944, without incident although several Sonar contacts were made with some depth charge activity, but no hits. We picked up our Pilot and proceeded directly to the Brooklyn Navy yard after unloading all our depth charges and ammunition to a waiting Navy barge attached to a Navy tug. We were scheduled for immediate attention to our storm damages, removing the three torpedo tubes and adding more anti-aircraft weapons. I remember the Navy Yard was active 24-hours a day, at a fierce pace. It had the largest traveling cranes I ever saw, moving on huge wheels and tracks along the various docks. They looked like the head of a hammer, reaching to the sky, hence their name, hammer head cranes. As soon as the Ramsden tied up, the workers swarmed over the ship with cables, hoses and equipment. The work they had to do was already coordinated, and they went at it. The Captain had announced Port and Starboard liberty as we were coming to the Navy Yard. All going ashore were washed, polished and ready to go almost as soon as we tied-up; they never moved so fast, except at General Quarters!

One of the entrances to the Navy Yard was called the Sand Street gate. There were many "Ladies of the Evening" standing around looking for dates. Many sailors walked arm in arm with them toward the bar-lined street. While at sea, I had celebrated my 18th birthday on February 15 and had saved some money for liberty. Large billboards on top of the buildings around the docks advertised the best prices and materials for custom tailored uniforms, with special prices for summer uniforms, whites, or heavy-weight blue serge for winter dress outfits. All of the tailors guaranteed 24-hour delivery. The wool winter uniforms were rayon lined with appliqués inside the cuffs and the back, with anything your heart desired. Most sailors had dragons on the part of the cuff that could be rolled back, all in bright and flashy colors. I asked a few sailors which uniform shop was the reliable one and they all mentioned the same company! I went to the shop where they took my measurements, gave me the price of $35.00 and arranged delivery for the next afternoon. Sailors opted for the custom made for better fit, and the heavier quality serge material held a press better. Navy issues were one size fits all; the uniforms looked like they needed a draw string at the waist and had no bell in the leg. The tailored uniforms just looked so much better than the regular issue, and it was easy tell an old salt from a boot camp arrival. I picked the uniform up the next afternoon and the fit was just as promised.

I mentioned the Sand Street entrance to the Brooklyn Navy Yard because later in life an old work mate in civilian life, Jimmie Dunn, mentioned that was where he met his wife, who was a member of the U.S. Navy WAVES (Women Accepted for Volunteer Emergency Service). He was on the Battleship Texas for the invasion of Europe in June 1944, and later the invasion of Okinawa, south of Japan, the next year in April 1945. He was a natural comedian and a fantastic baseball player. His hero growing up in Camden, New Jersey, was Lou Gehrig. Jimmie played baseball in Phoenix with his high school coach who had also moved to Arizona. They played ball every Sunday morning, until the coach passed on several years ago. Later in life Jimmie entered into the Senior Olympics in the Phoenix area and was never beaten in any race he entered. He always said, "At my age there isn't much competition left."

When Jimmie retired from the Post Office, the crew had a party for him at a local Italian Restaurant. I had never met his wife, Dot, before. She complemented him by her happy go lucky view of life. I thought it was a golden opportunity for a joke. When we were introduced, I looked at her in a quizzical way and asked her if she had ever been at the Brooklyn Navy Yard. She said, "Yes, why?" I said, "Didn't I see you at the Sand Street gate?" She knew exactly what I meant. In an instant, she cracked up and almost rolled on the floor. Jimmie almost had a convulsion! Sadly, they have both passed on.

The Brooklyn Navy Yard operated 24-hours a day. Getting the Escort ships back into service was high priority. I came back from liberty one night, probably close to midnight. The ship was overrun with civilian and military workers at various jobs. I walked into my sleeping compartment and a worker was asleep in my bunk. To make matters worse, he had his greasy shoes and greasy coveralls on. I grabbed him with both of my hands and rolled him onto the deck; it wasn't difficult, because I had the lower of the triple tier bunks. He awoke with a start. I told him to get back to work or I would turn him in. I got no protest from him. I changed my greasy mattress cover to a clean one so I would pass inspection. From then on, when I left the ship any other time, I put the fire cover on the mattress.

Another time a worker was selling chances on his paycheck, worth about $75 with his overtime hours. All day, for 50 cents, he took anyone's name and ship, and he paid off to the lucky sailor if the ship was still in the yard. He must have made a bundle. I think back on safety in the yard at the time. Sometimes the crew would find that work done in the ship's interior involved the pipes and the walls, which were covered with white-painted asbestos. It wasn't until forty years later that health science determined the dust released caused of lung cancer, Mesothelioma. My twin brother, Gerry, was exposed to it during his 23 years of Navy service. The asbestos dust was everywhere onboard, on the bunks, on the decks and in the air. We would sweep it with a broom, further spreading this deadly rock dust. Years later, it was proven that the wives of the ship builders who worked with it or around it were dying of the disease just from washing their husband's clothes.

All the work on the ship had been completed, including replacing the quarter-inch steel shield that almost completely surrounded the forward 3-inch/50 that had been flattened by the storm waves coming over the bow. Six pieces of heavy I-beam were shaped and welded to the deck and then welded to the new steel shield. If that didn't work, nothing would. The other work was the removal of the three torpedo tubes amidships. It was decided that the addition of more anti-aircraft weapons made more sense and additional 20mm and 40mm weapons took the place of the torpedo tubes. Other work was done in various areas and we were getting ready to return to our escort missions. With the Mediterranean area being heavily supplied, escorts were needed badly. We moved out to the outer harbor, met the ammunition barge and filled all the magazines and depth charges; it was heavy-duty labor and took most of the day to load.

Air Cover in the Ocean Gap

German submarines, U-boats, were being supplied and refueled between Europe/Africa and the United States in an area south-southwest of the Azores Islands in the Atlantic. This area was chosen because it was in the gap not protected by anti-submarine hunter-killer aircraft. What the Germans soon learned was that we were now sending out Escort Aircraft Carriers, CVEs. By the summer of 1943 the CVEs were built on freighter hulls. One class was the Bogue class; others in the class were the Card, Core, Croatan, and Block Island. They were about 500 feet in length and about 15,000 tons. They had a range of 27,000 miles and were capable of making 15 knots. The aircraft they carried were 18 torpedo bombers and 16 fighters. The Carrier came equipped with

5-inch/38 surface or AA guns and 20mm and 40mm anti-aircraft weapons. Before the Escort Aircraft Carrier, air protection was limited to short range coverage from Charleston, North Carolina, and the Naval Airbase on Hamilton Island in Bermuda.

Convoy UGS-36 United States to Bizerte, Tunisia

The next assignment for the Ramsden was a convoy to Bizerte, Tunisia. We started out as 26 ships and four escorts from New York on March 10, 1944, to Norfolk, Virginia. We joined 79 ships and 12 escorts at Cape Henry, Virginia, the southern end of the opening to Chesapeake Bay. The convoy formed up at sea and consisted of 105 ships and 12 escorts. The first evening the seas were rough, but the ships in the convoy had all formed up into 12 columns wide and eight columns long; four Destroyer Escorts and one Navy Destroyer made up the front Sonar screen. Way off to the starboard flank were two Destroyer Escorts, the USS Ritchey DE-385 leading and the USS Savage DE-386 following in line. Leading on the port flank was our ship, the USS Ramsden DE-382, followed in line by the British Destroyer, HMS Tomick. Following at the rear of the convoy and completing the Sonar and Radar screen were three Navy Destroyers, the USS Edwards DD-216, the USS Alden DD-211 and the USS Whipple DD-217. The ships being protected were obliged to maintain a distance of 500 yards fore and aft and port and starboard of each other. We were a huge Allied vessel convoy, a prime target for the Germans. An attack was just a matter of time and every sailor knew it.

Station keeping for the ships was maintained with Radar. The merchant ships in the middle of the convoy usually didn't have Radar, and it was difficult for them to keep station; each had a wake light to help keep the ships in columns from colliding. It could only be seen by the following ship, with difficulty, and did not compromise the safety of the convoy at night.

The Convoy Commander made sure that the escorted ships maintained a tight formation, especially during the day and as soon as dawn approached all the merchant ships strived to tighten up the formation. Our communications were restricted to blinker signal lights and Morse code. All the escort vessels had a short-range radio called TBS, meaning talk between ships, but its use was minimal; with atmospheric help the TBS transmissions could skip over the open waters for many, many miles and compromise our security.

The only ships that were a liability in a convoy were the older freighters. Their engines were constantly breaking down, forcing them to drop out of the convoys. A vessel dropping out of the protection of the convoy was almost certainly going to be attacked by the German subs who were trailing to the rear of big convoys to pick off the stragglers. Each day a ship or two, even the newer LST's, would have some problem and one of the destroyer escorts would come along side, find out the trouble, the time to fix it and return to its convoy station.

It would take about three weeks for the convoy to cross the Atlantic, if we maintained speed. Fresh water was usually rationed. One could wash up at the sinks, but showers were turned off until the Captain was sure that the supply was sufficient for the whole crew. Members of the Black Gang, the engine room crew, were allowed to shower off the coal dust after their shift was over. Strict observance of the water hours was absolutely mandatory. The crew was obliged to wash their clothes in a bucket with salt water and an item called salt-water soap; you couldn't raise suds if you rubbed it all day long. Most of the crew tried to adjust, but a few didn't try. Many of the sailors had Athletes Foot fungus on their feet. The skin between the toes would become inflamed and cracked. It seemed as if there was no cure, and a few had to be hospitalized with horrible and painful feet. The fungus was usually spread by walking barefoot in the shower. It was Navy policy that a trough partially filled with a weak solution of bleach was walked through before and after a shower. Most sailors had wooden clogs they wore in the heads, and the bleach solution kept the exposure down significantly. One Radioman had a serious case of Athletes Foot and he kept washing his feet in the sinks in the heads. The Skipper found out and ordered him to stop immediately and to use a laundry bucket to wash and treat his feet. I had always walked through the bleach solution and after drying off I powdered my toes and feet with the Quinsana anti-fungal powder sold at the Ship's Service Store. Quinsana was considered a must in every sailor's kit. It was such a good product I always kept some around years after I left the military.

Our practice drills during the daylight hours continued unabated, to keep an edge on our skills. Quite a number of the crew wrote letters every day, mostly to their wives or girlfriends. I tried to write to my mother at least once a week, but it was difficult to find many different ways I could say "I miss you and hope everyone is OK."

The weather the first week, except for the first day, had been sunny and bright. Then we hit a winter storm. The seas became rough; the waves were breaking over the bow. The flat bottomed LST's were tossing and turning, but they were capable of using water for ballast to keep them lower in the water. It helped some, but it still was rough considering they had cargo above decks and on their tank/cargo deck below. The LST's ability to regulate ballast for different circumstances was what made it invaluable for landing operations and made it one of the two truly amphibious ocean-going landing craft of WW II. The weather continued to worsen; sometimes we couldn't tell the rain from the ocean spray coming over the ship. The cooks and bakers shut down the galley and only served baloney sandwiches. The waves were 30 to 40 feet high and the DE's and DD's spent more time in the air than in the water. Sometimes the ships would disappear from view; it felt like we were riding on a roller coaster. There were times the bow was buried in the water and the stern was up in the air. When the screws would be clear of the water, the motormen working the throttles in the engine room had to back off the power, so as not to damage the engines. The officer at the con had to be alert and relay orders to the engine room. We had to have faith in the ship weathering the storm, especially when trying to sleep in a bunk, with feet wrapped around the chains that held it.

Torpedo Junction

Two weeks had passed and the Convoy had traveled approximately 3100 miles. Our Radar picked up what appeared to be four ships headed our way. The IFF Recognition Code was correct. The three British ships joined up, a British Aircraft Carrier and two British Corvettes, the HMS Speed and the HMS Colombo. They dropped behind the convoy bringing up the rear, almost beyond the horizon. We were now in an area the military called Torpedo Junction.

The weather changed to sunny as we passed north of the Madeira Islands off the coast of Africa. The crews, topside on most of the other ships, were working without shirts, happy to be through the storm. Sixteen days and 3300 miles out, now approaching the Strait of Gibraltar, one of the escorts picked up a submarine on Sonar and made a run toward it. The escort dropped ten depth charges in all and returned to the convoy. All ships were in a high state of alert and we could see the crews of some of the convoy ships, all topside wearing their life jackets. From that moment on, the crews of the escorts and the armed ships were on four hours on/four hours off shifts. General Quarters was automatic at 0530 hours and 1900 hours, one hour before sunrise and one hour after sunset, for the duration of our time in these enemy waters.

On March 30, the convoy of over 100 vessels began to break its 11-column formation and formed into four columns to enter the Strait of Gibraltar, with the British Carrier moving into the middle of the convoy. The ships in the convoy were spaced 500 yards apart on all sides. The escorts had a tremendous area to cover with Radar and Sonar to protect the convoy from the constant threat of submarine attack, especially when the Germans knew about our convoy. Late in the afternoon, a British sub was spotted rising to the surface. The convoy had been alerted that it was in the vicinity because it was a member of a hunter-killer group. It was surfacing so no vessel in the convoy would mistake it for a German U-boat. The convoy passed through the Strait of Gibraltar during daylight for maximum visibility of enemy aircraft. We were now in the Mediterranean and within range of German bombers.

Convoy UGS-36 Is Attacked

The German Luftwaffe attacked around 0300 the morning of April 1 when the convoy was about 15 miles off the coast of Algeria. The Destroyer Escorts were on the outer edges, forming a screen. The crew was sleeping at their gun stations; everyone was on edge, and some later recalled their knees were shaking. The Radar picked up an intermittent blip on the screen; it could have been a sub surfacing. One of the escorts dropped depth charges in the area of the blip, about one mile from the convoy. The air attack began with magnesium flares dropped on the convoy from German scout planes. The flares illuminated our vessels and all our ships were given the command to fire up into the night sky. The destroyers fired 20mm, 40mm and 3-inch/50 weapons, while the British Carrier fired its powerful, booming, anti-aircraft weapons, the concussions being felt by the crews of the other convoy vessels. The tracers and the magnesium flares lit up the water; the hum of airplane motors was heard. One of the Merchant Marine vessels was hit and there was a fire on its deck. The gunnery crew on the Ramsden saw a German bomber by the light of the flares and directed their firing at it. The bomber was hit, lost altitude and skimmed across the water. Our Ordinance Officer, Richard H.

Welton, yelled over the Ramsden ship speakers, "Amen, Brother!" During the battle, a torpedo dropped from a bomber just missed the Ramsden, going port to starboard, ahead of our bow. The Captain and gunnery crew saw the glow of phosphorescence caused by its propeller. If it had been few feet closer it would have hit the bow of the Ramsden. Other ships reported seeing torpedoes in the water. Ship number 93, the Robert E. Ingersoll, U.S. merchant vessel, was torpedoed on the port bow, caught fire, dropped astern, but did not sink. The battle lasted less than an hour, with so much ammunition being fired at planes port and starboard, we were in danger of shooting at our own vessels. The Luftwaffe bombers, about a dozen of them, called off their attack and returned to their base.

Later I heard that some German bomber survivors, who got out of the downed plane and into a rubber raft, were shooting off their flare pistols to be picked up. Our Captain, through an officer on the bridge who could speak German, told them to stop shooting the flares and they would be picked up at daybreak The All Clear sounded at daybreak and we proceeded to pick them up. Only one German was found onboard the rubber raft. We were told the Chief Boatswains Mate climbed out on our propeller guardrail to reach down to grab the German on the raft. But the turbulence from the screws sucked the survivor off the raft and chopped him up in the screws. The Chief standing on the rails witnessed the death and was indelibly shaken. We found out later the body of a German pilot was picked up out of the water by the rear escort.

In the morning, six planes were seen in the distance far off to port. The Convoy Commodore ordered all ships having barrage balloons to fly them. The balloons were like small, airborne blimps, tethered to the ships by heavy cables. They were defense weapons for protection against low-flying aircraft. The idea was that the blimps had dangling cables that would entangle plane propellers. Before sunset, all ships with smoke screen equipment were ordered to lay down a smoke screen to protect the convoy from another nighttime attack.

The Harbor at Bizerte, Tunisia

The Ramsden and the convoy arrived at Bizerte, Tunisia, at 1012Z, Monday, April 3, 1944. The convoy had traveled 4410 miles from Norfolk, Virginia. The General Quarters drills of our Captain Joseph E. Madacey, our Gunnery Officer Richard H. Welton, the Gunners Mates, the officers and the crew served us well when the chips were down.

The harbor was a sight. There were over 50 ships sunk, capsized or half sunk. Some were blown up and others were without a bow or without a stern. The Allied forces had bombed all the ships when they chased Rommel out of Africa. Included in the wreckage were two American LST's sunk during German air attacks, one blown to pieces and the other buckled in half. The town was smashed to bits and it seemed as though it was just a mass of steel girders standing upright. We had established a Navy Base in Bizerte and the United Service Organizations, U.S.O., was there to support the troops.

Ed Toczylowski, who with a few of the crew members that kept the younger guys on the straight and narrow, recalled the flat beer in Bizerte tasted "like you had poured it at 0800 and drank it at 1700." Prior to leaving the ship for liberty, the Army Shore Patrol would frisk each sailor for cigarettes, and only one pack was allowed to be taken ashore. Cigarettes were being sold on the Black Market for a dollar or more a pack. We were also told not to sell a uniform or dog tags in North Africa. Once ashore, we kept in groups of four for safety.

Terrible News Arrives of the USS Leopold DE-319

The worst news was when we heard the report about the Coast Guard manned USS Leopold DE-319. On March 9 she was in a convoy and had been torpedoed; most of the crew had not made it to safety and were dead. That was the ship I was supposed to be on, but I was sent to the hospital after another sailor broke my nose while we were in training at the Naval Operation Base at Norfolk, Virginia. One of the Ramsden crew was thinking out loud and said, "When you add up the hull number it was 13, an unlucky number." I asked him, "What do you get when you add our hull number 382?" His face had a strange look and he whispered, "13." That was the last time I heard that story.

The following is the terse Naval Communications report of the death of a gallant ship and its crew:

Official Navy Department Communiqué No. 511, March 20, 1944

The USS Leopold, Destroyer Escort 319, manned by United States Coast Guard Officers and Enlisted men, was sunk on March 10 as a result of an underwater explosion in the Atlantic. The next of kin of all the casualties have been notified. (End of Communiqué)

The USS Leopold DE-319

The USS Leopold was one of the first Destroyer Escorts to be sunk in the convoy defense program. It was sunk on its second voyage by an acoustic torpedo while it was attacking the German submarine U-255, 400 miles south of Iceland during the night of March 9, 1944. The coordinates were 58 44N, 25 50W which were to be her resting place in the North Atlantic. A sister ship, the USS Joyce DE-317 under the command of Lt. Commander Robert Wilcox, was also attacking the German sub. The Joyce came close to the Leopold, but had to turn away repeatedly to avoid the torpedoes. He transmitted to the Leopold's survivors, "We're dodging torpedoes, God bless you. We'll be back."

The Commanding Officer of the Leopold was Lieutenant Commander Kenneth Phillips. His ship was sinking; his men had to survive in the frigid waters until they were rescued. Destroyer Escorts had only one small Motor Whaleboat; the only other flotation devices were personal life jackets and large rectangular life rafts with heavy netting in the middle. That meant the majority of the crew had to swim in the frigid water.

The USS Joyce finally picked up 28 survivors; 171 men, including all of the Leopold's officers, died in the waters. After World War II, the USS Joyce always held its annual reunion with the survivors of the USS Leopold. The USS Leopold to this day is carried as an active ship and crew "At Sea" in the United States Coast Guard, as an honored tradition for all Naval Forces.

In April 1944 the Joyce avenged the sinking of the Leopold. The tanker, Pan Pennsylvania was straggling behind its Britain-bound convoy and was torpedoed by the German sub U-550. The Joyce and the USS Peterson DE-152 rescued the tanker's surviving crew, and then the Joyce detected the U-boat on Sonar as the Germans attempted to escape after hiding beneath the sinking tanker. The U-550's Nazi engineering officer later told his Allied captors, "We waited for your ship to leave; soon we could hear nothing so we thought the escort vessels had gone; but as soon as we started to move, BANG!"

Headed Home

The Ramsden departed Bizerte on April 11, 1944, with the other escorts and headed back through the Strait of Gibraltar. Most of the

British escorts, the Carrier and the Cruiser were assigned to stay with the convoy, now heading to the invasion of southern France. They were now at the peril of the German Luftwaffe. We were to report back to Norfolk, Virginia.

On the way back, I talked to the Communication Officer and made a request to attend the Fleet Radar School in Virginia Beach, VA. He said he would entertain the request and let me know later. In a few days he got back to me and told me he and the Captain approved the request and that the school was an accelerated training program for three or four weeks. He told me that I would be assigned to the 5th Naval District while I was at the school and be stationed at the Coast Guard Barracks at Little Creek, Virginia, a couple of days before leaving for school. I really didn't know what I could learn; it seemed that I did all that the other Radarmen did, but I knew that I probably couldn't get a Radarman rate without the school. The other Radarmen had been to the school before their assignment and said it was worthwhile. It looked like this was the right choice to make.

Nineteen days later, after an uneventful trip back across the Atlantic, we arrived at Norfolk. I packed my sea bag that night and the following morning I was transported to the barracks at Little Creek, adjacent to the Army Mine Depot and the Navy Amphibious Training Base, Camp Bradford, VA. The following Sunday I was to report to the Radar School for the start of a new class of 120.

Little did I know that this was my last voyage on the Ramsden! I had hoped that she would still be in Norfolk when I completed the school. During the following thirteen months, which were to complete her career in the Atlantic, the Ramsden made the crossing fourteen times, putting into Cardiff, Londonderry, Glasgow, Plymouth, Portsmouth, Le Havre and Cherbourg. Her career in the Atlantic was interesting, and at times dangerous. On many occasions submarine contacts were made and the Ramsden and her sister escorts dropped many depth charge patterns to destroy or divert the submarines from making torpedo attacks.

Coast Guard Barracks, Little Creek, Virginia

The Coast Guard Barracks had the look of a temporary facility. It wasn't fancy and was in reality a receiving station with in transit personnel. The food was great after being on the Destroyer Escort that was not able to reprovision from shore-based military commissaries. The men on temporary-duty had no schedules other than to be ready for further assignments. We had liberty every day from 1300 until 0700; I usually hung around for the evening meal. I would end up at the U.S.O. in the downtown area. Being thin of wallet, I had hoped to return to the Norfolk Naval Base, about 15 miles away. The Norfolk base had its own recreation area and beer was only 25 cents. It had first run movies every night and a Ship's Service Store, the Navy's equivalent of the Army's PX. In larger military installations such as Norfolk, they resembled a department store and the prices were in line with the military pay scale of that period. The barracks in Little Creek had a writing lounge and that was the sum of it. My stay was only for three days when my orders came through from the 5th Naval District Office to report to the Hotel Cavalier in Virginia Beach for training.

The Navy Fleet Radar and Sonar Training School

The Navy Radar and Sonar Training School Program was conducted in the posh Cavalier Hotel on the shores of the Atlantic in Virginia Beach, Virginia. The hotel was a large multi-storied red brick building. It had a large lobby, with furniture reflecting some opulence from a bygone era. The Navy controlled access to the interior of the building, to the upper floors where the students lived, and especially to the uppermost floor where the mostly secret Radar and Sonar equipment was installed. The roof of the building was a forest of antennas for the various systems. The hotel was built around a large atrium area with a glass roof that covered a large indoor pool. The pool was drained and I think it was being used as a classroom. The glass roof could be seen from every room around the perimeter and served as a light and airshaft. The hotel was about seven stories high, if my memory serves me. Most rooms had eight occupants in four double-decker bunks. Each room had a large, modern ceramic tile bathroom. The bathroom had a small rectangular window that could be opened to refresh the air in the room. The rest of the windows were sealed, so as not to compromise the air-conditioning in the building. The side facing the ocean to the east was Officers Country. The north and south sides offered spectacular views of the shorelines. My quarters were at the back of the hotel, with a view to the atrium and the glass covering the indoor pool; the rooms on the opposite outer corridor showed downtown Virginia Beach. The dining room was converted to large banquet type tables and benches, and looked as a normal Navy mess hall would, but there were draperies and the art work on the wall. In one corner was a grand piano, which seemed to be out of place.

The Radar training day started at 0600, with chow at 0700 and classroom instruction starting at 0745. Lunch was at 1130 and the afternoon session commenced at 1230 until 1630, with a 15-minute coffee break in the classroom. Mostly first and second-class Radarmen ran the classes; they had gained the experience at sea under combat conditions. Unknown to the instructors and the students, I too gained my experience at sea under combat conditions. I had an ace in the hole regarding the subject matter. It wasn't a breeze, but there were no surprises. The first few hours were dedicated to the secrecy aspects of this new electronic weapon and its tremendous contribution to naval warfare, particularly in Anti-Submarine Warfare, Navigation and Aircraft Detection. The Radar equipment could be compared to the computers of the 1960's; each new version was better than its predecessor, and its capabilities grew by leaps and bounds.

The first Radar sets were large and bulky and a great deal of time was spent calibrating the sets after turning them on. A log had to be kept of the start and shutdown times, so that the technicians could keep track of the hours on particular parts, such as the vacuum tubes, that had a specific life span. The idea of solid state, transistors and printed circuits, was beyond possibility and comprehension at that point in time. The secret of Radar was the invention of the Magnetron Oscillator. Its position in the main transmitter case was marked with red lines painted on the outside. It was to be smashed with an axe to prevent it from being seen by the enemy if capture was imminent. Later, a tube about the size of a ¾-inch pipe and eight inches long was incorporated into the case and a thermite, explosive magnesium cartridge was inserted and connected to electrical terminals. If one was abandoning the ship, a switch above the exit door was thrown and the equipment would melt down after the initial small explosion.

Our classes were accelerated, making learning the material extremely difficult. This was secret technology and any notes taken had to be turned in after class and locked in a safe; if you had a bad memory you were lost. Getting to class on time was mandatory and going to class early was the only possibility to review your notes. After the first week, the use of a Plotting Board to ascertain the course and speed of a detected object was the most difficult. The senior Radarmen on the USS Ramsden DE-382 showed me a fast way to do this, without using time-consuming math. Time to solve a problem could be the difference between life and death. A simple pair of naval dividers, flip-flopped on the plotting board gave me the answer in almost a split second, and it was super accurate. The plotting board was not only used to find the course and the speed of a vessel or plane, but to plot the fastest intercept course and the time required to intercept.

Every two or three days the class was tested and anyone who fell behind was not there the following day. Unless you were bunked in the same room with the sailor, you would never know what happened to him. There was no time for individual instruction; even with my experience it was challenging.

One day at lunch, an officer sat down at the grand piano in the dining room. He began to play and everyone in the room stopped eating. He was terrific and played a few hits of the day for about ten minutes. His name was Eddie Duchin, a famous pianist and orchestra leader. He was the Commander of the Sonar training section at the school. He played once more while I was there; for me, it was the thrill of a lifetime. He hung around after lunch and shook hands and signed a few autographs, before we all had to leave. He was quite a guy, not one bit aloof because of his celebrity.

After training day was over, shore leave was granted until midnight. The only attraction in our area was an amusement park, with the usual mechanical rides and prize booths. It was usually filled with teenagers and sailors looking for a good time. The rides weren't expensive and the park had a beer garden that was usually the center of attention. I managed to get to the park a couple of times during my stay.

Several of the rooms on my floor were occupied by British sailors and after becoming acquainted, several of us would meet in each other's room to tell sea stories or just to spend some idle time. They were all very nice and, like all servicemen away from home, spoke of home and wives and sweethearts. We all swapped details of our homes and lives. We introduced ourselves; when it came my turn I said my name was Smith. They all laughed and called me Dodger. They said, in Britain, anyone with the name of Smith was always thought of as "Dodging the Law." Henceforth their nickname for me was Dodger. I suppose it fit, considering how I was trying to hide my Lazy Eye. We were all surprised that the U.S. was paying the Brits $20.00 per day while they were attending this U.S. Navy training school. At that time my base pay was $66.00 per month. I never figured out that deal.

One morning when we went to breakfast, we heard that someone in the room next to us jumped out the window in the bathroom and plummeted through the windows that covered the unfilled pool below. The Navy never figured how the guy could get out the window and get far enough out to land on the covering over the pool. Investigators even filled a sea bag with the sailor's weight in sand and pushed it through the window twice; they never could get the distance the victim's body traveled from the side of the building. One of the British sailors mused, "Maybe he did it from the roof." Because of all the secret technology in our building, the Navy said it was a murder mystery and not a suicide; I guess they were stuck with it. Naval Intelligence questioned us all as a matter of form. We never heard any more about it.

With little to do ashore and less cash to do it, I turned down invitations to go on liberty. If you couldn't carry your weight, you were wasting everyone's time. One evening I went to the Lab where all the hands-on training took place. It was full of all the Radar and Sonar equipment being taught plus all the latest types. The techs were working to get any instruments that needed repairs or service ready for the next day's classes. Several of the techs needed a third hand, so I volunteered. They taught me to operate most all types, some I never knew existed. Several models were used as portable systems, to be setup after a landing; they had their own gasoline generators for power, were in several different containers and had their own separate mounting stands. The containers were all weatherproof to protect them outdoors. These portable models were used until permanent Radar systems could be installed after the hostilities ceased. All the seagoing military ships had Radar of various types, as did aircraft. The aircraft radar that had a PPI scope with three tube types in one envelope intrigued me. All the operator had to do was flip a switch and have a different view; such Radar I would never see on any ship I would ever serve on. The Sonar I learned to operate would be beyond my rating, but it was nice to know how they all worked. The techs knew their jobs; they had to trace circuitry, replace component parts, continually check and replace vacuum tubes. I thought this was how Thomas Edison's workshop must have looked when working on new machines. Some officers came by occasionally to check progress on the repairs, but none paid any attention to me. I had a standing invitation to come by the Lab; they appreciated a volunteer, and it made their work faster and easier.

The three weeks came and went so fast. We had a final exam and I came out 7th in a class of 120. Here I was, 18 years old and I was pleased with my success; the other Radarmen on the USS Ramsden had taught me well, although my determination to learn everything I could was a factor. We had a general assembly where the Officers congratulated us and wished us well in our new assignments. We were shipping out the following Monday morning and we would be handed our orders over the weekend. When I opened my envelope all it mentioned was for me to return to the Coast Guard Barracks, Little Creek, Virginia, about a 45-minute bus trip. I was sure I was going to be back on the USS Ramsden as soon as it returned to Norfolk.

Coast Guard Barracks, Little Creek, Virginia

When I arrived at the Receiving Station, I turned in my papers. I asked if DE-382 had returned to Norfolk and no one seemed to know. About the second day I went to the Coast Guard 5th Naval District Office in Norfolk to inquire. After waiting around for about two hours a SPAR yeoman found my personnel file and told me she saw that I was attending the Navy Fleet Radar School, and I was transferred to the Coast Guard Barracks at Little Creek. The next part of my file that she read to me stunned me. It said my transfer from the USS Ramsden was permanent and it was notated NTR, Not to Return! I would be notified of my new assignment within three days.

I was in shock! I heard that the Ramsden had arrived back in port. I went to its berth and saw the Communications Officer. He said, "The decision is final," and walked away, no explanation, no anything. Anyone standing around was as embarrassed as I was. I returned to Little Creek, still in shock. The next day, I was informed that I was transferred to the Naval Amphibious Training Base, Camp Bradford, at Little Creek, Virginia, not more than a mile away. The USS Ramsden would continue its service career without me. It served in the war effort until it was decommissioned on June 13, 1946, and entered the Atlantic Reserve Fleet. When the Korean War started, the USS Ramsden was transferred to the U.S. Coast Guard and was recommissioned on March 28, 1952, with the Coast Guard hull designation WDE-482.

Camp Bradford, Naval Amphibious Training Base, Norfolk, Virginia

The Amphibious Training Base was devoted to training crews for the LST, the largest amphibious landing ship of WWII. I had seen the LST's in convoys to the Mediterranean. I had no idea that I would be a crew member on this type of vessel. The "Landing Ship, Tank," or LST, were naval ships specially designed to transport and deploy troops, tanks, vehicles and supplies onto shores where there were no docks or cranes. An LST could land on any shore that had a gradually sloped beach. The ship could offload heavy equipment for battles, or take on heavy equipment to be relocated for further battles. Heavy equipment did not have to be deserted after a battle anymore. Vehicles such as tanks could be put back in action more quickly using the LST's.

The American-built LST was 328 feet long, 50 feet wide and it could carry 2100 tons. Built into the bow were two doors that opened outward to a width of 14 feet. The lower deck was a tank deck, where 20 Sherman tanks could be loaded. Lighter vehicles were loaded onto the upper deck. An elevator was used to load and offload vehicles, artillery, and other equipment from the upper deck; in later models, a hinged ramp replaced the elevator. The compartments along the sides of the interior of the ship were designed for the crew living quarters, and extra spaces were capable of transporting an additional 160 troops. A number of LST's were fitted with flight decks for small reconnaissance aircraft. The LST was powered by two diesel engines, and had a maximum speed of 12 knots and a cruising speed of 8.75 knots. The LST's were lightly armed with a variety of weapons. A typical American LST was armed with seven 40mm and twelve 20mm anti-aircraft guns.

Beginning in July 1943, Coast Guard manned LST's participated in almost every amphibious operation involving American forces, and several landed British troops, from Normandy, France to the Philippine Islands.

After an LST's initial beaching, it was usually ordered to go alongside a larger vessel offshore to embark another cargo to be landed on the beach. This sequence was often repeated in the course of a single amphibious operation. When beach gradients didn't permit a close approach before the LST grounded, pontoon causeways, brought to the scene by the LST, formed a safe passage between ship and shore.

Many of the Coast Guard coxswains had learned handling rescue boats in the surf at lifesaving stations and applied that experience to handling the LST in the surf. These Coast Guard sailors could successfully maneuver landing craft through strong currents, reefs, sand bars and heavy surf. Their contributions to amphibious operations were immense.

Training at Camp Bradford, Virginia

It didn't take long for me to realize that the base was operating as a boot camp. We were all quartered in Quonset huts. These were arch-shaped, corrugated sheet metal buildings, with the ends closed off and a door in each end. Several windows were along each wall, and bunks were placed the full length of the floor on each side. The buildings were designed for easy and fast assembly. They were permanent, with concrete floors. They were new, comfortable and clean. Our toilet, lavatory and showers were at one end and adequate. When we arrived we had no crew assignments or training schedule. The base had several hundred sailors, both Coast Guard and Navy who were assigned to separate areas. I could not sense whether the competition between the Coast Guard and Navy would resurface again, and if the Navy sailors would again start referring to us Coast Guard sailors as the Hooligan Navy.

In all the time I was there, I never met anyone from my previous duty stations. The usual large mess halls were located nearby. No matter where I went, I heard sailors complaining about the food; I always thought the food was great, only that in some places it was maybe a little bit better. The hundreds of sailors would parade in formation around the side of a dirt-surfaced drill field, larger than a football field. After a couple of days, our training programs were set.

When I entered the service and was issued all uniform clothing, I was given a stencil, stencil brush, and black and white inks. For all sailors it was mandatory to stencil name, such as "Smith, F. A." and serial number, on every piece of clothing from the underwear to the outerwear, and in specific areas only. This was also required on any replacement clothing. In Camp Bradford we were inspected in formation by a superior officer. It was a shock when we were all instructed to unbutton our pants and lower them, so that the stencil could be seen on the waist band of our boxer shorts. The groans from the sailors were almost like a shout. The tone of the training was now apparent. I was still experiencing the occasional headaches; they would linger for a day or two. I went to our sickbay and got some Navy aspirin which helped, but upset my stomach. I figured it was caused by the stress of the camp.

The only thing different about the regimen was the emphasis on aircraft recognition and a gas mask drill. The gas drill was with a military gasmask. We were required to enter a Quonset hut filled with chlorine gas, remove the mask, and hold our breath. As we stepped through the door into the room, we would bring the mask to the face, blow lung air into it, and then put the mask on. We had to walk the length of the hut and exit. The whole length of the hut had instructors wearing their masks monitoring everyone for safety. I don't know if this was found to be dangerous or affected anyone in later life. We had been warned prior to entering to remove any silver jewelry or things of that nature, because they would turn black. I couldn't see how anyone could keep from inhaling some of the chlorine gas. We did this twice during our stay.

Part of the daily routine was the usual marching on the drill field and calisthenics to keep in shape and give us something to complain about. Most all the sailors at the camp were sea-duty veterans, but maybe the introduction to vessels and methods was some sort of equalizer. There were always rumors in the service, and the Bradford Camp rumor was this Commander had been in charge of the Navy phase of the Sicily campaign, when the Navy opened fire on the night flights of our own 82nd Airborne prior to the landings, shooting down several American DC-3s loaded with the parachutists. I never heard of this again until I met a member of the 82nd Airborne, in Kingman, Arizona, after the war. He had also heard the rumor that the Officer in Charge during the friendly fire incident was transferred to a training command in Virginia. It could have been just rumors.

Being just a First Class seaman, Radarman Striker, my duty assignment was protecting a large helium-filled barrage balloon, the kind seen tethered above ships to protect them from low flying aircraft on strafing runs. It was attached to a heavy cable that was attached to a winch to raise it or lower it, and was used in demonstrations during training exercises. I never figured why it had to be protected. I was dressed in wool Undress Blues, canvas leggings, and white hat, and carried a 30.06 Springfield rifle while patrolling the area. About the only time I moved was when the shade from the balloon moved. I did this everyday for a week for two hours, in the middle of the day. I must say that I did my duty, because no one stole that balloon while I was in amphibious training!

The Aircraft Recognition Training was interesting. Prior to being assigned to the USS Ramsden, I had been trained in German plane recognition. Now I was going to the Pacific battles and had to be able to identify Japanese ships and plane types. In the training, silhouettes were flashed and students were singled out to call the names, like "Zeke," etc. The identification names were the same for all services. After a couple of classes, most everyone could rattle the names off instantly, but the ships all looked the same to me. I guess I was affected by my knowledge of the Radarman IFF (Identification Friend or Foe) system, located near his Radar and triggered by the operator. It worked every time I had to use it and was always accurate. If a friendly had the wrong code in at the time, lives were in jeopardy. The IFF system was an electronic system that sent a coded signal to an aircraft or a ship whose identity and intentions were in question. Lives depended on the object being able to answer the electronic inquiry from the sender with the correct coded response. The system was a two-way street and a friendly had the same prerogatives. The codes were changed many times during the 24-hour day, so it was critical that all concerned had the secret codes entered into the system correctly.

All the trainees with the exception of the ones stuck with the duty, were given liberty the whole weekend to see Norfolk. I had very little money, so I stayed on the base and visited the base beer garden where beer was 25 cents a bottle. After about two weeks, all the Coast Guardsmen were separated into their own Quonset huts. I didn't know anyone or their rates until we wore our dress uniforms and the rates sewn on their sleeves showed their area of expertise.

One day a young officer came into our quarters and introduced himself. I can't remember his name, but he had been a Chief Radioman aboard the Coast Guard Cutter Spencer WPG-36 that was one of the early stalwarts in the anti-submarine battles in the North Atlantic. We were sitting around on our bunks and asking him questions about the war and assignments. It wasn't unusual for the enlisted men to be in the dark, and the Chief was our only source of information. As the men started to drift away, I asked him about the crew assignments; he said most all billets were full up except the communications division. He was the communications officer in charge and he said he had no Radar men to assign. I must have looked shocked! I told him I was a Radarman striker from the USS Ramsden DE-382, with combat anti-submarine and aircraft warning experience on convoy runs in the North Atlantic and the Mediterranean. He took my name and serial number and told me he would check me out and get back to me the next day. He was true to his word and after lunch the next day, he sought me out. He came up to me and said he checked my records. With a big smile, he told me I was his leading Radarman and I would be responsible to train two others and a spare to fill the crew! Now I felt better. He was a good friend all the time I was aboard. He appreciated my efforts and was instrumental in getting me my radar rate and had me slated for 2nd class before I left the ship at a later date.

Most of the training was the usual type of exercises like damage control, firefighting and gunnery. The mechanical training would take place later. We were all taken to a boat facility on a pond open to the sea at one end. There were small landing craft tied up at the docks. A machinist mate monitored the engine and a seaman or a coxswain steered it. He controlled a throttle that looked like an upside down stirrup, mounted on a short shaft. It pushed forward or pulled back for direction, and twisted right or left for speed. The coxswain stood at the rear, usually exposed and the motor machinist was in the well near the engine. We all had one chance to operate the boat once around the lagoon, to acquaint ourselves with its controls. It was training but it was fun.

All crews had to qualify in swimming. We were taken in groups to a large indoor multi-pool swimming complex. The test was to jump into the deep end of the pool and swim about twelve feet to a wet rope cargo net that hung from a platform suspended from the ceiling. We had to climb the net, rest a second or two, jump off the opposite end of the platform, and swim to the shallow end of the pool. That was it. If you couldn't do it you had to return and take instruction. It was really hilarious watching some sailors take a running start on the pool deck to get as close as they could to the net and dog paddle the distance. It wasn't funny to the sailor who was afraid of the water or couldn't swim a lick. Most of us completed the exercise. Several in our group climbed up to the platform and because of the illusion of great height, couldn't make themselves jump down into the pool. After three requests, the instructors used a fire hose, full force, and knocked them off the platform into the water. We had qualified lifeguards along the sides; the pool was wide enough and nothing was hurt except the swimmer's pride.

Camp Bradford had two nine-man crewed, oar propelled, wooden lifeboats that could be used for recreation or competition. The ninth man was for steering. I was on one of the Coast Guard rowing teams; we practiced as much as we could. Our real intention was to go to one of the public swimming beaches, pull the boat partway up on the beach and girl watch. All we had on was our swim trunks and a t-shirt. Young and fit, we all looked good. We would row back to the lagoon, grab a shower, dress and go to evening mess. We had several races with other crews and were never beat. Girl watching might have been our motivation to be the fastest team.

Our amphibious training was fast coming to an end. With about a week left, we had a formal introduction with all our officers. The Captain was a full Lieutenant from the Boston area. He informed us that our ship was LST-759. It was being completed at the Dravo Shipyard on the Ohio River in Pittsburgh, Pennsylvania. We would have about two weeks of intensive training to operate the systems of the LST. We would be billeted at Carnegie Tech University in Pittsburg. As soon as it was determined we were all qualified to run the ship, a skeleton Navy crew, for the key positions, would accompany us as we travelled down the Ohio River to our destination of New Orleans at the end of the Mississippi River. For better or worse, our journey was about to begin.

Goodbye, Camp Bradford, Virginia

We packed our sea bags and laundered our day-to-day gear. We had no idea what the accommodations would be at Carnegie Tech. Some universities had temporary barracks for wartime classes. We rolled out at 0600. The uniform of the day was the usual dungarees and blue chambray shirt for breakfast, and a change to Dress Blues for travel after breakfast. The crew was full of chatter and rumors, as usual. We mustered in the street in front of our quarters, and marched to the mess hall. The food tasted great that morning, mainly because of the expectations of the journey and the cessation of gripes about Camp Bradford. We returned to our Quonset hut, stripped our mattress covers off the bunks, secured anything forgotten into the sea bag, and changed into our Dress Blues. We sat on the side of the bunks and waited for our transportation.

Navy buses pulled up to our area, followed by a Navy flat bed truck for our sea bags. Our hope was that we all arrived at the same place at the same time. Most of the sailors of our crew were experienced and had bought custom made Dress Blues. They didn't relish traveling on a troop train in their Sunday best. Our transportation took us to the rail yards of the Pennsylvania Railroad in Norfolk. The sea bags were transferred to the baggage car of a train that was comprised of two dining cars, a kitchen/ bunk car for the railroad personnel, two regular Pullman sleeping cars, and four strange cars that looked like converted boxcars. They had windows along each side, two sliding doors with windows close to each end on both sides. These four cars looked new, and when we boarded, we were told the cars were built for military personnel sleeping. Inside were six rows of triple-decker bunks separated by three-foot aisles between each row of six, with the same along the other side. A main aisle ran the length of the car. There was a toilet facility on each end, and a washroom along one end. A doorway at each end let passengers through to adjoining cars. I think it was approximately thirteen feet wide by about sixty feet in length. Because of the short supply of Pullman sleeping cars, the cars really filled a need. After the war these military sleeping cars were sold to the Railway Express Agency.

We were given permission to change to work uniforms, dungarees with a shirt. If we had been on a Pullman sleeping car we would have had to sit until the porters pulled down the beds and put linens on them in the evening. We were allowed to lie down and sleep if desired. The bunks were like the bunks aboard ship, with canvas bottoms laced to pipe frames, topped with a military mattress and a pillow and a blanket. All in all it made for a comfortable mode of travel. As on all Navy ships, Bos'n Mates were Masters at Arms, almost like a police officer. The Bos'n Mate would wear an armband while having that duty and if he told us to police the area, it meant clean it up. As a rule, no trash of any kind was allowed to accumulate and the sleeping compartment was almost spotless. As we pulled out of the railroad yard in Norfolk, the fans in the ceiling along the center aisle helped a little to freshen the air; travelling with 48 sailors in confined quarters had a definite odor. The crew opened up the sliding doors, pulled folding gates down and locked them for safety. The crew spent the time napping, reading, playing cards, and spreading rumors about where our LST was going. The two dining cars were for our use and the Bos'n came in and gave us our chow times. Each of the four military sleeping cars had about 48 occupants. The two dining cars could feed about 50 or more at a time, so sit down meals were divided into two sittings.

On our journey to Pittsburgh, we passed through parts of Virginia, West Virginia and eastern Maryland. The scenery was out of this world; beautiful forests and small farms were out in the countryside with larger farms near metropolitan areas. Most of the barns were painted red, and some were painted with ads for the local tobacco products, baking powder manufacturers and others. Once in a while, as we climbed through the mountains, we would see a barn that looked as if it couldn't carry the weight of the roof. The livestock looked mostly well fed and fat. The fences were in good repair. Occasionally little kids would run out of the houses to wave and yell. The sailors near the doors did the same and if a teen girl was out, the whistles were louder than the one on the train. The engines on the train were all coal-fired after we left the electric locomotives in the metro areas. The chug-chug-chug of the engines as we climbed the grades and the whistle before the country crossings made me think of home and what the future held. Sometimes the town residents, who were stopped at the crossing waiting for us to pass, waved at the sailors standing by the open doors. Some of the old veterans gave us a hand salute. It was the usual thing everywhere we traveled, from the Atlantic to the Mississippi. We experienced the patriotism and shouts of good wishes from all who viewed our progress down the Ohio and the Mississippi Rivers.

I'm sure our train traveled on other right-of-ways; sometimes we were aware of the engines being replaced. The train crews could only operate on specific tracks that they had been certified on. The steam trains all had to be watered and fueled; this was usually done when the crew reached the limit of their time or miles. The sleepers and the dining cars were all owned by the Pullman Company, which paid a fee for being hauled. Pullman in turn charged a fee to the passengers using their services, in our case, the U.S. military.

We traveled through the Appalachian and Allegheny mountains and through the seemingly endless beauty of the Monongahela National Forest. The train struggled with some of the grades as the smoke stack billowed huge volumes of smoke. At times we had to close the doors to keep out the heavy smoke; the air became much cooler as we changed elevation.

Darkness swallowed up the scenery, and the dormitory cars slowly became quiet. Our food service in the diners was always first class, with a couple of entrées, usually roast beef, ham or chicken, bread and butter, coffee or milk, and a dessert of cake, pie or a scoop of ice cream. The quantities were adequate and the porcelain dishes and heavy tableware was "uptown." Our lunch was a variety of large meat sandwiches of several choices. The waiters treated us as they would a civilian traveler. The dining cars had a supervisor who ran the show and looked elegant in his own special uniform. The car was always immaculate and the meals well prepared. Hot coffee was always available in a large container at the entrance to the diner.

During the daylight hours, eating in the diner was a real experience for most of the sailors. It became part of the great memories of my service days. Being on military bases sometimes had a dehumanizing factor, as individuals became part of a larger force. Not meaning to complain, we all realized military service demanded utmost cooperation and hard training, but it was a serviceman's prerogative to gripe. With so many personalities involved, conflicts flared now and then and had to be resolved. On this trip it usually involved card games that were played from dawn to dusk; the money usually disappeared when an officer was spotted on an inspection tour. The service had its share of "slickers." They were easy to spot and usually had the lion's share of the money at the end of the day. Wherever I travelled during the war, there was always someone with a cribbage board. When I was a kid, I would visit my Uncle Jim at the firehouse. The firehouse day room had several round wooden tables with four chairs, and each table had a cribbage board or a set of dominoes. It wasn't until several years later that I learned to play cribbage, so I avoided losing money to the slickers in the service.

The Steam Train Rumbles on Into the Night

Lights out on the train was around 2100, and by this time most of the sailors were reading, sleeping or writing letters home. The expectation of visiting a Pittsburgh and seeing our new LST was on most minds.

The next morning as we were at breakfast, we began to traverse the famous Horseshoe Curve on the mainline of the Pennsylvania Railroad, near Altoona, Pennsylvania. As we traveled the curve to climb a grade, the curve was so sharp that it gave the impression that we were passing our own train. I drank in these sights; being a flat-lander, raised by the seashore, I was intent on these new sights and sounds.

Welcome to Pittsburgh, Pennsylvania, the Smoky City

The Pittsburgh factories were all running at full capacity to provide the steel and other materials for the World War II effort. As we approached the Golden Triangle between the rivers, the smoke rising from the hundreds of smoke stacks mostly obscured the countryside. The train slowed to a crawl as we made our way through the huge rail yard filled with the hundreds of gondola cars loaded with coal and coke.

The train pulled onto a busy passenger train terminal. Dozens of engines, passenger cars and Pullman cars were lined up and ready to go. Most of the passengers were military personnel leaving for parts unknown. The depot was teeming with every branch of service as well as civilians. Travel for civilians was difficult. During the war, civilian passenger trains were required to turn away a civilian traveler to make room for a serviceman.

Civilian buses were lined up at the curb entrance to the depot and railway personnel loaded our sea bags onto flatbed trucks. We all carried our own ditty bags with our personal traveling gear. We boarded the bus and were ready to look at the town and its ladies. Our new home for a couple of weeks was to be the campus of the Carnegie Institute of Technology, later renamed Carnegie Mellon University.

The Halls of Ivy

The buses carried us through the wide, tree-lined streets of Pittsburgh. We passed the dense neighborhoods of blue collar workers and, as we neared the campus, the neighborhoods changed to single family and larger homes. Even with the hubbub of the war effort, the streets were clean and all the houses looked well kept. As we approached the campus, it appeared to be a collection of massive granite buildings. To me, it was the perfect image of a proud, major university. It was inspiring and beautiful. The lawns were well groomed and the old trees seemed to have been there forever.

The buses pulled to a stop in front of a line of granite buildings. We claimed our sea bags, filed into a building, and as our names were called in groups of four, we were assigned our rooms. The interior, though plain, had pictures and art lithographs on the walls of the rooms and in the corridors. The rooms were clean and well maintained; toilet facilities were more than adequate. We were instructed that the cleaning staff was us. The area training was to continue without abatement.

We were given our orders and welcomed by a Navy staff. We assembled outside in the street, to march in a column of fours to the cafeteria assigned to this area. The cafeteria was the usual large buffet type building, which would seat about 400 sailors at tables of four. A civilian contractor did the food preparation and serving.

Until LST-759 was ready for our crew and we were trained on the new equipment, our liberty was from 1500 each day, until 0700 the following morning. The crew would muster out in the street at 0645 each morning and march off to chow, precisely at 0700. Anyone not at muster at 0700 would have his liberty pass revoked for a weekend. We all learned the city and its bus schedules, so it was no trouble for the night owls to make the 0700 cut-off time. However, it was usually a hilarious situation in the morning, at about 0650. The formation in the street would be facing the end of the street, where the municipal bus line stopped. The usual late night revelers would storm off the bus and come running down the street to make muster or lose their privileges. Some came drunkenly stumbling up to join the formation, and some couldn't stop talking about their escapades of the evening, which was to be listened to but not believed. Because of the 24-hour operations of the war industries, most bars and entertainment areas were also open 24-hours a day. The sailors never missed a trick and ferreted out the best that matched their appetites and budgets.

In Pittsburgh, I met two of the nicest men it was my good fortune to know in all the years in the service. One was Patrick Kevin Healy from Jersey City, New Jersey. Pat was a 1st Class Quartermaster, who knew his job inside and out. The other was James Madden, from upstate New York. Jim was a 2nd Class Signalman and handled his signal flags and signal lights as if he had been doing it his whole life. They were in their early twenties and were gentlemen in every sense of the word. As the years flowed by to this day, I feel fortunate to have met them. Pat was a Catholic and always made it a point to remind me to come to Mass, whenever we had the opportunity. Jim was a devout Presbyterian and was leaning toward becoming a minister. When we went ashore, we usually traveled together, and they saw to it that I, the youngest in the group, didn't overindulge sampling the fine local beer and ales that came our way. They weren't killjoys by any means; they just knew when the party was over. Wherever we traveled they were just as interested in seeing the sights and touring as I was, although the opportunities didn't come up often.

The campus food was great and the environment made it seem as if we had traveled to another world. We went to band concerts on the grassy slopes near the University of Pittsburgh. The people of that city were the warmest since I was in Houston, Texas. It felt as if they had adopted us, they were beyond friendly. We discovered one of the best places to spend an evening in Pittsburgh was a Polish-American club. They had a bounty of food, live polka music and great beer. They were open 24-hours a day and the places were always full with the war industry civilian workers coming off their shifts. Depending on the time of day, they would have their families with them; it was a real wholesome, friendly atmosphere. At times a generous civilian would pay our bill. If we were sitting at a table, someone walking by would set a couple of beers on our table, wave thanks, and smile.

The Army Specialized Training Program

In one of the buildings on our dormitory street was an Army unit of rag-tag soldiers in ill-fitting uniforms. They were in an Army program called Army Specialized Training Program. We never learned what they were training for and why they were at a university instead of a military base. They were in various programs with various disciplines, and looked as if they had slept in their uniforms. Whenever they were lined up in the street as we marched to the mess hall, we would sing as we paraded by, "Tear down the service flag Mother, your son's in the ASTP." We sailors would repeat this about three times, until we were out of hearing.

Pat Healy and I went to concert in Schenley Park and while we were viewing the scenery, a couple of girls sitting on a blanket close by, called us over. They had a small cooler box of local beer. The park was lighted and much of the crowd remained after the concert. We chatted for quite a while. When they had to leave, we walked them to their apartment, bid them a goodnight and hoped we would see them at another concert soon. As Pat and I were walking back to Carnegie Tech, we saw a dairy with small trucks getting ready for the early morning milk delivery routes. We walked over and both of us bought a quart of ice-cold milk to drink on the long walk back. Pat and I sat on the curb, drinking and talking. A long black limousine of that era pulled up as we started to leave. The driver, in his late forties, asked us where we were stationed. We told him that we were domiciled at Carnegie Tech. He said he would drop us off if we didn't mind riding along as he picked up the receipts of several bars and roadhouses in the area. A very attractive woman accompanied him; she appeared to be in her late twenties.

Pat and I sat in the back seat. Limos in those days had a lot of space between the back seat and the front seat. They had jump seats or folding seats that came out of the back of the front seat. The whole floor was covered with fully loaded moneybags. The driver said to move the bags around if they got in the way. He made no secret that the girl was his girlfriend and he was married. He said that if we were to be around for any length of time he would fix us up with a couple of his girls. Pat and I looked at each other with a worried look and began to wonder what we had gotten into. The driver told us that he owned all of the places he was collecting from and took a different route each night so he wouldn't be knocked over. We stopped at several nice looking places. When we came to the last one, our host tossed the moneybags into the car, and another man came out of the business and handed Pat and I cold beers. The floor of the car was now really loaded with the moneybags. We drove to a large garage where several young men came over and unloaded the car. Pat and I had no idea how much money was in the bags, but were glad to see them go.

Our business friend wanted to know if we knew anything about the care and handling of wooden boats; Pat and I said we did. He drove us to the banks of the Monongahela River, where a boat shed was built near a large marina. It was more like a two car garage that was built to extend over the water. He parked his car and we walked into the boathouse. He turned on the overhead lights. Suspended over the water on one side was a very expensive mahogany and chrome speedboat. An electric hoist connected to a long I-beam held the boat over the water. We supposed that this was for winter storage, although it was now summer. His problem was the boat was leaking, not bad, but still a source for concern. He wanted our suggestions to eliminate this. Pat and I thought the best preventive was to keep the boat in the water so the planks wouldn't dry out and to have some water in the bilges during the winter when it was on the hoist. He thought that was a great idea and said he would do it.

On the garage side was a large Indian brand motorcycle. I asked and he said it was his. He had owned one ever since he was a kid and loved to ride it. He said he would take it for a spin with me on the buddy seat. He cranked it up a couple of times and the roar of the engine was deafening. I hopped on the back and he took off. The road was damp and there were street railroad tracks along our way. Whenever he crossed those tracks, he leaned the bike over. I had been through a German Luftwaffe attack, but this scared the living daylights out of me! In Pittsburgh, a couple of the main roads were tunnels through the mountains; he drove through one so fast that the railings on the emergency walk ways looked like a picket fence. I put my neckerchief ends in my mouth to keep it from blowing away. This was about 0200, and I thought we would wake up the whole city. The ride probably lasted only about 15 minutes, but it seemed like forever. I made a vow to myself that this was my first and last time on a motorcycle. We returned to the boat shed, he locked the building and he drove Pat and me to Carnegie Tech. We thanked him, he gave us his card with his number and we promised to give him a call if he could help us in any way. His girlfriend gave us both a hug and wished us well.

Frank A. Smith, Jr.

I don't know about Pat, but I wasn't in a hurry to meet up with our driver friend again. Pat laughed all the way to our dormitory. As I got ready for bed, I took off my neckerchief and noticed that I had bitten right through the ends that I had clenched in my mouth. Plus, I now had a hole through the side of my shoe.

Twin Toddlers, Francis Anthony
Smith, Jr. and Gerald James Smith;
Boston, 1927

Twins, Gerald J. Smith and Frank A.
Smith, Jr.; Boston, 1942

Frank A. Smith, Jr., Catherine Cullen Smith (mother),
Barbara Marie Smith (sister), 1942

Frank A. Smith, Jr.

Gerald J. Smith, OSCM USN

USS Ramsden DE-382

USS LST-759

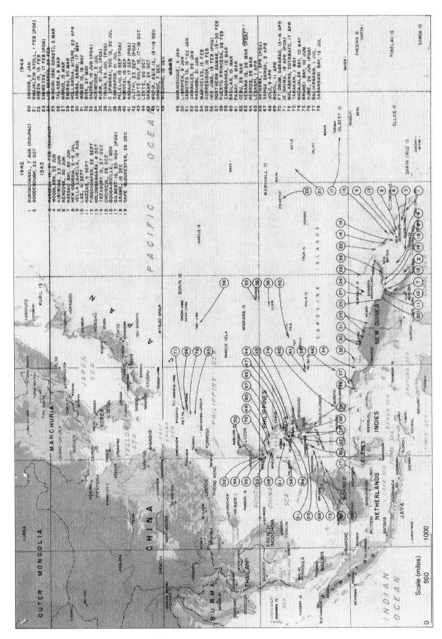

Allied Landings, August 1942-August 1945,
United States Department of Army

Marriage of Frank A. Smith, Jr. and Lorraine R. Brodeur;
Boston, MA, September 11, 1948

Headstone, National Memorial Cemetery, Cave Creek, AZ

MY NEW ASSIGNMENT, THE USS LST-759

The Dravo Shipbuilding Company on the Ohio River

Pittsburgh was a strategic location for shipbuilding alongside the local steel mills, and Dravo Shipbuilding Company served as leader in the production of over 60% of the entire Navy fleet of 1058 LST's. It took Dravo builders 219 days to construct and launch USS LST-1 into the Ohio River from its yard on September 7, 1942. Not only was it the first of a new, amphibious design produced on an assembly line, it was the largest combat ship ever launched on inland waters of the United States. Dravo continued completing one LST every six days during the war.

We Take Delivery of USS LST-759

The crew members were bused to see the LST for the first time. We saw the mast, and all gear that was normally attached to it, lying on the main deck. The LST had to be to be able to pass under any bridge along the way down the Ohio River. All of the anti-aircraft defense weapons, single 20mm guns and the heavier caliber twin and single 40mm, were installed.

All of the equipment necessary to communicate, navigate and propel the ship was installed. Anything else, though, that could be done to lessen the weight was left to be installed later at the Navy yard in Algiers, across the river from New Orleans. A skeleton crew of Navy officers and a full complement of Coast Guard combat veterans were to spend every waking moment preparing to have the ship combat-ready during the two-week journey down to New Orleans.

Thanks and Farewell, Pittsburgh

We spent a few more days traveling between the shipyard and Carnegie Tech, while the galley staff and the engine crew honed their skills. Many of the crew met girls in Pittsburgh and formed lifelong relationships. Others would leave with memories, which would become smiles to add warmth on a cold night. Several crewmembers had their wives in tow. The wives intended to follow the ship downriver to New Orleans, although no crewmember would be allowed ashore until the journey's end. We packed up our gear at Carnegie Tech, policed the area, and prepared the dormitories for the next LST crews soon to follow. The two ship yards were each turning out about one LST each week, a record time for shipbuilding. We marched to breakfast for the final time, and loaded onto waiting buses. Our ship, the brand new USS LST-759, was waiting to come alive with its brand new crew.

We arrived at the docks. The USS LST-759 was about to commence its maiden voyage down the Ohio River; all fuel and supplies were loaded and all crew was accounted for. The skeleton training crew was standing by with the permanent crew in all critical areas. The Ohio River Pilot was on the bridge with the Captain and other officers. The first of many civilian Pilots, he would control the navigation of the ship on the river. His expertise was gained by years of navigating other ships along the inland waterways. Others would relieve the Pilot from time to time. He would depart the ship and wait for other ships going up-river, normally long strings of barges. The Ohio River portion of our journey would cover over 1000 miles from Pittsburgh, Pennsylvania, to Cairo, Illinois, where the Ohio River would glide us into the Mississippi River. It was interesting to hear people from the area pronounce Cairo like "Karo" Syrup.

Our Ohio River Journey

As we traveled down the river, every town we passed through cheered us on and applauded our efforts. I don't know how many other ships of our type and other shallow draft craft bound for war passed this way. Our ship looked ready to go to battle, painted gray, flying the American flag. Traffic on the many bridges that crossed the river came to a complete stop and people left their vehicles to run to the railings to wave and express their good wishes for our safe journey. The younger sailors, who whistled at the sight of the young ladies at the first bridge, were warned that it wasn't an activity that would be allowed. The ship didn't have a regular PA system installed as yet. The Captain was on the loud hailer almost instantly. He spoke of the reputation of his ship, the Navy, and the respect that was to be shown to all along our way down the river. The Commanding Officer of the training crew decreed that in the Navy, "Only Boatswain (Bos'n) Mates and fools whistle."

Our Daily Work Routines

Being the leading Radarman, I was without that duty since the ship's Radar was to be installed when we reached the Naval Base outside New Orleans. Being a member of the Communications Division, I didn't have Deck Force duties. I needed something to do for these two weeks. Patrick Kevin Healy, our Leading Quartermaster, had a tremendous job to do on top of his other duties. Each ship had a large, eight-inch thick loose-leaf manual titled "Notice to Mariners." This manual and others like it contained all the notices and warnings pertaining to navigation of the ship in all the waters of the world. The notices warned of hazards marked with buoys, channel hazards, shoal waters, lighthouse flashing sequences. The manuals were issued in small single-spaced print and corrections or additions to a particular site or location had to be changed as soon as received. The corrections were cut from sheets labeled Additions, Corrections and Deletions, and pasted over the print in the manual. New information was received constantly. New pages were included when it was determined that the pasting would jeopardize the use of that particular page of the manual. This was the tedious part of the military. The sheer volume of the changes was enormous. Pat asked me if I could help him, and I was grateful to be busy. Being without any real duties until we arrived at our destination, it was the opportunity to learn something I knew little about.

The major problem was all new ships, such as our new LST, were supplied with a manual that had no prior corrections. It was tedious and sometimes mind-numbing work until the many boxes, which were numbered and dated in sequence, were emptied. The work had to be done to protect the ship and the crew from marine hazards. Much of the information was extremely confidential and the waste was shredded. Pat pitched in when his regular duties allowed. I was happy to have something to do. The senior members of the ship's various departments were involved with the same type of updating. When the manual was fully corrected and up to date, the new corrections and updates came at regular intervals and it was easy to keep up with the flow.

Some Ohio River Cities and Views Along the Way

With all the cities we saw along the way, the places with the most industry and the largest populations were the most memorable. Some of the cities were familiar to me from school or associated with celebrities of my day: Steubenville, Ohio; Wheeling, West Virginia; Parkersburg, West Virginia; Huntington, West Virginia;

Portsmouth, Ohio; Louisville, Kentucky; Evansville, Indiana; Cairo, Illinois.

Cincinnati, Ohio

Little did I know that this major city in Ohio would have another role in my life, when my middle daughter, Elizabeth, and her family would live in Cincinnati. But, during WWII it was just another river city on our way to the South Pacific. The city sits on the northern bank of the Ohio River. As we passed under a bridge crossing the river from Cincinnati to Kentucky, I was struck by its similarity to New York's Brooklyn Bridge. Years later, I found out two bridges were designed and built by the same man, German-American John Roebling. That Roebling Bridge in Cincinnati, which our LST-759 passed under in 1943, was built in 1866 as the longest suspension bridge in the world. The Brooklyn Bridge, built 30 years after the Roebling, is a mirror image. Both are architectural treasures.

USS LST-759 Enters the Mississippi River

Our 1000-mile trip down the Ohio River from Pittsburgh, Pennsylvania to Cairo, Illinois, had come to its end. As our ship entered the Mississippi river at Cairo, Illinois, the river averaged from 3000 feet to 5000 feet wide with a depth of about 15 feet. The Pilots for this river had a daunting task to navigate this part of our voyage. As soon as we entered the Mississippi, it wandered to all parts of the compass and would at times turn back on itself. Soon after we left the Ohio River, we had the state of Kentucky on our portside and Missouri on the starboard side. Almost as soon as we had reached the Kentucky state line we began to head north and Kentucky was on our starboard and Missouri was on the port. Before we crossed the Kentucky state line into Tennessee, we changed directions north and south four times. The river almost straightened out as we made a turn to the south at New Madrid, Missouri. The Ohio River was like an arrow by comparison.

We saw so much waste disposal along the Ohio and Mississippi Rivers. The towns of any size would draw water from the river up stream of the town and dump their wastewater at the town limits down stream. It was easy to see that the volume of water coursing down the river was the only real wastewater dilution the shore-side inhabitants could hope for. The water must have dispersed the contaminants and reduced the threat. The pipes that spewed the crud were very large and increased in size as we passed through larger industrialized areas; the smell of the noxious outflow was very strong. When we passed through forested areas, where the thick woodlands came up to the river's edge, the banks were like high dirt cliffs. The swift river water had undermined the banks and whole sections of trees dropped off into the river, to float downstream creating navigation hazards.

We began to pass through hundreds of riverside cities and towns of various sizes: Caruthersville, Missouri; West Memphis, Arkansas; Memphis, Tennessee; Helena, Arkansas. Further down the river we passed Greenville, Mississippi, and crossed the Louisiana state line. Lake Providence, in northeastern Louisiana, was 170 miles north of Baton Rouge, Louisiana. Barges of various lengths tied together, hauling of coal and sand, were moving in both directions along the river, not only for the war effort, but also the raw materials and goods for the country. Next we sailed past Vicksburg, Mississippi on the east bank and I thought about Civil War soldiers and their battles. Now we were sailing to battle in another part of the world.

The Mississippi River continued with switch backs and hundreds of forks in the river; just one wrong turn and the ship could be aground. The Pilots knew their river, but our ship did have a few bumps along the way.

The Paddle Wheel Steamboats on the Rivers

It seemed as if most of the larger cities on the river had paddle wheel steamboats. Many were tied up to the shore in various degrees of repair. The ones that were restored and renovated were a sight to see; cities used them for moonlight cruises and restaurants. It was easy to imagine the importance of the old paddle wheelers in bygone days.

As we passed the Mississippi state line, the towns became more numerous. The small towns were blending together into one long city; the river made large turns that gave us the opportunity to see much of the area leading into Baton Rouge.

Excitement Was Building

After our long river journey from Pittsburgh, the excitement was beginning to build for us sailors, our imaginations working overtime. While the journey down the river was great, we were ready to get off the ship. Knowing that we would be two or three weeks in the Navy yard at Algiers, across the Mississippi River from the New Orleans was a dream come true. We had seen the wonders of Pittsburgh, and now we were ready for the shore activities in New Orleans.

New Orleans, Louisiana

As with the other larger cities along the rivers we traveled, the scenery before us changed to factories and industrial areas. The shorelines in most of the areas were covered with what looked like the black asphalt used in road construction, from high up on the banks to beneath the water's surface. The skyline changed to multi-storied buildings and skyscrapers. The activities on the river had increased ten-fold, and the oceangoing ships seemed to be everywhere. Naval vessels, mostly Destroyers and Transports, were being loaded and prepared to go to sea. Our Pilot directed LST-759 to a berth at the Naval Support Activity base at Algiers, on the west bank of the Mississippi.

U.S. Naval Support Activity, Algiers, Louisiana

My knowledge of Naval Bases were the huge Norfolk, Virginia Naval Operating Base and the other large bases I had visited from New York to Charleston, South Carolina, as a Radarman aboard the USS Ramsden DE-382. The dock at Algiers gave little clue of the activity ashore, other than a few cranes working on other ships close aboard. Even though the LST-759 had prepared in Pittsburgh for the shallow water part of our voyage, our propeller had been damaged and repairs had to be completed. Also, the mast, the antenna systems for radar and radio, the signal lights, the cables for that equipment, and the halyards for our national flag and signal flags, had to be raised and stayed. Among the many things to be done was the Degaussing of the ship to help it defend against magnetic mines and torpedoes. The last and one of the most important jobs was loading all of the ammunition we had to carry for all the 20mm and 40mm anti-aircraft weapons. The guns were for our protection and for defending the task forces we would join.

Carrying a Landing Craft Tank and Her Crew

The Algiers Navy Yard crews started welding strange brackets to the sides of the ship, just above the water line. The brackets were installed about three feet apart and extended almost the entire length of the ship. Another set of brackets was welded close to the deck line, also the same distances. We were told that they could be bolted together to hold pontoons to form a dock at a landing sight.

Other crews were welding brackets to the top deck and the brackets were bolted to huge 12"x12" timbers that extended just beyond the entire width of the ship. We had been selected to carry a 114-foot long and 33-foot wide, 286-ton amphibious landing craft designated as an LCT, Landing-Craft-Tank. An LCT was not a commissioned ship of the Navy, although it had an Officer in Charge and a crew of 14 enlisted men. The LCT was able to carry five Sherman Tanks or 180 tons of cargo for 700 miles at a top speed of seven knots. It had three Gray Marine diesel engines geared to three propellers and came armed with two 20mm anti-aircraft weapons and two .50-caliber machine guns. The LCT was hoisted aboard by a huge crane in the Navy Yard and placed on the timbers that would be the skids to slide her off when our ship launched it at the invasion site. The LCT was lashed to our deck by huge cables and turnbuckles. When it came time to launch, the skids would be slathered with heavy grease and all but one of the cables would be released. The remaining cable attachment had a massive pelican hook on the end opposite the launch side. The pelican hook was a heavy, hinged affair that passed through a heavy ring, and was held by the pressure against its hook. The LST would flood its tanks on the launch side and empty its tanks on the opposite side, thereby creating an angle toward the beach. After it would be determined that all hands were safely out of danger, a boatswains mate with a heavy sledge hammer would hit the retaining ring that held the pelican hook closed. This would release the hook and the LCT would slide into the sea. All compartment doors in the LCT were to be sealed tight because a tremendous amount of water would come over its low side. A huge wave of water would act as a cushion between the LST and the LCT and to prevent damage to either one. The LCT crew would be on our landing craft and would board her soon after the launch. The Naval Engineers that devised the launch procedure were very clever.

New Orleans Shore Liberty

The sights that the crew saw from Algiers across the river to New Orleans were magnetic. We knew we would be docked at Algiers for about three weeks. The officers knew that shore liberty was the only thing on our minds. As soon as the ship and its equipment were secured and the Captain received his orders, the officers were called to a meeting in the officers' wardroom. About 15 minutes later the Captain set Port and Starboard liberty. One half of the crew could go ashore until 0700 hours the next morning; the other half would commence liberty at 1300 hours the next afternoon. Normal routine was established, such as security, meals and cleanup. Before the last line was secured to the dock, a panel truck pulled up to the gangway and the driver from the civilian dry cleaning store was prepared to pick up our Dress Blue uniforms and return them in the morning. I often wondered how local businesses got the ship's information. Most times the Ship's Service Store made the arrangements, and received money to the benefit the personnel. It was always nice to be able to have our uniforms cleaned and packaged prior to leaving, to be ready for the next shore liberty.

Bourbon Street, New Orleans

Access to New Orleans from Algiers Naval Support Base was by a regularly scheduled ferry. The area was below sea level and bayous and swamps were everywhere. Along the shore were large signs that announced No Anchoring, Cable Crossing and No Anchoring, Asphalt Mattresses, meaning the banks were reinforced with asphalt to prevent erosion. Most of the personnel working at the Algiers base lived on the New Orleans side. Some workers lived on the base, in a few small towns, but as a whole, New Orleans was the place to be. It was the only place we sailors wanted to be.

The business area was just a short walk from where the ferry docked to let us off. Any of the crew who could, arranged for leave if they were close enough to home, and took off, to return by a specified date. Being from Boston, which was a long way from New Orleans, made it impossible for me to go home and stay within the time constraints imposed. Those of us staying all wanted to see famous Bourbon Street. I wanted to find a nice restaurant that offered a real non-military meal, such as a big juicy steak with a baked potato and a large cold glass of milk. The food coming down the Ohio and Mississippi Rivers was great, but a nice juicy steak was not on the menu. I found a place to eat and had cold local beer instead of the milk. As soon as the wrinkles were out of my belly, I began walking to reconnoiter and find out where the action was.

Action meant different things to different people. A ship full of unmarried sailors covered the whole spectrum of desire. Where was the Best Bar? Where was the Best Music, the Most Girls, the Cheapest Drinks, the Best Free Entertainment; you name it, some sailor was seeking it. Having some money, I had the opportunity to sample some of the best beer, south of Boston. One thing that intrigued me was the dark brown streetcar, rumbling down the middle of the street. The streetcars reminded me of home; the fares were cheap, and I took off by myself to see the city.

I bought a ticket to the evening moonlight cruise aboard the stern wheeler, listened to the music, had a beer or two and returned to our ship's quarters after the cruise ended. My funds were limited and going on a date was out of the question. Throughout the days of liberty, I toured the whole city from end to end, went into every bar and saloon, every honky-tonk. I really enjoyed the music places along Bourbon Street and usually stood inside the doorway against the wall, out of harm's way. The city had hundreds of military personnel milling around, and it was usually safe to stay with the crowds instead of going off solo. The officers usually gravitated toward the major hotels downtown, such as the Roosevelt and the Hotel Jung. Most of the enlisted found these hotels too expensive for what we were earning.

A group of us sailors went to a place called The Wonder Bar, away from the downtown area. We were all sitting at the bar, and a floorshow was taking place in the lounge area. It had a stage with a small orchestra, and several young women in costumes were singing and dancing. Most of us stayed in the bar because there was a cover charge inside the lounge plus the drinks were more expensive. We all enjoyed the show as much as we could through the large doorway off the bar. When the show was over, one of the girls walked into the bar. As she passed behind me she cleared her throat and began speaking in a very male voice. I was in shock. Being the youngest in our group, the look on my face must have been priceless, and everyone at our table all burst into laughter looking at me. I had been the only one who didn't know we were in a club for female impersonators. They had me fooled; the costumes, the makeup, the singing, though, were really sensational.

The pace began to quicken on the ship; it seemed as if all the painting and modifications were done. My Radar and Radio Transponders were being checked out and the RT Radar Tech and I had been on the mast checking all the cables and cable stays for our equipment. We had to verify that all the installations were seaworthy and correct. The radiomen were all back from leave and were at full speed checking, checking, and checking. No one spoke openly of safety, but our lives would depend on everything being correct. My Radar Tech's name was Bob Baird. We were fortunate to have him; he knew everything the Navy knew as well as the manufacturer of the equipment. He could look at a blueprint of the equipment and travel through a schematic as if it had been his own idea. We never had a moment of trouble with any of the equipment as long as he was in charge. He was our resident brain and a great personality to boot.

After all areas were tested, we moved to an area down river where the ship was wrapped from stem to stern with large diameter cables. All clocks, watches, compasses and anything that could be affected by magnetism had to be removed from the ship while we were at the Degaussing station. The ship was being demagnetized to give it some protection from enemy magnetic mines. Permanent cables, installed around the ship during construction, could be energized with various voltages as we passed through the different magnetic areas while at sea. The ship's navigator was always aware of these areas, because it affected his computations as he plotted our courses around the world. He would refer to a controller that looked like a large, square metal box with a meter at the top and a large round hand control knob at the center to control the voltage that passed through the cables. Lieutenant Carroll Pfeiffer was our navigator, and this was just one of his many responsibilities. He took them all seriously; we never missed an ETA, estimated time of arrival, with him as our navigator, and Quartermaster Patrick Kevin Healy as his assistant. Little did we know that Pat Healy would receive a Wartime Appointment to the United States Coast Guard Academy, in New London, Connecticut, before the end of the war in the Pacific.

A day was spent getting squared away after Degaussing. The next morning the ship was maneuvered checking the compasses and setting the gyrocompass for all headings. We maneuvered up river to the Naval Supply Depot and all hands worked to load all the food and stores we would need for our trip through the Panama Canal to San Diego. The frozen food locker was loaded as well as all the dry stores and fresh foods and vegetables we would eat. The small Ship Service Office was stocked with the candy bars and dozens of other items the crew could buy, such as toothpaste, Athletes Foot remedies, writing paper, and anything the Navy did not provide for personal use.

The following day we moved to the Naval Ammunition Depot and a couple of Navy rail boxcars were waiting with our consignment of arms and ammunition. The ammunition ready boxes were now installed at all 20mm and 40mm anti-aircraft weapons and were loaded with magazines; the storage magazines below decks were fully loaded with the reserve ammunition.

The following morning we returned to a remote area of the Naval Supply Depot and railcars were waiting on a siding dock with a crew of stevedores to load and secure the thousands of cases of beer onto our tank deck. Yes, good old American beer. Marine Guards were at every entrance to the tank deck; any entrance was blocked or locked. Thousands of cans of beer in 24-can cases, with names I never heard of like Alpen Brau and Rolling Rock and a dozen more, were packaged in olive drab boxes in olive drab cans. The beer drinkers on board were salivating and their eyes were as big as saucers. You could almost hear sailors thinking, "How can I get into the tank deck and get a case or two or a can or two?" All thoughts of Duty and Honor were forgotten; it was going to be a long trip to San Diego.

We knew that we were ready to leave when the local dry cleaners' truck came screaming down the dock with the crew's fresh, cleaned uniforms all wrapped in brown paper and tied with string. The driver presented the bill and was paid out of the Ship's Service Funds to be collected from the crew when time allowed. I didn't open my package, I just took it and stowed it in my locker, until another liberty would be announced.

Leaving New Orleans to Join Pacific Forces

The Captain used the loud hailer to signal the Setting of the Special Sea Detail; our public address system was not fully functioning as yet. Bill Baird and I were in the process of running cable to the speakers around the ship, not only for emergency announcements, but for Armed Forces Radio music and for a 33-1/3 and 78 rpm record player, to be bought with funds at the Ship's Service Store. The deck force went into action and the Chiefs and the Bos'ns Mates had all the seamen at their duty stations. All lines were singled up, the bridge was manned and the engine room was ready to answer all bells from the bridge. The Skipper was on the flying bridge with the Navigator Carroll Pfeiffer, the Executive Officer, and two seaman lookouts. Pat Healy, our Quartermaster, was in the wheelhouse tending the Ship's Log, as well as his other supervisory duties. The wheel was manned as well as the Engine Telegraph to the engine room. Jim Madden, our senior Signalman, was at the flag bag aft of the bridge, ready to hoist the flags that signal the ship's intentions.

All lines were finally cast off and USS LST-759 was into the Mississippi River as it flowed to the sea. The ship had been commissioned on August 25, 1944, and now we were leaving on September 26, 1944. We had boarded our Pilot at the Algiers Naval Base and as mentioned in prior chapters, he was an expert on the river and knew all the sand bars and snags, the twists and the turns along the way. The Pilot was the final authority during our journey to the sea; this was the time when even the Captain was under his control. It was understood that he was the expert in this situation, and he was respected for his service.

As soon as the ship left the vicinity of Algiers, it was plain to see that the services of a Pilot were needed. Our direction changed from due east, to south, to west, to southwest, and finally to southeast as we arrived at Pilottown, and then southwest to a channel leading into the Gulf of Mexico. The dredged channels were at least 45 feet deep and we passed several large ocean freighters and tankers as we very slowly made our way to the sea. It was estimated that we would drop off the Pilot at his headquarters in Pilottown in approximately 8 hours; we would follow a buoyed channel to the Gulf of Mexico and be on our way.

The Gulf of Mexico and the Caribbean Sea

Although we were on our own, our proximity to U.S. Cuban bases and other U.S. Naval Air Force facilities provided air support and anti-submarine protection. My Radar was picking up aircraft blips at all hours of the day. The route we were taking to Panama was through the Straits of Yucatan between the Yucatan Peninsula and the Cuba. The Straits were 120 miles wide and deep water all the way.

After we left the Mississippi and were about three hours into the Gulf of Mexico, I went out on deck, looked over the side and down into the water. It looked as if we had passed over a fence. An almost straight line stretched across our bow and as far as the eye could see; it was clear blue water on one side and muddy water to our rear. Our salt-water evaporators could now replenish our fresh water supplies. Fresh water was a mostly rationed commodity on smaller ships, and we were fortunate that our newer model LST-759 had evaporators. The older ones had to scavenge fresh water wherever they could. In the Pacific, Fresh Water Tankers had to be deployed, not only for islands that had no reliable water supply, but also for smaller combat ships without the ability to distill their own water.

Being the Senior Radarman and a veteran of several convoys, the mostly new officers relied on the information I relayed to them, especially during the hours of darkness. The Communications Officer, who was a veteran Chief Radioman at the height of the submarine battles in the North Atlantic, thanked me for training the Strikers, apprentice Radarmen. It wasn't long before my confidence in them was sufficient that they were allowed to perform on their own. Only one of the apprentices, the Relief Striker, gave me second thoughts. When on Radar watch the operator was expected to continually monitor the Radar Screen; we had no time to read, to visit or stray from the station. A Radar operator was lucky to be able to light a cigarette. I hoped this Relief Striker would fall into line with the rest of us.

Our course to traverse the Straits of Yucatan would cover about 600 miles from New Orleans. The route was a major artery for shipping. The ship was on constant alert against German submarine attack. The crew was on a four hours on, eight hours off schedule. Everyone on the Radar gang, except the Relief Striker, was relieved of the usual seaman details such as chipping paint, standing gun watches. Although all of my crew had other General Quarters stations, my station was in the Radar room even if I was off duty at the time. If one of us was the Radar operator during chow call, we would be relieved for chow by one of the group.

We had our usual calls to General Quarters during the days and the nights. All weapons had to be manned and ready. The Skipper had his stopwatch out on every drill, and the division officers felt his ire when we didn't meet expectations. This constant drilling was the same on every naval vessel; the sailors who took drills seriously were more likely to survive.

The Radar on LST-759 was in the rear of the chartroom, off the regular bridge. The door to the bridge opened into the room, which contained a very large table along one wall for the large charts used by the Navigator and the Quartermasters. Several large, locked drawers about four inches in depth were mounted on tracks as part of the chart table cabinet. Mounted on the wall above were several special radios. Pat Healy could use the radio to check the time for the ship's chronometers; accuracy was so important when the Navigator was using his sextant to shoot the stars and the sun to ascertain the ship's position. Pat would be standing beside Carroll Pfeiffer with a stopwatch and call, "Mark." Mr. Pfeiffer would read the angle on the sextant, and then retire to the chartroom to make his mathematical computations to determine the ship's position. He would usually have a plain sheet of chart paper taped to the tabletop, so it wouldn't and couldn't be moved. No one was authorized to enter the room except the enlisted Radar crew, the Radio Crew, the Quartermasters and the Officers. Pat Healy would come in occasionally to check the Navigation radios or pickup the "Time Tick" used to check the clocks. The Time Tick was transmitted at regular intervals from Washington, D.C. One of the radios was close to the end of the table and closest to the Radar set. Occasionally, Pat would tune in a stateside commercial station for some of the current music and share his earphones with me.

The Radarman wore a set of sound-powered phones and had immediate access to the lookout on the flying bridge. Next to the position was a speaking tube that went to the bridge; just depress a signal button mounted at the tube and it would alert the Officer at the con who would answer. At night when the ship was darkened, all doors opening to the outside were equipped with an automatic switch that turned the lights off in the immediate vicinity; this was to prevent any light from the ship shining out over the water. Some interior areas were only lighted with red lights to protect night vision.

At sea, the Radar operated 24-hours a day. A Radar log was kept of the hours Radar equipment was used, and the time it was down for a malfunction. All repair parts were logged as well. Bill Baird was a wizard with all the electronics and kept everything in working condition. He shared his knowledge with me and didn't treat me as the 18-year-old I was.

The ship could travel between 75 to 100 miles per day, depending on wind and the sea currents. The estimated running time to pass through the Straits of Yucatan was about eight days. I happened to be on Radar watch as we approached the straits. The distance between Cuba and the Yucatan peninsula was 120 miles. I picked up an electronic image on the Radar screen that amazed me. The picture on my screen was a perfect image of about one-third of the island of Cuba to the east, and part of the Yucatan peninsula to the west. I was seeing at least 60 miles on either side of our ship! I called the Officer of the Deck and he came down and was equally amazed. He returned to the con, called down to the officers' wardroom, and the Captain and some of the other Officers to view the Radar image. The Navigator came by and his calculations had us right on course and right on time. That night I was very proud of the Radar equipment and the operators.

By morning we had passed through the Yucatan Channel into the Caribbean Sea, and a new course was set for the Panama Canal; we had approximately 1000 miles to go. This portion of the journey was made more complicated for the Navigator; many small islands dotted this part of the Caribbean and the sea depths varied greatly. We were out of sight of land most of the time. Our estimated time of arrival at the Canal was approximately 10 days after we passed Yucatan. Having already been to the Canal when we escorted our first convoy on the Destroyer Escort USS Ramsden, it would be the first time I actually made the transit across to the Pacific Ocean. I had great expectations as well as did the whole crew.

The weather was calm with a few showers now and then to break the monotony of the constant training drills and the never-ending maintenance. We had boat drills, which required the partial lowering and securing of the large four LCVPs, landing craft vehicle-personnel, on the aft part of the ship. The gunnery crew practiced live firing of the 20mm and 40mm anti-aircraft weapons. Two of the weapons were twin 40mm's, one on the stern and the other on the bow, each aimed remotely by an operator with an electronic sight. He was strapped to the gun sight which he moved with large bicycle handle bars; when he moved that weapon moved. The twin 40mm weapons generated tremendous smoke and vibration. They could be fired for great lengths of time; the barrels were encased in a circulating water chamber to keep them cool and to prevent burnout. The twin 40mm weapons were operated by six-man crews and all could be operated manually in the event the remote operator was incapacitated. We had four more single barreled 40mm weapons, one on each side of the bow and one on each side of the stern; they were operated manually. The sides of the ship were lined with 20mm anti-aircraft weapons operated manually by three-man crews; these weapons were high output and used a huge amount of ammunition. Around each weapon were large containers, called Ready Boxes; each contained loaded magazines for that particular gun. The ship's magazines below deck had thousands more; the magazines were reloaded when time permitted. The shells used in the magazines had to be greased as they were placed in the container and every fifth shell had to be a tracer that blazed as it traveled to the target so the sailor firing the gun could see the track.

The ship's personnel were organized into divisions. Our sleeping quarters were one deck below, along both sides of the ship. Each division was split and co-billeted or mixed in these compartments, so that in the event of a disaster, no one division would be wiped out and unable to function. The only enlisted crewmembers having private quarters were the Chiefs. The Officers had their wardroom, galley and mess cooks that prepared and served them their meals. Each two Officers had their own sleeping compartment, but most of the time the Officers were singled up if we did not carry additional visiting Officers. The LST-759 had room for carrying combat personnel, so most compartments had empty billets.

Toward the stern of the ship, the first compartment below deck entered was the mess hall, which was used as a day room for reading or writing. Forward of that was the Head, bathroom, which contained several sinks along the outside bulkhead and several showers, toilets and urinals on the inner bulkhead. If a sailor was assigned to the first sleeping compartment after the Head, it was bad luck, because it was noisy and well lit most of the time. When not carrying troops and their equipment, we had sleeping room to spare. Most activity in the compartments was curtailed at 2000 hours to allow the crewmembers with the Mid Watch, midnight to 0400 hours, to get some sleep. There was always a card game being played that the Master-at-Arms had to shut down.

When we were close to the 16th parallel and 80-degrees of longitude, our course changed to almost due south, for a straight shot to the Panama Canal. We were somewhere near 450 to 500 miles, about three days away, assuming that we were making about 10 knots per hour. Usually the crew had little news of our progress and rumors were rampant. In the olden days of the Navy, a water cask was called a Scuttlebutt; it was where the crew congregated and where all rumors started. In the Navy of my day, Scuttlebutt, rumors, started at the ship's water fountain.

After we came to our southern heading, Radar echoes became more numerous as we neared the Panama Canal. Aircraft from the Navy and the Army were on patrol 24-hours of the day. Our IFF (electronic Identification Friend or Foe) system was working perfectly; it was a two way street and our system was as important to us as theirs was to them. This area was like a funnel for the ships to transit the canal and would be a priority target for any German submarine that could slip through the security nets. Destroyers and Destroyer Escorts patrolled the seaways with their Sonar screens 24-hours a day and their presence was quite visible.

Our Radar picked up land about 100 miles away as we approached the Canal Zone. We saw many LST's, and Merchant ships of every description and country of origin, all fully loaded with war material. Most ships were at slow speed or were keeping station as we neared the breakwater. We saw several submarines at the sub base as we past Coco Solo on the way in. The closed submarine nets blocked and protected the entrance to the canal. Several hours after we arrived, the pilot boat came alongside and our civilian pilot came aboard to take us through the submarine nets, which were opened and closed by a tug attached to the nets. During our wait outside the submarine nets and all during our passage through the nets, we were under the Pilot's control. Our junior signalman was at the flag bag and senior signalman Jim Madden was at the blinker light, sending and receiving messages for the ship in Morse code from Harbor Control tower. All this signal traffic was pertaining to the Captain's new orders and imminent meetings prior to our passage through the canal on our way to San Diego.

We Enter the Panama Canal

The Panamanian Pilot, dressed as an Officer in a white uniform, with his hat bearing a gold badge similar to a Navy Officer, took command of our ship and directed us to a long pier that had several LST's tied up in nests. It took us about one hour to complete the process. The Captain and the Pilot saluted each other, shook hands and the Pilot boarded another pilot boat on our port side and headed out to escort the next ship. With all the LST's tied up and smaller ships at anchor, it was evident we would be joined with others for a transit through the locks, and form up a convoy to San Diego. We would move out in about four days. This would give the crew two liberties while here, much to the delight of the men.

Captain addressed the crew and gave us his usual pep talk, salted with admonitions that we were to be in a foreign country, subject to their laws, and our behavior reflected on the ship. Port and Starboard liberty was established for the time we were to be tied up. The first group of sailors to go ashore was all dressed in their whites in what seemed an instant. Liberty passes were handed out and away they went to the usual unknown adventure of shore leave. Several of the rated men went ashore to augment the Shore Patrol. They wore black bands with SP in yellow letters and wore their authority, shown by the 24-inch billy club, hanging on their web belt. An Officer or a Chief carried a Colt .45 weapon.

The first of the crew to return after the first liberty party carried gifts for the folks back home. The most purchased item ashore was Chanel No. 5 perfume. I often wondered if it was the real stuff or counterfeit. Many sailors had found the Red Light District soon after getting downtown.

The next day I dressed to go on liberty with the second half of the crew. I unwrapped my blue uniform that had been delivered by the New Orleans dry cleaners just before we shipped out. I was stunned when I saw it! Mine had been the spare service uniform I bought for $35 from the tailor in Brooklyn. The uniform returned to me in New Orleans was a custom tailored heavy serge jumper and pants with rayon lining. It had multicolored dragons embroidered on the inside of the button cuffs and the waist area. It was a perfect fit. None of the crew sent out word complaining of the mistake, and we were a long way from New Orleans to find my uniform. I hope the sailor who got mine would not lament the loss of his dragons. I rewrapped the uniform and put on the uniform of the day in these tropical ports, my Dress Whites.

Having been ashore in the Canal Zone before, I answered questions from sailors who were visiting for the first time. The canal during this time was managed by the U.S. and was considered to be part of the United States. The Canal Zone was bordered with a large chain link fence that was patrolled and protected by U.S. Army troops, Army Air Force, and Navy sea and aircraft vessels stationed in the zone. Close to the canal were tall streetlights with an extra bright blue light atop to identify the zone limits. In many places along the way these secure areas bisected populated areas. The U.S. government canal authority employed native Panamanians who lived and shopped in large cities along the canal. Identification cards had been issued to the population. They were required to show ID to cross the canal at guard points. All military also had to show ID for entry into the zone. The Canal Zone was a highly protected military transit area.

I went into town with a group of sailors, and I got a haircut. Many commercial buildings and large department stores were along the broad streets. The stores were full of merchandise; restaurants and sidewalk vendors seemed to be everywhere. The menus were a mix of Latin flavor and All-American. Servicemen seemed to outnumber the local Panamanians.

I strolled by a tattoo parlor and saw one of our crew getting a tattoo. He was having the names of every major port he had visited added to his arms, including Panama and San Diego. He was just about finished, so I waited for him and we set off to have some beer. He told me that he wanted to get the Purple Heart when we got into battle. I warned him that most of them were given posthumously; that didn't seem to bother him in the least.

As we entered the first bar, pretty young girls came rushing up and asked us to buy them a drink. I took off by myself after a couple of good cold draft beers and toured the area. I strolled in and out of some department stores, and ended up at the El Gato Negro, the nightclub that I had visited on my last trip. I found most of our crew there, drinking with the ladies on their laps. I had enough trouble affording my own drinks, and after a couple, I left, and wandered back to the ship. I met several of the crew with the same idea. When we got back to the ship we learned we had been refueled and reprovisioned. It looked like we were ready to sail and our liberty was going to be cut short.

Gatun Locks

There was activity all around the ship early the next morning. The Skipper announced that we would start transiting the Canal at 0700 and enter the Pacific Ocean approximately ten or eleven hours later. The crew was disappointed to leave so soon and would have to wait for San Diego to get back to the bars.

At 0700, we entered Limon Bay, Cristobal, and a Panamanian Pilot boarded the ship. We proceeded southbound towards the Gatun Locks. It consisted of three chambers, which raised our ship from sea level to Gatun Lake, a height of 85 feet. The LST-759 was moored to electric towing locomotives, running on tracks on each side of the lock. All six of the Canal locks were similar in dimensions and method of operation.

We Follow the Setting Sun to the Pacific Ocean

It took about eight hours for LST-759 to make the transit. At the end we saw Panama City off to port. Seeing the city was a disappointment to the crewmembers. Shore liberty would have been so much better if we had been able to walk the broad boulevards, shop at its stores and surely it would have had a greater variety of watering holes for sailors. As the isthmus slipped astern and the ships that transited with us caught up, we began to form up into a semblance of a small convoy. Several Destroyer Escorts formed our screen for the 10 miles per hour the slowest ships could maintain. Several Destroyers, not needed for anti-submarine escort duty, took off and were soon out of sight, on their way to San Diego, I presumed. The only thing the crew knew for sure was that we were going to San Diego. Destroyers were patrolling the Canal entrance area and several aircraft were seen and heard close by, mostly during the day, and a few at night.

LST-759 Enters the Pacific Ocean

The journey to San Diego would be close to 3000 miles. Again, imaginations were working overtime. We didn't have any money, but we would be paid in cash prior to arriving. We were looking forward to being at the Naval Base. Beer was 25 cents on base, first run movies were 10 cents, and a better selection of souvenirs was offered at the Ship's Service Store at the base.

The weather to San Diego was calm with a few scattered squalls of rain. The Pacific Ocean was what I had always imagined, calm and beautiful. The North Atlantic from my experiences was ruled by the mountainous storms we encountered during our USS Ramsden convoy duty. I'm sure LST-759 would see bad weather, but all we saw up until this time was a peaceful Pacific.

It was to take about eight days to cover the distance from the Canal to San Diego Bay. Our journey to San Diego was a first for most of the LST-759 crew. Most were from the Midwest, South and the Northeast. The sailors talked about Tijuana, Mexico. The city had a reputation for bawdy shore leaves. All this sailor scuttlebutt hinged on the LST-759 staying in port for a while. Our course kept us well out to sea to avoid some of the shoals and small islands along the way. My Radar picked up the Central American and the Mexican coast occasionally, but no land was seen from the deck. Our small convoy had no mechanical problems and set speed according to the slowest ship in the convoy. We were the slowest ship, at about eight knots, because we were fully loaded, including thousands of cases of well-guarded Midwest beer.

Beer Liberation

The LST-759 had several large stacks, or air intakes, just forward of the bridge. They were about 12 feet high and had climbing irons welded to the outside and the inside. At the bottom of the stack was a huge electric fan to exhaust the air in the Tank Deck when tank and vehicle engines were loading or leaving the ship. To supply the air for the engine combustion and to exhaust the fumes for safety, air was pulled through passageways and other stacks forward on the ship. I think we had about six stacks to exhaust and about five for fresh air intakes. The tops of the exhaust stacks were fitted with canvas covers to protect from the weather.

The thousands of cases of beer were stacked almost to the overhead, ceiling. All entrances were locked and patrolled. The guards must have thought, "There was no way the beer could be liberated." A shipload of sailors with unquenchable thirsts and devious plans thought otherwise. Most of the canvas covers were off to passively ventilate the tank deck and were loosely tied or hanging from one of the climbing irons. While working with one of the covers, one of the crew looked down into the stack and, between the huge fan blades, saw down the stack to the cargo of beer, lots of beer.

It didn't take much imagination to see that a slight person could slip between the blades and frame, stand on the cargo and pass a case to someone standing on the motor and hanging onto the interior climbing irons. Passing the case of beer to others on the exterior climbing irons would be simple. The temptation was even greater because the officers had a liquor ration and beer in their fridge in their wardroom, and the enlisted men had fresh water. A plan was devised and "Midnight Requisition" was born. The only way it would work was if no sailor got greedy or careless. No one did, and a trail of empty, liberated beer cans were left floating from Panama to San Diego to Pearl Harbor. The discipline was amazing!

Our small convoy, composed of several LST's and their escort vessels, was nearing our destination of San Diego Naval Operating Base. My Radar began picking up the coastline and Navy patrols intercepted us south of the border between the U.S. and Mexico. Navy Patrol planes were in evidence at all hours of the day and night. San Diego was a major training base on the west coast and a major staging area for all ship movement west to Pearl Harbor, and south to the Panama Canal. Patrol craft of every description with their Sonar and Radar swept the area 24-hours a day to protect the Naval Base.

Naval Operating Base, San Diego, California

We formed up single file and approached the submarine nets protecting the huge harbor. The Escorts continued their Sonar sweeps for submarines as the Navy Tenders opened the nets. We had picked up the usual Pilots who assumed control of the convoy vessels to move us to our docking areas. We passed through the open nets and to starboard saw the Naval Airbase at North Island. We made a turn as we entered and saw a lighthouse on the mountainside bluffs, to port. It was the Cabrillo National Monument, dedicated in 1913.

We entered the main channel, passing the large Submarine Base on our port side. There were moorings along the length of the Naval Air Base at North Island. One of the spots contained an Essex-class Aircraft Carrier sporting a new coat of paint; she looked as if she was making ready for sea. Her deck was full of planes tied down with their wings folded. We could see other planes through the openings in the hanger deck. A bee hive of activity was around her; two Navy tugs were close to the ship. It appeared as though the crew were all at their stations and a host of sailors were on the flight deck as if to have a final view of the area as they departed. In Navy language, the Special Sea Detail had been set.

The Pilots took our ship and the other LST's to the long docks at the Naval Base. We tied up into a nest of six LST's, each side by side with the first LST tied to the dock. We were the last to tie up to this particular nest and we were the outer ship. It made for a long walk over each ship to the dock, but had the advantage of being able to load supplies and fuel directly from barges brought alongside.

There was no immediate Liberty Call. The Captain and other Officers had been summoned by the Base Commander at Naval Headquarters for orders. The crew thought that liberty would be granted when the ship's Officers returned. Meanwhile, our signal gang had been busy since LST-759 made port. The harbor was controlled by a tower that resembled the kind seen at airports, and the signal lights were giving information in Morse code to all the ships entering the base.

The Officers returned later in the day and told the crew Shore Liberty would be granted the next day. Crewmembers not on duty were given the run of the base and allowed to visit the large Ship's Service facility and recreation area, meaning cold beer was available at a reasonable price. We could also shop the merchandise at the Ship's Service Store, which was restricted to military service members; our ID had to be presented to the guards on duty at the store.

Our Electronic Technician, Bill Baird, had been given the job of altering the ship's PA system to receive broadcasts and music from the Armed Forces Radio Network. We had installed the major wiring system for the PA system coming from New Orleans. The necessary equipment to make the changes was paid for out of the small profits of our onboard Ship's Service Store. Our store was small but there was money from selling candy bars, cokes, tooth paste, cigarettes and other items.

Welcome to San Diego

Bill Baird asked me if I could help him with the PA system. I was happy to help. I didn't have any duty watches; the Radar was secured. Our Quartermaster, Pat Healy, hadn't received his Notice to Mariner changes yet for the notebook, which I usually helped him to correct. Pat was always busy ordering new maps and supplies for the navigator, preparing the Ship's Log, having duty at the gangway now and again, and occasionally having Shore Patrol Duty ashore. He was too busy to come with us to search for parts.

Bill got permission to use a jeep from the Base Motor Pool so we could hunt down the parts for the PA job. We couldn't draw from the Naval Supply Depot on the base for this project, so Bill checked the phone book for Lafayette Radio and Electronics in the San Diego area. We naturally toured the city before we headed to Lafayette, scoping out watering holes and music spots. The city was flooded with sailors in uniforms, and the popular places were easy to spot. Even though our trip was regarded as a work detail, we were required to wear Undress Blues; no Navy personnel were allowed off base in dungarees or work clothes.

At Lafayette Radio and Electronics, Bill found everything we needed for the job and he paid with cash supplied by our Ship's Service Officer. We bought an amplifier, a two-speed record player, switches, boxes and wiring supplies to make a first class installation. It would be installed at the Quartermaster desk on the bridge, with remote switches and boxes for the Radio Room to patch into the radios. The 33-1/3 rpm phonograph records of the day were onboard as well as recordings of popular radio shows supplied by the Armed Forces Radio Network.

Liberty in San Diego

Bill and I worked with the installation after morning chow. The installation was so good and professional, that after we painted the outlet boxes gray and bound the wiring, it looked like the ship builder's construction. We had tapped into the wiring at the PA junction so we could isolate different parts of the ship, so as not to disturb any compartments. The Captain was delighted with the installation. We found out his taste was in classical music and at the beginning he had complete, absolute control of everything that played over the new system. The crew complained through their Division Officers, and soon Bing Crosby, Dinah Shore, Guy Lombardo, Mills Brothers and Harry James music was broadcast the majority of the time.

During World War II, cactus needles were popularized as less damaging to the record surfaces and giving better reproduction to the music. The Captain felt that cactus needles were better for his private collection of classical records than steel stylus needles. The Captain's needle preference required the cactus needles to be sharpened. He had a miniature, hand held sharpening device. I had never seen anything like it before or since. It had a mini drill chuck that secured the cactus needle, and above it was a small disc with a ring of super fine sandpaper along its rim. He would lower the ring, spin it with a finger and the needle would turn as it was sharpened.

It didn't take long, but Captain had a box of hundreds of cactus needles that had to be sharpened for playing records.

All Ashore

We all had looked forward to liberty. In our travels and scuttlebutt from other crewmembers, we were told that San Diego was one of the greatest places to go ashore for liberty. Right off the ship, I went to a small restaurant with fresh fruit in the window. I was with a couple of shipmates and we went in for a snack. I had seen honeydew melons in the window and decided to order half a melon. At home in Boston, my family had cantaloupe when it was in season; expensive honeydews never came to our table. The melon was juicy, cold and sweet. I spent the rest of the afternoon checking out the bars and having a few friendly brews with my group. Payday was a couple of days off and as usual I was short. The others hung around for the Trianon Ballroom to open for Big Band music; I headed back to the Naval Base.

I walked in to the Ship's Service Store for souvenirs to send home, and see the super-large recreation area. Beer was 20 cents and the new movie was 10 cents. While in the store I began to feel odd and hot. I went to the head and was my face was red; I began to itch all over. I went into a Sick Bay and a Navy doctor checked me out. I took off my jumper and T-shirt; I was covered with welts. I was allergic to the honeydew melon! I was given a shot of adrenalin and told to go back to the ship, lie down and not be alarmed at my increased heart rate. I took a tram to the ship, crossed over the other LST's and went aboard 759 and hit the sack. My heart was beating so fast it shook the bunk. I finally fell asleep and when I awoke the rash was disappearing and I swore I would never eat honeydew melon again! I had another day to explore.

The weekend was coming up and we could get a 48-hour pass. Many were headed to Mexico for the evening. Pat Healy, the

Quartermaster, and Jim Madden, the Signal Man, insisted we go to Los Angeles for the weekend. They had heard of The Stage Door Canteen; it was run by the Hollywood Actors and Actresses who danced with the servicemen or entertained on stage. The food was free and the music was Big Band. We didn't even know where it was or how to get there, but sounded like a good idea so we put in for the pass.

The Stage Door Canteen

The first Stage Door Canteen was created in New York City by Broadway stars supporting the war effort. The nightclub took its name from a popular 1943 movie that was a favorite of service members. The motion picture was seen around the world at every military and naval base and on ships fortunate to have a projector. The canteen was staffed with an all-volunteer force of celebrity actors, actresses, top-of-the-line entertainers, and Big Band orchestras. Hollywood stars John Garfield and Bette Davis helped to create The Stage Door Canteen in Los Angeles for the same goals. The nightclub welcomed enlisted personnel and non-commissioned officers. I will never forget being able to see so many stars in a truly glamorous setting.

Hitchhiking to Los Angeles

The three of us left the ship before noon. We had asked others for the best way to get to Los Angeles. We were told buses would be full, the train schedules erratic, so head for the highway and get a lift up the coast. We decided to give it a try. Being young and in uniform, we hoped any patriotic citizen with a car and the gas would welcome such a fine group. We walked and waited by the side of the road for most of an hour. Several trucks stopped but were turning off just a few miles up the road or crossing the desert to Riverside. A middle-age gentleman with a late model Dodge sedan stopped; we told him what we had in mind and he thought it was a good idea. The Stage Door Canteen was the most popular attraction in the Los Angeles area and was strictly for servicemen in uniform. Our driver told us we made the right choice.

He drove us into the Los Angeles area before he had to turn off for home. When we left, we chipped in $5.00 each and shoved it in his pocket as thanks; he protested but he was a workingman and it helped with the gas. He gave us directions to the Los Angeles City bus lines or its streetcar lines to get us to the nightclub.

The Stage Door Canteen, Hollywood

By the time we arrived at the Stage Door Canteen it was getting dark. As we turned the corner, we saw a line of servicemen from every service and every allied country, enlisted and officer alike, in a line stretching for most of a block. We had arrived at a good time and our chances of getting in looked good. Big Band dance music filled the air. Wartime blackout conditions were in force and the windows were covered. The doorway had curtains and a twisting corridor with more curtains to stop the light. When we finally entered into the huge ballroom-type building, we saw famous actors and actresses and many others we would come to know over the years. We were all hungry after our trip from San Diego. Food was served in a buffet line; it was delicious and served by the stars themselves. They asked us about our hometowns and told us they appreciated our efforts. We were star struck; our mouths were wide open and most of us stammered when we tried to answer. As we passed down the serving line, we could see into the kitchen. I saw several men washing the dishes; one in particular was an action hero from Westerns. Tall and brawny Rod Cameron was slaving away at the sink, sweating in the heat of the kitchen. We found an empty table and ate our meals of fried chicken, mashed potatoes and gravy, vegetables, a roll with butter and a choice of soft drink; it was a gala affair. It was difficult to imagine that this went on seven days a week; the Hollywood stars were out in force showing their support for the troops.

Floor Show at the Stage Door Canteen

After we ate we took our trays to another line to be cleaned and returned to the kitchen. We moved to the other end of the huge hall and found seats to view the upcoming entertainment. We had great seats and were not too far from the curtained stage. There was a loud fanfare, the curtains opened and in the center of the stage was a huge spotlighted guillotine. A famous Master of Ceremonies named Ken Murray came forward, had great words for us all, and thanked us for coming. He told us that everything was donated by the film industry, the actors and actresses to show us a good time. He told us they realized we were all going to be in harm's way soon and it was their way of saying thanks. We all stood and applauded as they all paraded across the stage and waved.

Ken Murray, a famous celebrity showman and comedian in his own right, introduced a famous motion picture action hero of the era, Chester Morris. He spoke of his career and his motion picture friends that we all knew. The audience was lit up and receptive. He told us of his interest in magic and he hoped there wasn't anyone in the audience squeamish at the sight of blood.

The spotlight turned to a guillotine and he walked around it, fiddled with the cables that held it. He put a large head of cabbage on the block under the blade, told his assistant to pull the cord, and the blade came plummeting down as the audience gasped. He came forward and called for a volunteer to participate in the exhibition. A young sailor jumped forward. Morris asked him if he had a will, of the boy's next of kin. The sailor was beginning to get nervous and the audience was chuckling. Morris took him behind the machine and the boy knelt down and placed his neck in the lower block, he closed the upper block that form fitted his neck. He placed a large vegetable on each side of the boy's neck. Morris went to a chest, opened it and took out a large sheet. He unfolded the sheet and it was stained with what looked like blood. He spread it on the floor in front of the sailor's face with a flourish. Morris walked to the side of the guillotine, reached up and grabbed the cord and with an exaggerated gesture pulled it.

The huge blade came whistling down. The vegetables on each side of the sailor's neck were sliced in two, but the sailor was unharmed. Morris went back and released the neck blocks and he and the sailor received thunderous applause and a standing ovation from the servicemen and women. Morris gave the sailor an autographed 8x10 glossy and stood around for about 20 minutes signing autographs and handing out his picture for souvenirs.

After the show the Big Band moved to center stage and played the music of the day including Jitterbug music. Some of the servicemen and women put on an exhibition dancing to the music. There was slow dancing, mostly the Fox Trot with some Waltz sets and the usual mix of Latin steps for the real dancers. Several celebrity actresses danced. The only problem was that they would take a few steps and there would be a line following them across the dance floor to cut in. It was all done in good fun and gave us all memories for a lifetime.

It was after midnight when we decided to head back south to San Diego. The three of us made our way back to the highway and an older gentleman picked us up. He had been drinking, and he directed one of us to drive while he fell asleep in the passenger seat. The vehicle was full of gas so we had no worries. We arrived in San Diego by early morning, woke him up and drove to the Base entrance. He took it from there. We walked through the Navy Yard which was as busy as if it was the middle of the day. We returned to the ship and had to turn in our Liberty Cards. We hoped we could retrieve them that afternoon; we had another day and a night of our 48-hour pass to use up.

Being a Sunday morning, Pat Healy and I went to Mass at the recreation center, which was full. The Mass reminded me of the one I had attended in French Morocco, which was in an old Catholic cathedral. It had no kneelers and everyone stood for the Mass and only sat down a couple of times. The priest was a Navy Chaplain and the altar was a table set on the stage. His homily was brief and he simply said, "Behave and remember the folks at home." We returned to the ship for a hearty breakfast. We all went back to our separate compartments and hit the sack to rest up for another night on the town.

Sailor's Night Life in Wartime San Diego

The ship was connected to the Base fresh water supply so the sailors going ashore were able to use the onboard showers. The smell of shaving lotion spread through the ship as any sailor with a liberty pass was heading out for shore. Earlier I slipped into the ship's laundry to iron my uniform before the mad rush. The Sunday evening meal by tradition was cold cuts for sandwiches because the cooks needed time off too.

We headed for the gangway to pick up our liberty passes and leave the ship for town. We walked through the Navy Yard to the main gate and had to show our passes to the Marine guards. The Navy had open-air shuttles to town and they were filled with sailors. When we unloaded, some of us just strolled around and followed the crowds. We headed for the Trianon Ballroom to check out the action and the music. The band was playing and it was great to just stand around and listen. The Trianon Ballroom had bars along all four walls and chairs and small tables lined up around the perimeter of the large dance floor. It was tailored to the military population and admission was one dollar. Military personnel were required to be in uniform at all times. We had a table of six and ordered pitchers of beer. The Shore Patrol was always walking through the crowd and no problems were expected. The local girls were beginning to fill in the scenery. For the first time I saw a civilian group of Zoot Suiters. They wore exaggerated suits fashionable in New York and major cities around the country.

During the later hours at the ballroom some of the military all liquored up began to make loud comments to the Zoot Suiters. Someone shouted out, "Draft Dodgers!" The arguments turned into a real bar fight. Our table was close to a rear entrance, and when the furniture began to fly, we bailed out into a back alley, walking hurriedly down the street. The Navy Shore Patrol and the San Diego police streamed into the building; we could hear the ruckus way down the block.

The next day, Bill Baird, our Electronic Technician, asked me if I had any trouble with ranging when operating the Radar. I told him that I didn't have any difficulty but it was a problem training others. Ranging used the Radar screen to approximate the distance between objects and the distance between anything in relationship to the ship. To be accurate a Radarman had to be consistent every time he reported distance between objects. My ranging had developed with practice and my accuracy was never questioned. Bill asked me if we could use a Range measuring device on the equipment. He said he was nosing around the Supply Depot and thought that he found an attachment for the Radar system that would simplify Ranging and would eliminate guesswork. He thought that its availability was unknown to the smaller ships and it would be out of stock as soon as its value was recognized. We agreed to modify our Radar.

Bill got the equipment ordered and authorized. He was such a fantastic technician that he got whatever he requested. He had a truck deliver the equipment to the ship. We dragged it to the Radar room and opened the crate; it contained the installation manual and necessary schematics from the manufacturer. He took the manuals and spent the rest of the day and part of the next studying them, digging through the dozens of pages of schematics. He was so thorough he even ordered a supply of spare parts for the machine.

The next afternoon Bill got started and by the next day the Ranging modification was installed. In military terms we gave it "The Smoke Test," which meant that we turned it on and hoped it didn't blow up in smoke! Whatever Bill did, the Radar functioned perfectly. What the modification did was to allow the operator on duty to turn a small hand wheel on the set and move an electronic dot up to the blip on the screen. The distance would be displayed electronically on the screen. It was amazing and so easy to perform! All the Radar operators would be accurate when giving distances, especially when keeping stations of 500 yards between ships in the dark of night. As soon as Bill showed the officers the improvement, they hailed it as the greatest thing since sliced bread.

It was fortunate that the job went smoothly, because we were to sail out to Pearl Harbor in two days. We received all our spare parts and stowed them in large metal boxes we welded to the wall and the deck. I must say that I was in awe of Bill's genius during the installation process and was happy to assist with whatever he wanted to get done. He was overjoyed that it worked out so well.

All of the LST's in our nest had been reprovisioned. It was easy for the crew to see the large potato locker, located on the upper boat deck on the port side, was filled to capacity. Navy fuel barges had topped off all the fuel tanks. The power and fresh water hookups would be cast off at the last moment.

Cold and Refreshing Coca-Cola

The most popular soft drink of the day became the most popular soft drink in the military world. Sugar rationing was enforced in the civilian world, but the Coca-Cola Company received unlimited sugar, as the almost sole provider to the military, a real advantage over other popular drinks of the day.

Prior to our departing San Diego, our Ship's Service Store, a small storage room on the lower deck, stocked up on everything from Athletes Foot powder to candy bars. One of the biggest sellers was Coca-Cola. Coke was so popular that the storage of all the bottles became a problem for the little store. The store committee bought a Coke dispenser, the type seen in drug store soda fountains of the day. It was a beauty and a coup for the crew. It was bright red with Coca-Cola logos on all sides; a pump introduced CO_2 into the system. The large red container had a coil inside and that had to be covered with ice from our refrigerated spaces. It was easy to store the syrup in gallon containers. It was the nearest thing to home on the ship. Our Ship's Service officer was always on the prowl for good deals. In war movies of the day, every outfit had someone called "The Scrounge," and we felt that ours was the best.

Shipping Out to Pearl Harbor

We departed San Diego Naval Operating Base at 0600, steaming in a westerly direction. We formed up into a small convoy with several Destroyer Escorts providing our Radar and Sonar screens. A Navy blimp flew anti-submarine patrol overhead and stayed with us for about an hour. We passed south of San Clemente Island, 60 miles from San Diego.

The vast distances that had to be covered by slow moving supply ships was really beyond comprehension. At times, with the thousands of miles that had to be covered, it was easy to go half-screwy from having been away from civilization for a long period. Wherever we traveled we always delivered our cargo, to be used at the moment or stockpiled for future use, and then we went back and reloaded with more. Most of the time LST-759 carried troops and machines for the war effort.

Westbound Across the Pacific Ocean

Our destination of Pearl Harbor, Oahu, was a plodding 13 to 14 days from San Diego, about 2300 nautical miles. The speed of the convoy was as fast as its slowest ship and our cruising speed was somewhere between eight to 10 knots. The ship's diesel engines sound never seemed to miss a beat; the oily exhaust smell was carried away with the breezes and we learned to ignore the engine noise reverberating off the steel bulkheads. To this day, if a public bus is near me and I catch a smell, my thoughts instantly return to the LST. I think the sailors felt the vibrations of the engines and instantly recognized any change in its tempo.

The LST-759 had cargo that included jeeps, trucks, cranes, amphibious vehicles, tanks, bombs, ammunition, 55-gallon drums of petroleum products for every type of vehicle, stretchers, barbed wire. You name it, and we carried it. The 55-gallon drums of aviation gas were sometimes on the top deck and exposed to careless smokers who forgot it was a hazard. The Skipper assigned areas and times for smoking. It was standard operating procedure to hear officers announce the designated smoking areas and hours several times during the day. A fire at sea would be a life or death battle because there was nowhere to hide.

Being the leading LST-759 Radarman was not really such a big deal for me. About the only managerial duty I had was to post the times for the on-Radar watches, which were in four-hour increments, such as four on and eight off while in a non-combat situation at sea. This changed when we were at General Quarters under air attack or if the convoy was involved with anti-submarine activity. If any of the officers had any complaints with my personnel, it was passed down to me and I had to correct the problem. During a call to General Quarters at sea, the ship's Radar and related equipment was my prime duty station and the other operators had to man combat duty areas. Most of the crew, with some exceptions in the engine rooms, filled other combat positions. Occasionally I would spot check the Radar operator on duty at night, to make sure he was alert to the other ships in the convoy.

All daylight hours were spent on ship maintenance, to paint and treat rust from the salt water. If one were to ask a sailor what he did during the day, he would most likely say, "Chip and paint." At times the decks and the bulkheads looked as if a strange disease had attacked the ship; the area was then given a final coat of gray paint and pride was restored.

In the evening, sailors wrote letters. All letters were submitted unsealed to the officers. It was usually the junior officers who had to read and censor each letter for any breach of security. It was a standing complaint among the enlisted men when censorship was discussed.

I borrowed books to read from the library on the ship. Books were donated by major publishers and distributed by various organizations ashore. Current best-sellers were available; any steamy romance novels were an instant success and passed hand to hand. Educational textbooks were always on the shelves for the browsing. Older crew members who had been in college used their off-hours to study, when they had the time. Most of our officers had at least two years of college or graduate degrees.

Other officers who came from the enlisted ranks of Chief Petty Officers and Warrant Officers were given wartime promotions. They were called Mustangs, the highest compliment to an officer. It meant that they came up through the ranks and were the experts in their naval career areas. Our Communications Officer was a Mustang, and knew his job; the LST-759 was fortunate to have him. He trusted my Radar knowledge and work ethic. He was great to work with and we never had a bad moment as long as I was on the ship. He would have been scooped up and assigned to a larger ship, but demand for amphibious crews was so great. Promotions in the enlisted ranks came fast to the peacetime sailors who were desperately needed to train the reservists flooding the training bases.

The weather on the way to the Hawaiian Islands was mild compared to my convoy duty in the North Atlantic. The sun was shining and the sea was as smooth as glass most of the time. Standing on the bow, I could see dolphins just ahead of our bow pressure wave. They were with the ship most everyday. I hoped that this was a good omen. In the dark of the night, standing on the stern, I could see the bright phosphorescence in our wake churned by our propellers. It seemed bright enough to be seen from the air as we traveled west to Oahu.

On November 7, 1944, we approached the island of Oahu and the Pacific Naval Operating Base at Pearl Harbor. We passed through the Molokai channel and paralleled the famous beaches of Honolulu. We recognized Diamond Head because it was in every photo or motion picture we had seen about Hawaii. The whole area was under 24-hour surveillance on the sea and in the air. Anti-submarine aircraft droned around us, patrolling everywhere. Our convoy began to form a single file to enter the anti-submarine nets protecting the entrance to Pearl Harbor. The Navy net tender opened the steel nets as we approached. The Escorts provided a constant Sonar screen around us to prevent any Japanese submarine from slipping into the harbor under cover of our convoy ships.

Naval Operating Base, Pearl Harbor

On our starboard side we could see palm trees, white sandy beaches and the pink Royal Hawaiian Hotel. The landmark Aloha Tower lighthouse stood high, inside the entrance to Honolulu harbor as we passed. We were to dock at Pearl Harbor, about six miles west of Honolulu.

I remembered I already had a connection to Pearl Harbor. Ensign Robert Lawrence Leopold of Louisville, Kentucky, was a crewmember killed in Pearl Harbor by the Japanese attack on the USS Arizona. It was Ensign Leopold who was honored on October 18, 1943, by the naming of the Destroyer Escort USS Leopold DE-319. The Leopold would have been my ship if not for being punched in the nose by another sailor before we were to sail out of Norfolk.

As we looked out over the rails at the harbor around us, few scars remained of the death and destruction of the Japanese attack just three years ago. The Pearl Harbor base was reconstructed and operating at full wartime capabilities. We passed Hickam Field, Pearl Harbor Naval Air Station and Hospital Point on our starboard side as we entered the channel. Pearl Harbor was divided into three large anchorages called East Loch, West Loch and Middle Loch. East Loch was split with Naval Air Station Ford Island separating it into three areas that included the Naval Submarine Base, a naval supply base and the naval ship repair facilities.

Along the southeast side of Ford Island was the aircraft carrier USS Saratoga CV-3, teaming with activity. Hundreds of ships of all types, Cruisers, Destroyers, Minesweepers and Destroyer Escorts, were tied to the docks inside the harbor. All anti-aircraft weapons were uncovered and ready for a call to General Quarters. We all felt we were on the brink of an adventure; very few of us thought about the possibility we would never return from the war. Across the channel were the docks where the thousands of sailors, bound for liberty in Honolulu, loaded and unloaded from the open, brass-railed liberty boats. Our crewmembers had their necks on swivels trying to drink it all in.

Hundreds of LST's were moored in nests to conserve docking space, many with 160-foot long LCT's mounted on their decks, to be launched at an invasion site. Some of the LST's had pontoons welded to their sides, ready to be cut off and used as docks to land cargo ashore. We were nested north of Ford Island; there were so many amphibious vessels it was easy to mistake one for another. The Harbor Control Tower ceaselessly flashed its signal light to raise one ship or another. The serious business of war was the business at hand. It was not until years later I read that a few months prior to our arrival, on May 21, 1944, an explosion on one of the many LST's docked in West Loch, Pearl Harbor, caused a massive chain reaction of explosions among the nearby vessels, sinking six LST's and killing 163 military personnel.

Liberty in Honolulu

Our crew was as anxious as any of the nearby sailors about to enter a new liberty town. The Naval Base was humming with activity; so much was going on it seemed as if it was organized chaos. Ships were loading and unloading cargo on a 24-hour basis. Acres and acres of wooden packing cases filled every available site within view. Oil tank facilities lined the southeastern hillside and Navy yard tankers were filling the tanks of all the hundreds of ships in the harbor. There was activity everywhere. Welding torches with their blue-white light flashed at the Navy yard and dry docks in the southern portion. Ships of steel had to be repaired no matter the hour and the clang of welding hammers never ceased. I don't remember if we ever shut off our diesel engines. We seemed to be supplying our own electricity with our on-board generators and our fresh water was available; where it came from I never knew. It was a pleasure to shower with fresh water when it was available.

Our Radar was secured while we were in port although large Radar installations were visible and rotating; our radio crew still copied Fox, which were groups of five character letters that comprised a coded radio message. The completed message would be typed into a code machine that would translate into an English language message. Sometimes one of the officers would convert a short message by hand from a codebook. The code breaking was done in private and in an area unable to be observed.

One of the first orders of business was for the Captain and the Executive Officer to attend a meeting at CINCPAC, Commander In Chief Pacific, Admiral Chester Nimitz, with headquarters in the southeastern sector near the submarine base. With the arrival and departure of ships on a 24-hour basis, instructions and orders had to be speedily given to ensure that order was maintained within the Commander's area of responsibility. The Commander was in charge and no one lost sight of that no matter what his or her position was in the ranks.

Large air raid shelters with capacities of 500 or more were stretched out within the Naval Reservation. The defense installations were a series of mounds camouflaged with vegetation or paint. Our sailor's work uniform of the day was dungarees; our white dress uniforms were for liberty. The work uniform for the officers was suntans or gray chinos and no ties. The relaxation of the uniform rules was by Admiral "Bull" Halsey while he was engaged at the battle for Guadalcanal. He told the Marines and sailors that they couldn't fight, "all dressed up like dudes." We were given orders to dye our working T-shirts and hats from white to dark blue in order to present less of a target from the air.

The LST's were tied up to each other side by side; each had a gangway to cross over to the next with six or more ships comprising what was called a nest. Usually ships of the same type were tied up this way to facilitate personnel moving back and forth. Falling into the water between the ships could be hazard to one's health. In port it was usual for a ship to have a movie playing on its fantail or any space large enough for the crew to gather. Each ship had its own movie projector and screen and after dark it was sometimes difficult to understand the dialogue above all the competing noise. Each day, in keeping with a long naval tradition, the Ship's Service officer or clerk would try to swap the previous evening's film for another. The clerk would most likely stretch the truth to the breaking point as he extolled the virtues of last night's film. His job was to get rid of the bad film that he got suckered into trading for the previous night.

Our crew talked every waking moment about liberty in Honolulu. Anyone who had been ashore was questioned about where the best places were for ladies and drinks. Although beer was 10 cents a bottle or can, it was almost impossible to have more than a couple after standing in line for an hour to get into a bar. Liberty was usually from 1200 to 1800 and the curfew was on at 2200; martial law was in effect and Admiral Nimitz was the boss. At first, I just walked around and soaked up the sights and the crowds of military of every description. We grabbed a crowded bus to downtown, bus fare cost 10 cents, and we found a place that served draft beer from 1200 to 1600.

Our beer garden of choice was called Joe Fats Barbeque on Kalanianaole Boulevard. The road led to a Marine base and the rumor was that they had real Wisconsin beer at their large open-air recreation area; they were letting sailors buy two beers at a time, but the line was a mile long. We stayed at Joe Fats for the draft beer and French-fried potatoes; with about six thirsty sailors per table, a 75 cents pitcher of beer disappeared in no time. The beer was the best on the island. There were only two breweries on the island, and they must have been working overtime during the war. The Navy had an enormous beer garden, called "The Breakers," at the end of Waikiki beach. In a stadium-sized tent, the largest I had ever seen, beer shipped over from the states was served. Hundreds of servicemen filled the tent. Beer was 10 cents a bottle and servicemen could only buy one bottle at a time. If a sailor had more than one bottle on the table in front of him, a Shore Patrolman confiscated it. The place opened at 1400 and with such a long waiting line for each beer, it was impossible to get more than three or four brews. After a visit to The Breakers, our group went back to Joe Fats; we didn't get thirsty and the French fries were cheap.

Paper currency in the Hawaiian Islands was the same as Stateside except the word HAWAII was printed in bold letters on the back. It was a court-martial offense to use currency without this HAWAII printing on it. Regular dollar bill currency had to be changed at a bank or at various exchanges on the base. The reason was that if the Japanese captured the islands, the U.S. would cancel all the Hawaiian currency and it would not be accepted in the international currency markets. Coins were not affected. All paper dollar bills without HAWAII on them were shipped back to the mainland. Those Hawaii dollar bills are collector items now.

On the second day of liberty, I went to the business district and wandered through the department stores. They looked like any stores on the mainland, except the stock was sparse. I bought six pairs of white socks to wear with my white uniform; I thought the white socks looked better than the black uniform socks. The first time I wore them I was walking down the main street along Waikiki beach. A Navy Shore Patrol jeep with two patrolmen pulled up and I was told to get in the back. They said the white socks could only be worn with a doctor's medical permission in hand, and I was out of uniform! I could not believe this was happening again! I forfeited my liberty for that day, my liberty pass was confiscated, and they drove me to the main gate. They gave my pass to the guard, and he returned it to my ship as a disciplinary measure. I never wore the white socks again and have an aversion to them to this day!

The next day, leaving for liberty again, this time in black socks, I walked around sightseeing. Our crew had no idea when we would move out, but it seemed something big was being planned with all the amphibious ships; we hoped we would be a part of it. I walked through the high-class residential areas near Diamondhead and saw the palatial mansions. The only one I remember identifying was owned by the late tobacco heiress Doris Duke. I visited all the museums and tourist places. I sat on benches by the beach for hours watching the surf and the waving palm trees; just to be there was a thrill for an 18-year-old kid from Boston.

Big Band Music and Dancing at the Submarine Base

Over time, rather than joining the throngs in Honolulu, I thought it was easier to stay on the base and use the base's own shuttle system. One day I was walking around the huge base and heard Big Band music playing; it was coming from a very large tent with screen sides and weather flaps that could be rolled up. I went by and saw that it was an Officers' Club. The area had a few trees and shrubs around it; I leaned against a tree and enjoyed the scene and the great music. The officers were having a great time dancing and were being served cocktails by white-jacketed waiters. I made up my mind then that if I had another life I wanted to come back as a Navy Officer. I came and listened to the music almost every day.

Over the six weeks we were in Honolulu, we continued training. Near the entrance to Pearl Harbor was the Navy Seabee base. When the harbor was dredged and deepened it created a sharp shelf bordering along the shore. To practice loading and unloading procedures, LST's would pull up to the shore and drop their ramps. One day an officer from our ship wanted to use one of our four LCVP's, known as Higgins boats, to learn how to land on a beach. This particular landing area didn't have the gradual incline as most beaches had. He nosed the small landing craft up to the edge of the beach, lowered the ramp as if to disembark troops or jeeps, and as the bow ramp came down, he stalled the engine and the weight of the ramp pushed the boat off the edge of the beach. As it pushed back he couldn't get the engine restarted or crank the bow ramp shut. The bow ramp slipped off the bank into the deep water of the channel; the boat took on water and sank. The officer and a qualified enlisted man were the only occupants on the boat and they swam to shore. Everyone watching from the shore was laughing at the incident, and the LST-759 officer was the butt of many jokes until we departed.

Another time the LST-759 was maneuvering in a turn to return to West Loch and ran over the channel buoy as the headwind opposed the turn. The buoy and its chain were caught under the ship and all engines had to be stopped so the propellers would not be damaged. Navy yard personnel had to sail out to provide assistance and a few more jokes were made at the expense of the amphibious force.

JOINING THE BATTLE IN THE SOUTH PACIFIC

Operation Forager

Every amphibious ship sliding off the stateside production lines was being sent to the Pacific. Amphibious ships and craft were being built faster than the crews could be trained for their difficult tasks. The journey from the shipyards to the combat areas was sometimes the first trip most of the crews had ever taken. It was strictly on-the-job training at an accelerated pace, and skills had to be honed on the way to the scene. My ship, LST-759, had a nucleus of no more than 20 combat-seasoned sailors. Before we left Pearl Harbor a Navy reporter and a photographer came aboard and wanted some stories for hometown newspapers. Having had combat duty in the North Atlantic and the Mediterranean, they told me that I was the only enlisted man on my ship they photographed because of prior wartime combat exposure. The photo was published in the Boston newspaper, "*Record American*," with a caption reading, "Seeing lots of combat duty in the campaigns in the South Pacific." We spent six weeks at Pearl Harbor and then departed on December 16, 1944, for Tinian in the Marianas with a cargo of engineering heavy equipment and 200 personnel of Navy Seabees. We were to take part in Phase III of Operation Forager. I was fortunate to be in the communication division to find out information about destinations. Operation Forager was the military campaign to battle the Japanese for the islands of Saipan, Guam and Tinian.

Eniwetok Atoll and Engebi Island in the Marshall Islands

The LST-759 and other LST's formed up a small convoy and we departed West Loch and Pearl Harbor on the first leg of our journey to the southwest Pacific islands. We would be protected by several Destroyer Escorts and a couple of larger Destroyers. Having been in convoys with Destroyers and Destroyer Escorts providing the anti-submarine Sonar screen, it was nervous time for us all.

Eniwetok Atoll was to be our first port of call on the way to the Solomon and Russell Islands. I can't remember how long we were at sea before we stopped at Eniwetok for a couple of days. We sailed past several groups of islands that had been bypassed by our forces, and the Japanese armed inhabitants had no way to replenish their supplies or battle our forces; they were stranded. After the war, our government reported that over 13,000 Japanese military died of starvation while 7400 died of bombings and disease. It wasn't calculated how many American lives were spared by not assaulting the bypassed islands. Japanese subs were known to be in the areas and many were sunk after being detected by our Sonar and Radar patrols of DE's and DD's.

Our approaching convoy did not go unnoticed. About 36 hours from Eniwetok we were observed by naval air patrols and our IFF electronic identification was challenged many times. I had Radar targets at 75 miles, and we all went to General Quarters, with weapons armed, loaded, manned and ready. Our Captain informed the others in the convoy. The aircraft circled about five miles out, and out of firing range so we could ID them and they us. They were friendlies, on our side. We were all happy to see them as we got deeper into the combat zone. Early the next day Lt. Carroll Pfeiffer, our navigation officer, came by the Radar room and warned us to be alert because the atolls weren't very high above sea level and might be difficult to target from a great distance. He expected landfall about 0630 the next morning. Our own surface Radar picked up Eniwetok Atoll at 35 miles and we had a visual at 0637 hours.

Our small LST force had been in three columns and by prearranged plan shifted into a single column to pass through the southern entrance into Eniwetok lagoon. A couple of PC's (173 foot, steel hulled patrol craft with ASW detection gear, depth charges and light dual purpose armament) and a Destroyer Escort patrolled the entrance and provided anti-submarine warfare defense. The lagoon was enormous and covered over 300 square miles. There were about 50 ships at anchor, many tankers and a couple of Escort Aircraft Carriers with planes on their decks. There were several Fletcher-class destroyers and a "Four Piper" Caldwell-class Destroyer among the vessels we saw. The harbor control had our signal gang working overtime on the blinkers so no one could eavesdrop on a radio signal. We dropped anchor in a designated area.

I borrowed a 30-inch long spyglass, used mostly for long distance signal observing, from the Quartermaster and looked out at the small long islands. One island had an airbase with planes landing and taking off on a regular basis. The Navy Construction Battalions, nicknamed Seabees, had been busy; they had erected dozens of Quonset huts. This was an active military combat airport and naval anchorage. It was easy to see that the Japanese could ill afford to lose this strategic area. We had arrived on a Saturday and we were advised that a church party would depart for the shore at 0830 for at Catholic Mass to be held at 0900. Pat Healey and I signed up with a couple of others. Other Sunday services were available at the same time and Jim Madden and others signed on also.

It was nice to be at anchor, the vibration from the engines had stopped for a while. Sea birds screeched for our attention, maybe for food. The weather was hot, with a strong breeze. The Skipper ordered the crew to air all mattresses; every sailor took his mattress topside and hung it over the deck cables along the sides for about an hour or two; this was done on a regular basis for health reasons. One of the officers would inspect the canvas bunk bottoms down below for cleanliness. Sailors found with dirty bunks were ordered to remove and scrub the canvas bunks. Most of the dirt was from shoe marks on the canvas bottom from sailors who would fold back their mattresses to snooze or write letters. Folding the mattress back made a nice backrest and kept the cotton cover clean, but the canvas bottom suffered. Many sailors usually had a uniform spread out under the mattress, being pressed for the next liberty.

When we considered the cost in lives to assault and capture this atoll, it was difficult to go ashore and not think of the servicemen who made it possible. The Battle for Eniwetok had taken place about 10 months earlier, leaving 37 Americans and 800 Japanese dead. When the Mass was over, we strayed as far as we could in the time we had. I walked to the center of the part of the island where we were, and threw a rock into the ocean in both directions, thinking of the battle that had been fought the previous February. We returned to the ship as soon as our LCVP landing craft arrived to pick up the church parties.

Our commissary officer was busy procuring fresh foodstuffs from the many supply ships in the lagoon. I never complained about the food, it always seemed to be just what I liked and plenty of it. I had a buddy who was a cook who liked reading author Ogden Nash. This buddy's girlfriend in Chicago would send the novels to him via ship's mail. He passed the books on to me after he was done with them. When he was working nights baking bread or goodies, he would let me stop by. Whenever he had a break of sorts, he would throw a variety of canned vegetables and leftovers into one of the huge steam pots in the galley and made three or four gallons of what he called "slumgullion." With the spices he added it always turned out to be delicious and really hit the spot. When we were finished he would drain the kettle into a large rectangular serving container, put it on the crew's serving line and in short time it was gone. The evening treat was appreciated.

One of the treats that sailors looked forward to at sea was ice cream. Destroyers and Destroyer Escorts that were guarding around aircraft carriers would vie for the rescue of aircrews that had emergencies and had to ditch their plane into the ocean. A successful rescue was always paid off with ice cream from the carrier; this was a well-known tradition and competition for the ice cream was fierce. Being an LST, our ship had no expectations of capturing this reward, so our engineering department built the ship's own hand-cranked ice cream freezer. The recipe used powdered ingredients, and it required lots of muscle power to hand-crank the freezer. When volunteers were called for, everybody would eat it but nobody wanted to make it. My cook buddy asked me for help and I recruited a couple of other sailors to take turns on the cranking. It turned out hand-cranking had a delicious benefit. When the ice cream was served, we ice cream makers were served as much as we wanted, much to the complaints of everyone else. The three of us held onto that sweet chore as long as we had the opportunity and the supplies.

We were at Eniwetok for a couple of days until we received orders directing us to the Solomon Islands for training exercises. Along with a couple of Destroyer Escorts for a Sonar screen, we weighed anchor the next morning.

My Letter to Home after Leaving Pearl Harbor

My mother collected the letters I sent to her while I was away at sea. I had written this one after we had passed any critical islands, so the censors did not remove many sentences. Here is the letter my mother saved:

> *"Dear Mom,*
>
> *We departed Pearl Harbor in a fairly large convoy of LST's with a couple of Destroyers and some Destroyer Escorts who provided anti-submarine sonar protection and additional anti-aircraft gunnery support, if we needed it. Our LST has a tremendous amount of anti-aircraft armament consisting of 20mm and single 40mm, twin 40mm mounts. It seemed that we were traveling forever to the southwest. Our first stop was Eniwetok Atoll. We stayed for a few days and departed enroute to the Solomon Islands, notably Guadalcanal, where the Navy and the Marines started the campaign to take back all that the Japanese conquered on their bloody trip through the South Pacific.*
>
> *When we arrived it was practically in the middle of their Monsoon season, which means, out here that it is simply doggone hot when the sun was out and high humidity when it was overcast. It rained almost every day, mostly heavy, and I mean heavy showers. It is easy to see why the jungle comes all the way down to the sea. The smell of the jungle is strong with decaying vegetation and God knows what crawls around there. The amphibious ships*

spent most of the time just practicing landings and retracting off the beaches. The officers had their training situations to practice also.

We rehearsed until we were ready to receive our combat cargo, most of which we loaded ourselves. After we loaded the ammunition cargo and it was secured, we shoved off on a one-day trip to the Russell Islands another malaria ridden paradise, no Dorothy Lamour or Jon Hall in these parts, just mosquitoes.

We loaded up with LVT's tracked landing vehicles that were amphibious. The ones we had been carrying and these new ones were open on the top, they had automatic pumps in case they shipped water on the way to the beach, during an assault. They were capable of being swamped in a heavy sea. The assault waves were all using these since they were capable of crossing coral impediments around most of the islands. The vehicles were manned by Marine Corps troops and they were mostly veterans of many campaigns out this way and well-seasoned. Some had seen action in the Palau, Bougainville, New Guinea, New Ireland, New Britian and others. They spent most of their time cleaning their weapons and resting. The LST's were constructed with several berthing compartments along their interior compartments to handle the troops that operated the equipment used for the assault waves. The only trouble was we only had 2 meals a day when we had visitors.

Most of what we can write about has been pre-approved and passé so some of this may be old hat. You might know more than we do by what you see in the papers, although we hear Tokyo Rose on the radio, she has the latest music and we get a kick out of her exaggerations.

Give my love to all with a big slice for yourself,
Junnie"
(That was my nickname, since I was Frank, Jr.)

The Solomon Islands

The Solomon Islands, about 3100 nautical miles southwest of Pearl Harbor, were the site of bloody battles between American and Japanese military forces. Our stateside news reported these as the Island Hopping Campaigns of the South Pacific. At times, it looked like the Japanese would win these battles, but the tide turned at the ferocious, epic battle of Midway atoll in June 1942. The famous wartime names of Guadalcanal, Tulagi, Florida Island, Russell Islands, New Georgia, Bouganville and Savo Island were locations of critical battles to stop the Japanese from conquering Australia, New Zealand, New Hebrides and the Fiji Islands. If the Japanese had won those battles in 1942, they would have consolidated their victories in the East Indies and the Philippines.

Arriving at Savo Island

Savo Island was a tiny island among the Solomon Islands, about half way between Florida Island and Guadalcanal Island. It was in the middle of the navigation path called the Slot, a diagonal waterway through the Solomon Islands. In August 1942, the Japanese stealthily navigated the Slot during the night and defeated the U.S.

Navy, sinking three U.S. Heavy Cruisers and one Australian Heavy Cruiser. So many ships were sunk to the bottom of the waters between Guadalcanal and Tulagi Islands, the area became known as "Iron Bottom Sound." The battle was fierce, many lives lost. Naval strategists determined that just two more Destroyer Radar Picket ships could have prevented the Japanese from slipping through the Slot undetected. As it was, the six Destroyers patrolling that night missed detecting the Japanese force until it was too late.

We arrived at Savo Island sometime in December 1944. Our small amphibious task force was scheduled to make practice landings and do station keeping exercises in the bay between Guadalcanal, Tulagi and Florida Island. It was a sobering feeling to know that one of the most important naval battles in the South Pacific happened right where we were steaming in Iron Bottom Sound. Destroyed ships and some of the casualties were on the sea bottom beneath us. Our Amphibian Forces now had the task of maintaining logistical support to the Solomon Islands across the vast Pacific.

The Atabrine Cocktail Hour

When we started our training programs we spent most of our time maneuvering in Iron Bottom Sound between Guadalcanal and Florida Island. Guadalcanal had been captured and secured two years before we arrived; it had an AM radio station that was a link in the Armed Forces Radio Network. The best music this side of the U.S. was broadcast all day and it had the familiar format with the disc jockey and his non-stop banter. It was like a visit to home, and all the music of the day was appreciated.

The name of one of the crew health programs during our duty in the Solomon Islands was "The Atabrine Cocktail Hour." Atabrine was the trade name of an anti-malarial drug we all had to take daily to ward off the mosquito-borne disease that stayed with you for the rest of your life. The mosquitoes were everywhere in the islands, spreading malaria. We lined up once a day and swallowed the dark yellow pill in view of the Pharmacist Mate; it was a court martial offense not to take the pill. After a few days everyone had developed a slight yellow cast to their skin. It was also a court martial offense to not wear a long-sleeve shirt buttoned at the cuffs and dungarees, all to ward off the bites. It was a relief to be at sea running training programs, away from the stifling jungles that came right down to the seashore of the islands.

Occasionally, when we returned to the Russell Islands after exercises, we would anchor in the mile-wide channel between the two major islands. The Russell Islands were only 30 miles northwest of Guadalcanal and the area was chosen for training the new amphibious forces. The LST's took advantage of the opportunities for the improvement of operations and could test landings under conditions more rugged than the rehearsals we staged at the crowded Pearl Harbor base.

The locals, like the ones on Guadalcanal and the other Solomon Islands, would take coral dust and color their hair red, white and all shades in between. The only locals we saw or talked to were men. The women were sent to the hills to protect them from the military pushing through the islands. A local woman looked pretty good to sailors after a long session in the South Pacific, and the military figured we needed the friendship of the local populations, not conflicts generated from illicit passions. Souvenir sales were not prohibited though. The locals would come along side in their dugout canoes with handicrafts and exotic sea shells that some of the industrious sailors made into beautiful necklaces for their wives and girlfriends. Cats Eye shells and Cowry shells were in great demand; they were so beautiful when strung on a silver chain. The sailors who made the necklaces even sold them to other sailors on the ship. During the war, it was interesting to see the jewelry and crafts that were handmade by sailors who collected bits of metal, glass, and brass casings from war materials.

The local traders were sharp bargainers and one had to be careful not to get swindled. One of the cooks tried to buy some goods with a large, long can of Spam lunch meat that he snatched from the galley. He tried to buy the trader's entire supply of shells with the whole unopened can. The shrewd traders could read English, saw that it was a pork product and wouldn't have anything to do with it. This was strange, because we saw pigs in the many villages ashore. Spam was a valued product in Hawaii, but not in the Solomon Islands.

Merchant Marine ships with civilian crews were anchored around the islands; every available cargo vessel was used in the war effort to haul food and war supplies. Members of Merchant crews included sailors too old for military service and many of the younger ones classified 4F by the Selective Service as unfit or too young for the military. Merchant sailors were exempt from the draft as long as they did not take more than 30 days of shore leave. If I had not scooted by the Coast Guard eye exam, I would have been 4F when I finally reached draft age. Civilian crews had sliding pay scales for war zones. It was rumored Merchant Marine crews made more money than the military; it was an unproven and probably unfair rumor, but a constant irritation to servicemen. The Merchant ships were protected by the Naval Forces when they traveled in the convoys; the ships were assigned Navy armed guards who manned the Merchant ships anti-aircraft guns. The guards would tell us of the great food on the Merchant ships and the deluxe living quarters, compared to ours. Sometimes a bottle of hard liquor could be bought for $35.00 to $50.00 from an industrious Merchant Marine sailor; that was more than a month's pay for most of the enlisted men.

When not anchored in the lagoon, LST-759 was usually up on the beach with our bow doors open and the loading ramp down. One day I was out walking along the beach and noticed coconuts that had fallen from the beautiful palm trees that seemed to be everywhere. Other crewmembers talked about how good the coconuts were. We all carried a heavy knife in a sheath attached to our belts. I grabbed a freshly fallen coconut, and, rather than become a casualty of war from a falling coconut, I moved away from the tree line. The coconut was covered with a thick fibered husk about two inches thick at the widest part, and I wasn't making much progress stripping it from the inner shell. I was about ready to give up, when I looked up and saw a tall local man with coral orange hair and a sarong-type cloth wrapped around his waist. He was standing about 25 feet away watching me. On his belt was a wicked looking machete. I smiled and nodded for the lack of something to say. In very good English he asked me what I was doing. I told him I was trying to open the coconut. He said, "I will show you." He walked over, I handed him the coconut, and he held it loosely in one hand. He pulled the machete from his belt and in about four quick, powerful strokes, cut off the husk. When he was finished, he swung the blade and cut off the top of the shell, not spilling a drop of coconut milk. All this took about 20 seconds. He smiled as he handed it to me and went on his way.

I learned several things about coconuts that day, not the least was that the meat of a fresh coconut was soft, delicious and easy to eat. The older ones we saw in the produce markets of Boston were older; the meat was hardened and difficult to pry from the side of the shell. Unfortunately I also found out fresh coconut milk had a slight laxative effect! On some of the islands, the coconut palm plantations were a commercial cash crop for early conglomerates that owned most of the Pacific islands. It was rumored that the U.S. government had to pay the conglomerates for each coconut palm tree that was destroyed when Seabees cleared the islands for bases or assault.

The Russell Island Beaches

The slope to the Russell Island beaches was gradual and easy to land our amphibious vessels. Before we hit the beach, we would drop our stern anchor at a calculated distance in order to pull ourselves off the beach when it came time to retract. The two bow anchors weren't used at this time; cables were used to tie us to the shore. We landed on the island of Pavuvu, the largest of the Russell Islands. The shore was loaded with mountains of every kind of machine and packing cases full of war material. There were oil drums, gasoline drums, aviation gasoline drums, jeeps and trucks. I didn't see any Sherman tanks but I knew that they were there someplace. There were Amphibious Tanks with flame throwers up front, and tracks that propelled them through water and land. Amphibious Tanks were ungainly looking in the water, but they did the job. We got our first look at the DUKW, or Duck, as it was called. It was a huge six-wheeled amphibious truck with a propeller at the back and floated like a big fat boat on the water. The Tanks and Ducks were used during the assault phase of an amphibious landing, being off-loaded with combat troops from an LST. Ammunition large and small, 16-inch shells for the Battleships to 20mm and 40mm anti-aircraft ammo by the hundreds of tons were among the ammo supplies on shore. There was enough lumber to build a town and hundreds of kits to build the various sizes of Quonset huts seen on every base in the Pacific. I wondered what our assault cargo would be. Our present cargo was the top deck mounted LCT, and the side mounted pontoon-like six-foot wide by 32-foot long causeways that would be bolted together to unload cargo to the shore if tides or obstructions prevented a beach landing.

With all the new amphibious tanks lined up along the shoreline, I wouldn't be surprised if we would be assigned to a Tractor assault wave group, meaning we would launch the personnel and the tractors from our bow doors for the assault waves. The Pacific Island battles were a bloody campaign to eliminate Japanese bases and installations, eventually bringing Allied forces within striking distance of the island of Japan. Allied forces were being massed for a colossal assault of the Philippines, Taiwan and Okinawa.

Loading a Combat Cargo

Whenever we were up on the beach with the bow doors open and the loading ramp down, a desk was mounted on the bulkhead to check in cargo and supplies. At night, after all activity was done, we closed the loading ramp, as it was watertight and very secure. One night I got the duty and was just killing time as sort of a security guard at the opening. The rest of the security detail was topside on the main deck and we had direct communications with all departments. A Marine asked permission to come aboard; he wanted to speak to me. He asked me if we wanted some beer for the crew, he wanted to make a deal. He said he would supply four cans of beer for every fresh egg I could supply. I knew that we had a large supply of fresh eggs in our refrigerated spaces and they were in full case and half case lots; half a case wouldn't be missed, but I didn't know where to store the beer. Admiral Halsey allowed us to have beer on board, but it had to be consumed ashore in a recreation area. I had the keys to all the spaces and found the compartment holding the crew's beer. The Marine and his buddies did all the work moving the beer onboard, putting as much as we could in the compartment, but we had six cases left over, about 144 cans of beer. By this time I had an audience of about 10 crewmates with their tongues hanging out! The beer was warm and we went to the ice-making compartment that had brine tanks with removable tanks for making slabs of ice. We took the ice tanks out and dumped the extra beer into the brine; it wouldn't take long to cool down. Several sailors went in to the sleeping compartments and woke a few buddies for a silent midnight party. Everyone was quiet and the 144 cans beer began to disappear. I was relieved of my watch duty and guzzled along with the crew. With most of the beer consumed and no empties in sight, an electrician came into the compartment. He was a non-drinker and frowned on our impromptu Marine gift. The other sailors told him to take a hike and he left. No one realized that the electrician had gone to turn us in!

With about a dozen cans of beer left and the area made spic and span, the Officer of the Deck came down the ladder and caught us. He wanted to know who was responsible and I stood up. He put me on report, which meant that I had to be present at a Captain's Mast, a shipboard tribunal with the Captain as the judge and jury dispensing punishment to fit the crime. The Officer of the Deck took one of the beers, and made short work of it. We secured the party, cleaned up the space, and took the empties ashore to dump them in the bushes. The compartment was never as clean as at that moment and no one got drunk to cause a problem. The participants hit the sack and I was left to the Captain's wrath. My story was that we bought a couple of cases of beer from a Marine on the base and we drank it aboard, rather than going ashore in the mosquito-infested jungle. The Captain gave me 30 days without leave or three liberty days, whichever came first. The entry in my service record, under Efficiency Marks stated: Captain's Mast; Sleeping in; loss of three liberties. My Conduct was reduced from 4.0 to 3.9. The Captain was kind to report me just for Sleeping In, a minor offense. When I eventually left the ship the conduct mark was put up at 3.99. Being out in the middle of the Pacific Ocean in a combat zone the penalty wasn't severe or difficult to serve, and by God that was the best, the coldest, the most delicious beer we ever had! The Marines had a few fresh eggs and we had a few ice-cold beers. The participants will all have the same big smile remembering back to that hot, humid night. The supply department never figured out the expansion of the beer ration in the crew's storage compartment.

It is so difficult to write war experiences for my family to appreciate the activities and experiences of thousands of "boys" just like me. I have come to view my wartime service with humor and sadness at the same time. I hope anyone who reads World War II recollections can understand I may recall humorous events, but it was a terrible war with terrible loss of life. I tried to reassure my mother in letters to Boston, and my twin brother, Gerry, also in the Navy, did the same.

Our rehearsals and accelerated training maneuvers, while making our crew more proficient, were just marking time before we received orders to move out. It was rumored in Pearl Harbor that the hundreds of military ships at the base would be used in battles for Saipan, Tinian, Guam and Rota. These were chains of islands in the Marianas that blocked the way to the Philippines and the Japanese home island.

Shore activities were beginning to show signs of expedited loading of the LST's resting on the beach. On our LST tank deck were heavy metal plates with a large X cut out of the plate's reinforced center. The plates were for chain links to be inserted to secure heavy equipment. A crew of Seabees came aboard and built boxes around each one of the plates, so that chains could be dropped into the X plates. They then had us load the ship with five-inch naval ammunition in heavy boxes as well as the powder that would propel them. After the floor of the deck was covered, the only open space was the X-boxes. The Seabees then built a floor over the ammunition and tied it all together with other lumber. The next day a line of LVT's, amphibious tanks, nicknamed Amtraks, started to come aboard. They were maneuvered over the heavy lumber and secured by chains and come-a-longs, ratchet-like devices to take the slack out of the chains, through the X-boxes. After the LVT's were secured, every available space left over was filled with hundreds of cases of K-rations, field rations. There was no way that the equipment could shift in a heavy sea. The Amtraks were open at the top and would carry Marine or Army infantry to a landing. Our berthing compartments were more than adequate to accommodate the crews for the tanks. The addition of the extra personnel overwhelmed our galley staff and we would go to two meals a day until the tank crews departed the ship on landing day. By order of our Skipper, the early breakfast meal for the troops and the crew the day we hit the beach was the all-time favorite, steak and eggs.

My Nervous Smile

I got off on the wrong foot with the Skipper as soon as we left San Diego. He passed away in 2004, but I can still feel the nervousness of those days. Whenever he addressed me, I always had a nervous smile on my face; I knew this irritated him and I was at a loss to avoid or correct it. He was a college graduate, about eight years older than me, and everyone knew he loved music. However, I could not get my mind to calm down around him. The Radar System where I was on duty was next to the navigator chart table, in a compartment aft of the wheelhouse. The officers would climb the ladder from the Officers' living quarters, go through a doorway into the Radar/Chartroom and then through the secure doorway into the wheelhouse. Then they would exit the wheelhouse to the outside and climb a ladder to the Flying Bridge where the Officer of the Deck and enlisted personnel gave the orders to the enlisted men at the wheel, and the engine telegraph system in the wheelhouse below. The Skipper could appear at any time of the day or night to check the readiness of the crew and query the officers and crew on duty. Usually he came by when I was on duty. Occasionally he would bend over the chart table, look at the chart, check the figures of the navigator, and check our position indicated on the paper taped to the tabletop. He wasn't the least bit friendly to me and had a skeptical way of asking a question. Once he asked me something and my nervous smile caused him to explode. He said, "Smith, is it my face or my diction that causes you to smirk when I address you?" I said, "Sir, I'm sorry! It's just an uncontrollable nervous habit." I could never understand what tricks my mind was playing on me to make me so nervous around the Skipper. The way I ran Radar crew was without blemish; I had the respect and confidence of all the other officers who commented on my flawless technique and performance. That would have to be enough for me.

Several days after his irritation with me, the Skipper brought me a box, about the size of a cigar box. Inside were hundreds of cactus needles and a small hand-operated machine that sharpened the points of the needles; I was to sharpen each needle. He used the needles in his phonograph; he was convinced that they were the only needles good enough for his classical records. He never thanked me for sharpening the needles for him. After the war, I moved to Arizona with my wife, Lorraine, but never planted a single prickly-needled cactus in the 50+ years we lived here, probably subconsciously because of those phonograph needles!

Once, during the 2400 to 0400 hours watch, the Skipper came through on a surprise inspection of the Officers on the bridge. After the Skipper closed the door to the wheelhouse, I signaled an alert to the Officers with my call button in Morse code that spelled out "CAPT." The Skipper returned in about 30 minutes on his way back to his cabin, and as he passed behind me, he said, "Smith, I understand Morse Code," and went below. I almost crapped my pants and knew I had just dug a deeper hole for myself!

The Captain's Hat

The Skipper always wore his hat around the ship. It wasn't the usual overseas cloth cap most officers wore, it was the flat-topped hat with the black visor and above the visor was a gold strap with gold buttons at each end near the temples. Fastened to the crown was a large gold officer's emblem that identified the service. After many months at sea the gold had begun to tarnish and had a green cast to it. To another sailor this was viewed as being an Old Salt, indicating that the wearer was a longtime Man of the Sea. The Skipper was never without it, unless we all had our steel combat helmets on. During one of our trips he misplaced it. The rumor among the crew was that someone stole it, knowing it was his favorite. He took the loss personally and one morning all hands were called to General Quarters and all not on duty had to line up topside for the Officers to inspect lockers of everyone on the ship. While the crew was lined up, the Captain and most of the other Officers took the lock master keys, opened and inspected every personal locker. The surprise inspection was not that unusual; it was the way any contraband like booze brought aboard ship would be uncovered. The Captain's hat was not found after the lengthy locker inspection. I have no idea what would have happened to the offender if the hat had been found. Being at sea, there was no supply depot to replace the hat for some time. The next day the Captain wore the usual overseas cloth cap, but it was a size too big. It was months before he would have the opportunity to buy a new hat with gold braid. The crew had a chuckle and no one ever came clean on what happened to the hat. Could have been there was a well-dressed fish somewhere out in the South Pacific.

Leaving the Solomon and Russell Islands

Our ship was fully loaded with all the assault material we could carry. We had to hope our air support flying out of the island bases would keep the Japanese *kamikaze* suicide bombers away from our vessels. Maybe if the Japs were flying out of the Philippines they would run out of gas before our next beach landing. We had so much ammo and explosive fuel on board that it wouldn't take much to make us just a memory.

Early in the war, the Pacific area was divided into two areas, west of the Solomon Islands was the dividing line. General Douglas MacArthur was the Commander-in-Chief to the west and Admiral Chester Nimitz was Commander-in-Chief of everything to the east, including Pearl Harbor in Hawaii. MacArthur was headquartered in Australia after the humiliating loss of the Philippines to the Japanese in May 1942. He wanted to get back to liberate those islands, in part to avenge the horrible, brutal deaths caused by the Japs on the Bataan Death March. Stories were starting to emerge about the mass killings committed by the Japanese military under orders from Emperor Hirohito. I will not include specifics in my recollections, but the reader can find documentation of the millions of people slaughtered by their Japanese captors. The battles of the

Philippines, the tremendous loss of lives, the strategies, failures, lessons learned are all worth reading in the annals of military history. I wish I could include the stories in my recollections, but I could not honor the memories of those brave fighters in such limited space. Suffice it to say, the aggression of one country against another caused so many valiant people to lose their lives. It was paramount for the Navy to totally control the sea and the air before this could be done. The Fast Carrier Task Forces assembled in January 1944, under Admiral Marc Mitscher, were raising hell with the Japs and reducing enemy air forces and ship strength. Admiral Mitscher had become a brilliant Navy air attack strategist. The Japanese fleet was still a threat, but their carrier-based aircraft were taking a beating. American forces had heard that Japanese Emperor Hirohito had proclaimed elevated spiritual status to any Japanese civilian or fighter who chose suicide over surrender. Allied sailors and ground assault troops were witnesses to Japanese civilians throwing themselves off island cliffs and bodies, sometimes with their legs bound, floating in the ocean waters.

Ulithi Atoll Fleet Staging Area for the Marianas and the Philippines

Ulithi Atoll was in the western Caroline Islands in the Philippine Sea, and with our ship's top speed of about eight knots, it was a two and a half day run, about 450 miles as the seagull flies. It was almost a carbon copy of Eniwetok Atoll, except that Eniwetok was surrounded by a coral reef that had offered greater protection from intruders and had only two major entrances. Ulithi Atoll had about ten inhabited islands, but the population of younger natives had been shipped off by the Japanese to the island of Yap, 105 miles to the west near the Palau Group, to be construction workers. The Japanese used Ulithi Atoll for a submarine and a seaplane base, but the Japs had abandoned the atoll in 1944. Geographically it was a good staging area for the U.S. forces. The Philippine Islands, Mariana Islands (Saipan, Tinian, Guam and Rota), Bonin Islands

(Iwo and Chi Chi Jima) Islands and points north and west were accessible. Ulithi Atoll was taken unopposed by Americans in September 1944, and with the ports built by the Seabees, Ulithi had become a major U.S. fleet anchorage. In November, the Japanese attacked the Ulithi anchorage using *kaiten*, a mini-submarine torpedo manned by a single suicide pilot. The USS Mississinewa, a tanker anchored in the lagoon, was hit by the suicide bomber. The Mississinewa, fully loaded with fuel and crew, exploded, sending the vessel to the bottom of the lagoon. It would not be until 2001 that the wreck was rediscovered, its trapped, dead crew members honored, and its storage tanks drained. Also years later, it would be reported that any Japanese fighter who had volunteered to be a suicide *kaiten* pilot would have as much as 10,000 yen paid to his family.

The Ulithi lagoon was heavily guarded when we arrived; it was crowded with hundreds of ships of every description; there were aircraft carriers, battleships, amphibious ships, destroyers, and destroyer escorts, transports of every type, Navy oil and gasoline tankers for the thirsty task forces and the carrier based aircraft that were continually on the move. The lagoon always seemed choppy for small boats and the smaller ships at anchor bobbed in a constant motion.

The only shore recreation was at the northern edge of the atoll, on the island of Mogmog. An area on the island was cleared and a lagoon filled to have Mogmog become the shore recreation area. Swimming was limited to a short enclosed beach because of the sharks. The only shade was from the tall coconut palms. There were picnic-like tables with benches and Quonset huts for indoor activities. There were a few military style latrines, but hundreds of rows of large yellow funnels welded to pipes driven into the land were to be used as urinals. Most were being used at any given moment; just to find one and relieve oneself out there in front of God and everybody else was an experience.

The Navy, with Admiral Halsey's blessing and wisdom, allowed ships to carry beer for the crew, but it could only be consumed ashore in a regulated supervised atmosphere. Our ship's allotment was three cans per man at 25 cents a can of 3.2% alcohol beer. In those days, during the beer canning process, a formaldehyde solution was used to rinse the cans; ingredient labels weren't on anyone's mind in those days and the formaldehyde became part of the expected taste of the beer. Although our beer was stored in our refrigerated spaces, it was starting to get warm by the time we got to shore. The anchorage was a huge, sprawling distance, and it all depended on your location and the distance in the anchorage for the time it took to hit the beach. The crews had no knowledge of times of departure so a visit to the Mogmog beer drinking area was to be a four-hour round trip for warm suds. Non-drinkers and hustlers were selling their beer for a dollar a can; it was green beer in a green can and warm to boot. Drinkers were waiting in line to hand over their hard earned dollar; to many it was the first alcoholic beverage they had consumed for months and months. For sailors it was delicious nectar of the gods, and a taste from home. I saw several sailors who were tipsy, and in the heat and humidity near the equator, they must have fried their brains. Some really looked on the edge of falling face down on the beach.

Every picnic table had a crap game or a blackjack game going. The 55-gallon drums lined up in rows were filling fast with empty beer cans; we were all warned not to litter under penalty of losing the privilege. The only real shade was from palm trees and groups of sailors moved with the shade. We were warned about scorpions and coral snakes so not many ventured to sit on the ground. The old sailors and the hustlers took gambling money from anyone naïve enough to play with them; some did so well they carried around their winnings in a shoebox. Because we were in a combat zone, our crew came ashore in different stages. Crews had to man their weapons and Destroyer Escorts were out 24-hours a day on Sonar runs to defend against the Japanese. Air raid attacks from the Japanese *kamikaze* suicide planes were on everyone's mind.

Our ship had four LCVP's, called Higgins boats, suspended on gravity davits, two on each side, at the rear quarters of the ship. We used one as our ferry, mail boat, tug and ambulance. On the way back to the ship from Mogmog, with the crewmembers all beered up, one of our young officers was standing on the rear deck of the LCVP as if he was on top of the world commanding his ship, when the boat crossed another boat's wake. The Higgins boat zigged and the officer lost his balance, flying off the stern into the lagoon. This would have been hilarious except for the shark-infested waters; we retrieved him without damage, except to his pride.

The temperature hovered in the low hundreds and the humidity was oppressive. Air-conditioning was not a problem on most ships, they just didn't have any. With a full combat cargo, sleeping space topside was almost by reservation only, and even then it was uncomfortable. A breeze did blow whenever we were underway. Usually with troops aboard, they would stake out their territory and sleep in their trucks or jeeps if they were part of our topside cargo. We were carrying an enormous LCT piggy-back topside and that area was reserved for the LCT assigned crew. Our tank deck cargo was usually tracked landing vehicles and their crews would spread sleeping gear in them and stay out of harm's way; some only came out for the two meals a day or to use the head. The tracked vehicle crews had their own supply of food and snacks and they tended to be careless with their containers and wrappers. It was a monumental chore for the ship's security force to monitor the trash generated, especially below decks. The ship's crew treated the ship as their home but to some of the combat troops, they couldn't care less and considered the trash not their problem. The danger was we were loaded with volatile cargo, high explosive anti-aircraft ammunition, drums of gasoline and loaded fuel tanks in all the vehicles. Smoking was absolutely forbidden. Navy regulations had spaces and hours reserved for smoking. The times and locations were announced at regular intervals over the public address system. It was a General Court Martial offense to violate the rule. We heard from others that an ammunition ship, the USS Mount Hood AE-11, blew up at Manus in the Admiralty Islands. The repair ship USS Mindanao ARG-3, close by, had over 200 casualties from the blast. The explosion tore a hole in the harbor floor a block long and 30 feet wide; 34 ships in the harbor were damaged and the casualties totaled 743. It was paramount that all the troops onboard observe the Skipper's smoking rules. We all knew that we were sitting on a bomb that could easily be detonated by a moment of carelessness.

Convoys of amphibious ships were leaving Ulithi Atoll and others were coming in to take their place. We all began to wonder why we were not shipping out; it seemed LST-759 was being ignored for some reason. No orders to sail were forthcoming. Usually if we were going to make a landing, a military escort would bring a topographical image of the area in question and the battle plan would be explained. The island would be mounted on a 4-ft x 8-ft sheet of plywood and it would be painted the dominant colors of the area. It really was a work of art and reproduced what we would see. The beaches, hazards and landmarks would be explained and the landing beaches assigned to the ship would be pointed out. Our own officers would explain the times of the assault and the finer details as we proceeded along the way with the Task Force. But no model came onboard; we did not know when and where we would be going after Ulithi Atoll.

Six months prior to our LST-759 arrival at Ulithi, the battle of the Marianas Islands, northeast of Ulithi Atoll, was fought in order to cut air and surface communications between Japan and its southern holdings. Capturing the islands south of Japan had provided advance bases for surface and submarine operations, and airfields from which our B-29 Superfortress bombers would be able to bomb Japan, only 1500 miles away. The Battle of Saipan in June 1944 was one of the bloodiest and horrific engagements of the South Pacific. It is worth reading the documented accounts of the cave battles, the banzai suicide attack at Harakiri Gulch, the civilian suicide cliff deaths, the bravery and the decisions that took place during the battle for the island.

Saipan, Northern Mariana Islands

When the invasion of Saipan commenced in June 1944, the Japanese-owned island had 30,000 Japanese enemy forces and 22,000 Japanese civilians. Nearly all the 30,000 Japanese soldiers died fighting on the island and 3,426 Americans were killed with 13,000 wounded. The technique for all later Allied amphibious assaults incorporated the Saipan Landing Plan of 1944; it is seen as a landmark in Pacific amphibious history. Using the landing plan strategy, assault troops were transferred to the LST's at the final staging area and those troops were brought onto the Japanese fortified beaches on the LVT's, the tracked armored landing vehicles carried on the LST's.

We Leave Ulithi Atoll

We shipped out around January 1945 after a few days at Ulithi Atoll. We learned our LST was part of a resupply task force headed northwest to the Marianas. Our ships were to lend anti-aircraft support with our 20mm and 40mm weapons. We covered the distance without engaging the enemy, and as Saipan Island came into view, we could see a large factory building in a cove south of the capital city of Garapan. It was a sugar refinery and it had a tall slim smoke stack that was peppered with holes. It seemed as if every Marine, soldier and every passing ship used the smoke stack for a target, but it was still standing. It was recognized early on as a great place for the Japanese to station an artillery spotter; with all the holes in it, I'm sure the spotter had a short life span. We were instructed to beach the ship a few miles south of the refinery. The Marines secured the area, but Japanese snipers who hadn't surrendered were known to be holed up in caves in the hills. The sounds of skirmishes could be heard occasionally.

Several of our crew went to the bow of our ship when we landed on the beach. The crew sat at the controls of the twin 40mm ground and anti-aircraft weapon. On the beach Marines had Japanese prisoners engaged in a work detail. The Marines had their weapons at the ready and the prisoners were loading GI trucks with sand from the beach. When they moved up the beach, our crew spun the weapon around, following them with the 40mm trained on them. The prisoners started to talk wildly at the Marine guards. One of the Marines walked over and asked our crew to knock it off, the 40mm was making the prisoners nervous and the guards had their hands full as it was.

Close to the shore were fields of sugar cane; we had seen it as we sailed down the Mississippi River to New Orleans. The island sugar cane was still green. Military vehicles had gone through the fields and the crop was in various stages of damage. Several of us slipped ashore at dusk and cut a few stalks. We cut them into six-inch lengths and stowed them in our lockers. We would slice them into thin slivers and chew on them; they were just like a piece of candy. No one gave a thought at the time to the possibility that a stray land mine could have been in the field close to the shoreline!

Even though the organized Japanese resistance had ended on Saipan, the Marines and the Army troops still wore their full battle gear. They were on 24-hour guard duty in their own encampments. The Japanese holdouts would sneak down some of the gulches and lob a grenade into any group not on the alert. We heard stories that when it seemed that the islands were absolutely secure, starving Japanese soldiers were captured sneaking into the chow lines late in the day. Some Japanese were captured when the troops were showing movies outdoors.

The Captain arranged through the Marine Commander for members of our crew to get to the Saipan airfield and see the B-29 Superfortresses that were starting to make bombing runs to the Japan homeland. At that time B-29's were the biggest airplane in our world and a sight to be remembered. The Marines had to ride as guards on the GI trucks; two Marines were armed in the cab and four in the back. Some of the senior-rated sailors were issued side arms for the trip to the airport. I hopped in a truck as soon as we were allowed to go.

The B-29's were lined up in all stages of readiness and maintenance; the base was a beehive for the Army Air Force. The familiar Quonset huts of various sizes were going up by the dozens as soon as the Navy Seabee construction battalions poured a concrete slab foundation. The military cloth tents were present but being replaced every day with the huts. Going from a tent to a Quonset hut was always an improvement, especially not having a dirt floor.

The U.S. Army Air Corps Superfortress was an impressive sight. It seemed impossible to me for anything that size to get off the ground. When a B-29 would take off from the runway, it seemed as if the earth shook. One of the B-29's had crewmembers that were willing to show them off to us visiting sailors. The crew took us into the flight deck and showed us the array of instruments and controls that made the plane such a formidable weapon. To the rear of the flight deck was area that contained the communication gear and the state-of-the-art remote-controlled Browning M2 .50-caliber machine gun turrets. Just being able to direct their fire from a central point without hands on was a mystery to me. A long tube over the bomb bay area had a contraption similar to a mechanics creeper to get to the other parts of the plane and to the tail gunner's position and his twin .50-caliber machine guns. The crew was generous with their time and showed great patience with our questions. As other swabbies were coming into the airfield, our time was running out for the tour. The crew's flight rations were piled outside the plane and ready to be stowed away. We sailors were all dressed in blue dungarees, work shirts and dungaree jackets, our white hats dyed blue. One of our crew saw a large rations can of boned chicken. He grabbed the can, rolled it up into his dungaree jacket, put the jacket under his arm, and we all walked down the flight line to look at other aircraft.

Alongside the taxiway were the wrecks of several Japanese planes destroyed during the primary assault six months prior. I climbed onto a wing lying on the ground and saw the red ball Japanese insignia of the Rising Sun. I took my large knife from the scabbard on my belt and tried to cut the aluminum from the wing. After about 15 minutes I got a piece loose, a souvenir from a real Japanese Zero. Months later when I saw it in my locker, I thought who was going to believe that piece of metal with the red paint was from the enemy plane? I finally gave it away. In the Solomon Islands, the Japanese said that the Americans fight for souvenirs and the Japanese fight for their Emperor. I guess they were right because the Japanese fighters would booby trap bodies and equipment that did kill a lot of unwary souvenir hunters.

Further down the flight line at the airbase was a Navy twin-engine patrol bomber. There was no one around and we entered through a hatch below and went into the cockpit area. It had the usual dual controls, a radio compartment and a navigator's position. I think they doubled as weapons operators also. In the middle of a divided wind shield was a hole about as big as a quarter. The overhead of the padded cockpit area was covered with bits of hair and gore and damage could be seen in the whole area. About this time a Navy officer in green coveralls came on board and saw what we were about; he didn't chastise us for being there. He told us that the evening before, the plane and a crew of four was on a bombing run to the bypassed island of Rota. A Japanese anti-aircraft round came through the windscreen and exploded in the cockpit, killing or injuring both pilots. The Radioman gunner got the plane stabilized and level and pulled them from their seats. He got the plane turned around and flew it back to Saipan. The ground control talked him down and he landed the plane safely without damage. He and the navigator survived. Anyone who flew in a combat situation was required to have airplane stick time and his being familiar with procedures and the radio saved their lives. It was sobering to think of the two pilot officers who did not survive. We thanked the Navy officer for allowing us to hear the story. I often wondered as we all did, if the families ever knew of the heroics and the attempt to save the other crewmen's lives. We hustled back to our convoy trucks for a somber trip back to our ship.

Little did I know that my visit to the B-29 airfield would have an impact on my life years later. While I was working for the Mohave Butane Gas Company in Kingman, Arizona, in 1952, a friend named John "Jack" Hokanson was sitting with me at the lunch counter of the Casa Linda Café. Most of the owners of the businesses around town were World War II veterans; it is amazing how many businesses were started by returning war veterans. Jack mentioned to me that he had been a B-29 pilot in the Pacific. I told him the story about my visit on Saipan, and he almost fainted! He said, "That was me and my crew and we were loading supplies for our bombing mission to Japan the next day! After inventory we found that a large can of boned chicken was missing; the crew figured that one of the sailors liberated it."

Jack graduated from college in Minnesota just before World War II and moved to California. He was the finest trombone player I ever heard and before he went into the Army Air Force, he was a member of the National Broadcasting System Studio Orchestra in Los Angeles in the Radio days. After the war, he went through the J.C. Penney training system and was given the opportunity to manage the new store they established in Kingman, Arizona. He then bought and operated a Culligan Soft Water Company franchise. He also started a Home Decorating and Furniture Company. All his endeavors were successful. He became President of the Rotary Club, the Chamber of Commerce and was a terrific Commander of the American Legion. He had a wonderful supportive wife, Marge, and two daughters. He retired, sold his businesses and moved to Mesa, Arizona. In the early 1970's, the United States Air Force awarded him The Distinguished Flying Cross. It was presented at the American Legion State Convention, in Kingman, Arizona, by the Commanding General of Luke Air Force Base in Phoenix, Arizona. Jack passed away in 1995.

During his tour of duty, Jack and his crew were returning from a mission to Japan and another B-29 had to ditch. Jack and the crew, although low on fuel, stayed and circled the ditched crew's position until a Navy submarine on lifeguard duty north of Iwo Jima located and rescued that crew. Jack's plane landed at Iwo, which was barely secured, refueled and then returned to their base on Tinian Island in the Mariana Islands. Jack's story is just one of thousands of the World War II veterans, but depicts some of the heroic efforts during that time in history.

Fresh Water Problem Solved

Most of the islands in the South Pacific had limited water supply. A logistics challenge was providing fresh water to our assault forces. It required a large-scale salt-water distillation plant. The U.S. Navy refitted four U.S. oil tankers and Liberty ships to convert salt water and carry fresh water. The first two ships had a 42,000,000-gallon capacity and a major effort was made to rush into commission two LST distilling ships capable of distilling 120,000-gallons daily.

The converted LST's were called APB's, barracks ships, capable of carrying 120,000-gallons of fresh water and 235,000-gallons of diesel fuel. They also provided fresh and frozen provisions in excess of 450 tons. Berthing and messing was available around the clock for survivors of ships sunk in the assaults or small boats and crews separated from their ships for various reasons during the assault.

Tinian Island

The construction of the airfields on Tinian was the largest building activity the U.S. Navy Seabees construction battalion had ever undertaken up until that time. They built six huge bomber landing strips, each a mile and a half long and a block wide, along with 11 taxiways with hardstands, round parking pads, sufficient to park

300 aircraft. The Seabees dug, blasted, scraped and moved tons of earth and coral on Tinian. In addition they built Quonset huts and other service buildings. Every airstrip was completed on time; none required more than 53 days to finish. The B-29 airfield originally located on Saipan, was moved to Tinian when it was determined Tinian was a better base. The Seabees motto, "We build, We Fight" and their spirit attested to a group who were able to do any kind of work, any place, under any conditions. They were a remarkable group.

The LST-759 headed back to Pearl Harbor after unloading at the Mariana Islands. All empty, large attack transports and large attack cargo transports were dispatched to Pearl Harbor at best speed to pick up troops and all their equipment for another assault in the South Pacific. The Marines who fought on Saipan and Tinian were to be included in the attack force. All the Amphibious ships such as LST's, LCI's, LSM's and amphibious tanks and DUKW's were to be used in the assault. Our ship, LST-759, arrived back in Pearl Harbor with others on January 24, 1945, to resupply, load pontoons and LCT's, and start the trip back to the Solomon Islands.

Plans for the Assault on Iwo Jima Are Made February 1945

While we were heading back west, crossing the Pacific, Iwo Jima in the Bonin Islands was chosen for the next assault. Iwo Jima was a volcanic island with steeply inclined volcanic sand assault beaches, and no vegetation or protection. It was located between Yokohama, homeport for Tokyo, and Saipan in the Marianas. Iwo Jima did not have a harbor that could be converted to a naval base, but it did have three airfields and one could be converted to handle the B-29 Superfortress. The U.S. Navy submarines had established a line of protection between Tinian and Japan to rescue B-29 crews or any other American aircraft that had to ditch in their vicinity. In fact one of my neighbors in Kingman, Arizona, Raymond Rucker, was a

Navy submariner on the USS Bluefish SS-222 involved with patrol and rescue duty between Iwo Jima and the Japanese home islands. The USS Bluefish was responsible for sinking many Japanese war vessels. Ray was active in the Kingman community, and, sadly, passed away in 2009, survived by a large family and leaving behind a long list of accomplishments.

Some 900 vessels were assigned to the Assault on Iwo Jima, code named "Operation Detachment." The amphibious tank, amphibious tractor groups, and transport groups on LST's departed Pearl Harbor in January 1945. The route was from Pearl Harbor via Eniwetok for logistic support for some of the smaller amphibious ships and then Saipan and Tinian, where they had a final rehearsal for the invasion.

Assault on Iwo Jima

While our ship, LST-759 was arriving February 18, 1945 at the Solomon Islands with its load, those were the final hours before the Iwo Jima assault was to begin on February 19. Emil Thomas Reda of Maryland, a 2nd Class Motor Machinist Mate aboard LST-723, had a front row seat at the Battle for Iwo Jima. Years into the future he would become a relative by marriage to my brother's daughter, Julia Smith, when she married Emil Thomas Reda's nephew, Scott Reda in Maryland.

The Battle of Iwo Jima was fierce and bloody. It lasted for days. The Japanese threw everything they had at the assault forces. The battle picture taken on February 23, 1945, by photographer Joe Rosenthal of one Navy corpsman and five U.S. Marines raising the American flag on Mount Suribachi won a Pulitzer Prize for Photography and was the model for the Marine Corps War Memorial in Washington, D.C. On March 16, 1945, Iwo Jima Island was declared secure. During mopping up operations, 1600 more Japanese were killed and 900 additional were captured.

Casualties and Recognitions of Bravery

Military accounts report 30,000 U.S. Marines were engaged in the assault on Iwo Jima; 4600 were killed along with 800 Navy men. There were 20,000 wounded and of these, 1400 more died of their wounds, making a total of Navy and Marine Corps casualties of 6800 dead. The 36-day assault resulted in 26,000 American casualties. Twenty-seven Congressional Medals of Honor were awarded to Marines and Navy corpsmen, many posthumously, more than were awarded for any other single operation during World War II. Several months after the Battle of Iwo Jima, I met several Marine Iwo Jima survivors at the Oak Knoll Naval Hospital, in Oakland, California. They all said that during the battle, they wondered if there would be any Marines left alive to dedicate the cemetery on Iwo Jima.

My Letter Home—No Date (Probably April 1945)

"Dear Mom,

Most of the time the crew is ignorant of where they are or where they are going, we have a general idea, but most of the time we don't know the specifics. I suppose what you don't know can't hurt you or the Navy if the worst would happen. We found out from the Marines that we were to be part of the assault wave to hit Okinawa Shima Island 350 miles from Kyushu one of the home islands of Japan. We then had an idea how big this blitz was going to be if all the ships of all types were just the assault waves.

We returned to the forward combat staging area after about a week underway. Ulithi Atoll, although it was further north it was kind of a weather break, hot but not as hot as the Solomons and the Russell Islands. You can see how hard up we were when we considered Ulithi atoll an improvement. It's been said that if God wanted to give the world an enema, the hose would be in Ulithi. The Japanese knew what they were doing when they abandoned the place.

When we were entering what was the addition of new submarine nets, and even before, we saw so many ships, it seemed impossible to be able to count them all in a week of Sundays. I saw several types of Aircraft Carriers from Essex class to Escort Carriers and Jeep Carriers, Battle wagons, Cruisers, Destroyers,

Transports and Cargo ships and every type in between. Destroyers and Destroyer Escorts screened the atoll outside. Hundreds of Amphibious Ships, we marveled that they could muster so many ships in one spot on earth.

We stayed there for about four days and our assault forces merged into a massive amphibious assault force. The weather turned foul and anyone who didn't have their sea-legs or stomach was in for it. This will probably be the last spot to mail home. I know you wish us luck.

All my love to all,
Junnie" (Frank Jr.)

Okinawa Assault

Okinawa was the main island in the Ryukyus Island chain that stretches almost 800 miles between the Japanese homeland and Taiwan. If the Japanese considered our forces capturing Iwo Jima to be too close to Japan, Okinawa was even closer! The island was 60 miles long and the bottom third of the island was narrowed by the Ishikawa Isthmus; the majority of the Japanese population lived south of the isthmus. The northern two-thirds of the island were hilly, with mountains rising to 1500 feet. The southern part was wooded or cultivated. The main city was Naha in southwestern Okinawa; it was the capital and had a population of 65,000. The major concern was Okinawa's location in the western Pacific typhoon belt; typhoon season for the area was April to November.

The Pace Quickens

The staging area for the assault forces was at Ulithi Atoll. The six-week interval from the Iwo Jima assault permitted the ships damaged by *kamikaze* suicide planes in the Philippines and Iwo Jima to be repaired and returned to be added to the Okinawa campaign. The Amphibious Fleet would be the largest assault group the world would ever see. Hundreds of Allied ships of every description were headed to Okinawa Island. More than 1400 ships were to be involved in the operation. The LST landings were to be preceded by and covered by gunfire from battleships, cruisers, and light units of the U.S. Pacific Fleet. The carrier aircraft would provide close support for the ground troops. Unknown to us all, this would become the last battle of the South Pacific and one of the bloodiest not only for the U.S. Army and the Marines but also for the U.S. Navy.

One part of the fleet had started to move from Leyte Island in the Philippines as General MacArthur's forces had moved into the major islands of Mindoro and Luzon. Leaving the Philippines on March 19, 1945, was the Tractor Flotilla consisting of 22 LST's, 14 LSM's and 40 LCI(L)'s. The second group left San Pedro Bay, Leyte on March 21, 1945, and consisted of 20 transports and cargo ships.

A Minesweeper unit departed Ulithi Atoll 24-hours after the groups left Leyte. The rest of the Amphibious Support Force and the Gunfire and Covering Force left Ulithi on March 21, 1945. The Southern Attack Force, along with Admiral Kelly Turner's Flagship, the USS Eldorado AGC-11, departed Leyte on March 27, 1945. The Northern Attack Force left the Guadalcanal and the Russell Islands area on March 15, 1945.

It was reported that the group of Minesweepers being escorted by Destroyer Escorts looked like the world's biggest fishing fleet from horizon to horizon. I think the secret thoughts of the sailors were that they would rather be fishing. The Seaplane Base Group, the

Demonstration Tractor Group and Transport Unit Charlie, which was rehearsing in the Marianas Islands, departed for the Okinawa area from March 23, to March 27, 1945.

Pre-Landing bombardment was scheduled to begin March 25, 1945. The plan was to capture outposts prior to the main landings on Okinawa and put in place heavy artillery to support the attack. The Minesweeping Flotilla was to start sweeping the area on the same day. Mines would be a major problem. On March 26, 1945, the USS Halligan DD-584, assigned to screen the pre-landing bombardment ships, struck a mine 12 miles off of Okinawa, blew up and sank in an area not declared swept. Military historical records report that ships swept more than 500 mines and these ships also sank many more floating mines by gunfire. The USS Vammen DE-644 was damaged when it hit a floating log with a crude mine attached; the Japs had sown them in the area to look harmless but the explosion could disable a ship if hit in a strategic area.

Underway from Ulithi Atoll to Okinawa

The major amphibious forces coming from every point on the compass all staged at Ulithi Atoll. It was here we were all saddened to be told that 4600 Marines were killed at Iwo Jima as well as 800 Navy. Years later we learned that 1400 more Marines died of their wounds. Convoys for the invasion of Okinawa were made up, orders given and after four days our amphibious group departed on March 25, 1945. The weather at Ulithi was always windy and the waters were always choppy. As we started our journey north, the weather changed for the worse. The LST had a top speed at launching of 12 knots; hence the nickname "Large Slow Target." Our cruising speed was probably 8.5 to 10 knots tops. Our tank deck was loaded with amphibious tracked landing vehicles on top of tons of naval ammunition; all other available space was crammed with boxes of combat meals called K-rations. The tanks in all the vehicles were filled to capacity with fuel; it was no place to smoke and it was forbidden.

The top deck was home to the 150-foot landing craft called an LCT, landing craft-tank. It was chained and cabled to the deck and mounted on huge timbers it would slide over to exit the ship when it came time to launch. Along both sides of our ship, stretching from just aft of the bow, to just forward of the bridge area, were large pontoons, to be used as barges or causeways if needed during the beach landings. They were to be detached when needed at the invasion site.

The Marines would laze around in the amphibious tractors on the tank deck, reading to break the routine aboard the ship. They all had snack foods such as candy bars, and their own food supplies. The K-ration boxes, half the size of our current cereal boxes, were filled with tropical chocolate bars, lemon-aid powder, small cans of cheese and all the other goodies, including four packs of cigarettes. The Marines would throw their rubbish over the sides of the vehicles that were chained down on our ship's tank deck. With all the fuel and ammunition down there it was like sitting on a bomb. The tank deck had several tall vents above deck. In each vent was a huge fan to exhaust the combustion fumes when the engines were started. Two doors on the forward deck could be locked open and the outside fresh air was drawn down below and exhausted through the stacks. One day smoke started to pour out of the exhaust stacks; someone must have been smoking in the tractors and threw a butt over the side into the trash that had piled on top of the ammunition. The crew assigned to damage control was our fire department and all aboard were trained and knew what to do. It took about 15 minutes to put out the fire, but seemed like an hour. The smoke coming from the exhaust stacks made it look like a four-alarm fire back stateside. I crapped my pants that day! After the fire was extinguished, all the trash was cleaned up on the tank deck and NO ONE was allowed access except a fire patrol; all hoses were hooked up and ready at any moment. A fire at sea was the worst thing that could happen, you had nowhere to go, you had to stay and fight it. Even worse, our LST was a powder keg of ammo and fuel.

The nasty weather didn't improve one bit and continued all the way to the north. I came out of the Radar room and stepped out on to the deck for some fresh air. My position was above our deck cargo. I could see the bow slam into the waves and a very noticeable ripple would pass through the ship and spend itself out past the stern of the ship; I could actually see the tall flying bridge tip back and forth, as the ripple passed through. The ship architects who designed the LST's knew what they were doing. I had noticed the deck plates were formed and fitted to overlap and welded that way fore and aft along their length, rather than being butted and welded to form a continuous plate of steel. One could see that without the flex, the LST would have broken in two in heavy seas. It was still unnerving to see this ripple effect. Our main concern was to prevent any of our inner and outer cargo from breaking loose in the heavy seas. We hoped the weather would clear before we arrived; it would be impossible to land the LST in this weather.

Good Weather News

The Task Force Commander received a welcomed message from the Bombardment Group shelling the island that the weather was and would be ideal for the invasion schedule for Easter Sunday, April 1, 1945. We sailors were pleased to hear the seas would be calmer. Our Marines on board seemed unconcerned and continued the sharpening, dismantling and cleaning of their weapons; I guess it had a therapeutic effect. I noticed that one of the Marines was a Native American; he was a member of the Marine Tractor personnel billeted on board. He always seemed to have a concerned companion. It wasn't until many years later it dawned on me that he was one of the famous Navajo Indian Code Talkers, one of the best kept secrets of the war in the Pacific.

Three Days Before Okinawa

We expected air attacks from the Japanese about three days before we landed on Okinawa. We were prepared to shoot down their Zeroes. Our anti-aircraft weapons were manned 24-hours a day. When I slept I was fully clothed, shoes and all. We all wore life jackets and combat helmets as uniform of the day. All watertight doors in the interior of the ship were closed and dogged. The typhoon season was not supposed to start until May, but it was cold, rainy and stormy.

When we arrived at the assault area, all ships Radar equipment was to be turned off, for all but ships in the covering force. The reason was to thwart the Japanese from homing in on our radio-like emissions. With so many ships involved, Radar frequency emissions would be tremendous. The assault was headed for the western and southern beaches of Okinawa, the areas closest to the Japanese airfields. My usual General Quarters station was the Radar, but for this assault, the Skipper assigned me as the helmsman to steer the ship in the combat areas and the landings, if the Radar was secured. Occasionally while at sea, the Officer of the Deck would allow me to relieve the wheel and I enjoyed it. No Japanese planes came at us, but the water was mined; we hoped they all had been cleared. I remember our landing area was Yellow Beach Two. Ships had color identifying pennants. The tops of some ships were painted with their assigned color. The beachmasters were to set out a colored banner on their assigned beach when they landed. The joke for all the colors was, "Red Beach, Blue Beach, son of a Beach."

Letter to Home, Dated April 10, 1945 (Uncensored)

"Dear Mom,

I'm sorry I haven't written you sooner, but we have been very business-like around these parts, since April lst. As you probably know we have landed troops on the island of Okinawa, and most likely feel that my ship LST-759 and I were in on it.

Well, we participated and we carried a U.S. Marine Amphibious Tractor Group, who made up the assault wave. This landing was called "Operation Iceberg." "Love" Day, as this "D" day was called, occurred on April 1, 1945, as you now know. Everyone was tense to a major degree, as we were making our approach on the island the evening before, we could see the island on the horizon. I was wondering what the Japanese on the island were thinking when they saw our Task Force steaming so close to their home islands, or as Radio Tokyo called them "Our Impregnable Home Islands." They must have looked on us with awe and great fear.

They couldn't help but wonder how in the name of the Emperor we got so many ships together after the misinformation their homeland was handing out. We listened to Tokyo Rose on our radios and she was always telling the home folks of the terrible defeats their Army and Navy were handing to the American Forces.

The ships involved with the assault waves began to form up to go into the beach at about 0530, Easter Sunday morning. We had no Japanese air opposition at this time. At 0600, 7 Japanese planes came over and one tried a suicide dive on one of our cruisers. One came in at about 5,000 feet and started his dive. All the ships around us had already opened fire on him. He dropped two bombs and they landed about 1500 yards from us. He then tried his suicide dive on a Cruiser. There was enough anti-aircraft fire "flak" in one minute to make about five LST's like ours, he puffed smoke and his gasoline exploded when he hit the water. Two more planes came in and tried the same thing, but the flak finished them off, they were still scoring zero.

The ships containing the assault waves came within 6000 yards of the beach and we opened our bow doors and lowered our ramps into the water. The Amphibious Tanks were launched and each was filled with its compliment of Marines, armed to the teeth. To the rear of us were more Battleships, Cruisers and Destroyers shelling the landing beaches. You could never imagine the thrill we had seeing our ships just blasting the living daylights out of that place.

There were ships as far as the human eye could see, and over the horizon. It seemed that it would be impossible to count them in a week. The shore bombardment ceased at 0700 and planes from our carriers, out of our sight, came and strafed and bombed the beach. Then the LSM(R) landing ships rockets, which had been converted from landing craft to fire salvos of rockets, came within 600 yards of the beach and steaming parallel to the beach, gave the greatest display of fire power we had ever seen, to say the least it was awesome.

The first waves of amphibious tractors with the Army and the Marines hit the beach on time at 0830, they landed dry and standing up. The only opposition they met was light mortar and artillery fire. The beach we were assigned to was called Yellow Beach Two close to the major airfield Kadena. The troops captured the airfield in less than one half an hours and it was undamaged. A Japanese plane landed on the field and as the pilot got out he was eliminated as soon as his foot hit the ground, it was like life; sometimes somebody doesn't get the message.

Four more Kamikazes came in on their suicide missions but the sheer force of the flak sent them down in flames.

The next day we started to unload part of our cargo, which was heavy naval ammunition. The ammunition was used on larger ships, such as Destroyers, Cruisers and Battleships, mainly for anti-aircraft but also for close in support of the troops. We spent most of the time getting rid of this volatile cargo without any interference for most of the day.

On day three, the Japanese Kamikazes came in again and all the amphibious ships, close to shore and the rest behind us filled the sky with exploding metal and they went down in flames, without hitting any ships.

Day four was overcast and it was difficult to see sky above it. We were still in the unloading phase all morning and afternoon. After lunch on the fly was over and I returned to the area, all hands had to help with the unloading, I looked up as I was passing some ammunition to one of my mates, and saw a plane dive out of the overcast about 1000 feet above us and about 1500 yards from a large transport ship. Another LST opened fire on him, with all AA guns manned; the rest of the assault forces did likewise. The plane came in low now and tried to get between the ships. The LST that started the firing hit him about 200 above the water, the plane hit the water, cart wheeled and exploded. With everyone firing at this Kamikaze so low, I don't know how friendly fire didn't kill us all. At the moment all you see is the plane and not your surroundings.

The Kamikaze attack happened so suddenly I was transfixed. Our AA weapons were standby-manned but not with the regular crews. General Quarters was sounded and all the regular crews ran to their stations. We didn't have to wait long; another Kamikaze came over us in a dive, out of the overcast. It appeared that the pilot had spotted a Battlewagon; I believe it was the old USS Texas BB-35. The plane was in its dive and all the ships opened up on him; he pulled out of his dive, started to burn, did a tail spin, hit the water and exploded, about five minutes later another came in and was diving to take out a clearly marked Hospital Ship, painted all bright white with a large green stripe all around from bow to stern and a huge Red Cross amidships. We opened up on him with every 20mm and 40mm weapon, we hit him and he hit the water and exploded and we were credited with the kill. We all thought that the Hospital Ship would be sacrosanct, but the game had changed.

The kamikazes came everyday, between the hours of 4am to 8am and 4pm to 8pm when all the ships would be silhouetted against the water and the horizon. Our carrier-based planes were meeting them but with the sheer numbers of them some were getting through. We heard that the Destroyers and other gunships on Picket Duty over the horizon as our covering force were getting slammed by the Kamikazes with a great loss of life even though they were shooting many down.

I'm heartily sorry to hear that Uncle Owen died. God was kind of late taking him though. After being in a home for 18 years and not able to get around after his stroke, he was in a prison of himself. He enjoyed our visits when we were kids. I hope he just went to sleep. He always seemed to be able to laugh even though his speech was affected.

I received your letters dated March 3rd and March 16 and Gerald's letter dated March 3rd also.

I hope everything is OK at home and with you. Give my love to all.

Junnie (Frank, Jr.)"

(By now, Gerald and I had turned 19 years old on 2/15/1945)

The Bombardment Group

As the LST's in the assault waves moved toward the landing beaches at high tide, they all had assigned areas that they were to occupy. The LSTs that contained the Tractor Groups were the closest to the landing areas. They all had their bow doors open and ramps lowered to debark the amphibious tractors and the Marines and Army troops. The tractors pulled away and made circles in the area until all the groups were unloaded and ready to make their way toward their assigned shore points. The Japanese had hidden suicide boats, piloted by two men and had a torpedo in the bow or drums of explosives on board. Many were discovered in shallow coves and destroyed before they could be utilized.

While all this activity was taking place, the Battleships and Cruisers behind us, barely discernable in the mist and smoke of the pre-landing bombardment, fired heavy shells at the island. I had been able to be relieved from my duties on the bridge and to view the battle. When I stepped outside, the Battleships, maybe the USS Texas among them, were firing and the shock waves made my pants flap as if a strong wind was blowing across the ocean. It was an amazing, unforgetable scene of sights and sounds.

After the tractors left and were circling in the landing pools a Marine was discovered hiding in our carpenter shop, crying. Several of the crew escorted him to the bridge. The Captain used the loud hailer to have one of the tractors return to the side of the ship. The Marine who was in full combat gear when found, was made to leave our ship by way of a cargo net thrown over the side. Not a word was spoken to him by the other men or the officer on the tractor. Later we found out that he had been a bus driver at a Marine Training Base in North Carolina for several years, and that this was his first exposure to combat. He just lost his nerve. We never heard anything more about it. Fear is a terrible thing and it made this guy lose control.

The Big Boys, the Battleships I could identify at that time, were the USS Texas BB-35, USS New York BB-34, USS Tennessee BB-43, and USS Nevada BB-36. Some others were lost in mist and the smoke of battle, and several cruisers and destroyers I couldn't identify, were all belching smoke and projectiles in the pre-landing coverage. It was an awesome demonstration of military power.

The Artillery Parachute Flares

The forces on the beach, with artillery, fired parachute flares to light up the battle area and expose any Japanese lurking in the darkness. The flares were used during all hours of darkness and even illuminated the harbor area. Sometimes the Destroyers or Destroyer Escorts were called to make this fire support. The flares were really spooky; as they drifted down they swung with the breeze and the shadows moved as they swung. If anyone was nervous, the moving shadows didn't help, on land or on the sea. One's imagination was working overtime, and it must have been hard for the Marines to discern dead enemy bodies from those staying still in the shadows. There are Fourth of July displays nowadays that use this effect for celebration, but on the Okinawa beaches this display had a deadly purpose.

Japanese Deadly Suicide Kamikazes

We had several two-way, voice radios with battle circuit frequencies on the bridge. They were tuned for communicating with the beach troops and the Command and Control staff of Admiral Kelly Turner aboard his flagship, USS Eldorado AGC-11, and Rear Admiral, J.L. Hall's staff aboard his flagship the USS Teton AGC-14. It was fascinating to plug in earphones and listen to calls for air strikes and covering fire, with some vulgar language at times.

Several suicide *kamikaze* planes broke through the picket lines; two of the battlewagons were damaged. One torpedo bomber missed the Battleship USS Idaho and slammed into one of the Battleship USS Tennessee anti-aircraft batteries, killing 23 and badly burning 106 sailors. The Tennessee continued in the operation.

The U.S. Coast Guard-manned LST-884 was hit by a *kamikaze*. Three planes flew at the LST, two were shot down, but one suicide plane struck the cargo hold, just forward of the bridge. It went through the carpenter shop into the main cargo compartment of ammunition. The fires were out of control and the commanding officer ordered Abandon Ship as the ship was rocked with explosions and fire. Twenty-four Coast Guardsmen died and many were badly burnt and wounded.

Admiral Turner ordered all ships in the covering force to stay underway, but to maintain station and coverage of the troops ashore and to keep all guns on call. One *kamikaze* suicide raid had over 185 planes, 150 regular fighters and 35 torpedo bombers. Most were shot down by the carrier air patrols and the ships on the picket line to the north and the west. It was impossible to stop them all. The ships in the assault forces had their hands full, especially when the planes came in low and tried to get between the ships.

With the Radar off except for the ships on the picket line and the major ships in the area directing the operation, we all felt helpless, knowing that the *kamikazes* were coming but never knowing the direction or amount. The carrier air patrols were bombing the fields on Formosa and any of the surrounding islands that had airstrips. We had smoke generators mounted on our sterns and we were making smoke every morning and afternoon as soon as we heard the *kamikazes* were coming. The smoke generators were on most of the ships and they all used a soybean oil concoction that made a thick white smoke when heated; it was eerie to climb to a higher part of the ship and see a Navy in the clouds. With the optimum atmospherics the smoke would rise and cover the area, and underneath one could see enough to detect ships or boats close by.

Another suicide tactic was the *Ohka kamikaze* suicide glider plane. In Japanese *ohka* meant Cherry Blossom, their symbol of hope. The American sailors nicknamed it *baka* bomb, the Japanese word for Fool. The rocket-propelled glider was a human guided 2600-pound bomb; it was carried in the underbelly of a large aircraft, released close to the target, and guided by its suicide pilot at a steep angle with speeds up to 500 miles an hour. Our Navy had not seen these suicide weapons until the Battle of Okinawa. On April 12, 1945, the USS Mannert L. Abele DD-733 was fiercely attacked by multiple *kamikaze* planes. Then one aircraft, a *baka* bomb, approached the destroyer at a tremendous speed and steep angle; the artillery could not defend the ship and it was struck. Another *baka* bomb struck the ship and it split in two from the hit, sinking in minutes. There were 81 sailors killed, and LSM(R)-189 and LSM(R)-190 dodged enemy fire to rescue the survivors from the waters. It was difficult to imagine a person sitting on a bomb, guiding it to a target and ultimate vaporizing death, but those memories were all dredged up again when the New York City World Trade Center towers were attacked on September 11, 2001.

Two ammunition ships, the Logan Victory and the Hobbs Victory, both manned by Merchant Marine crews, were hit by the suicide planes. The crews abandoned ship; the ships drifted all day burning and exploding and had to be sunk by gunfire.

Our Top Deck Cargo LCT Landing Craft Tank

The weather turned nasty and caused much damage to some LST's and other amphibious craft hitting the concealed, underwater coral projections and pinnacles at low water. We were all waiting to launch the LCT we had carried across the Pacific Ocean. The crew was Navy and they were ready and anxious to get out on their own. We had been selected to carry this amphibious behemoth, which measured 114 feet long and 33 feet wide. It weighed 286 tons. It was not a commissioned ship in the Navy and its only designation was its hull number. It had an Officer-in-charge and 12 to 14 enlisted men. It was propelled with three Gray Marine diesel engines, geared to three propellers. It was able to carry five Sherman Tanks or 150 to 180 tons or 5760 cubic feet of cargo for 700 miles at a top speed of seven knots. Best of all, as far as we were concerned, it had some anti-aircraft firepower, with two 20mm machine guns and two .50-caliber machine guns. It was cabled to timbers on our deck; the timber brackets were welded to other brackets welded to the deck. The launch crew slathered the timber skids with heavy grease. At the time of launching, our ship pumped water into its ballast tanks on one end; this caused the opposite side to rise and the heavy side to lower. When our ship was at its greatest possible inclination, a sailor blew a whistle and the cables that had not been released were cut by axe. The LCT slid into the sea. A huge wave of water rose up and it acted as a cushion between the LST and the LCT, and preventing any damage to either vessel. It was sensational to witness. The previous day we detached the pontoons along both sides of the ship, and they were being used as barges with large outboard motors, or for pontoons or docks to get cargo to the beach.

As soon as we released the mighty LCT, its crew went immediately to work transferring cargo and vehicles to the beach. We had a small, tracked crane as part of our cargo. We were able to lower a cargo net with supplies over the side to whatever amphibious conveyance that came along side. Our five-inch naval ammunition was unloaded to LCT's over our bow ramp and by cargo net to LCM's, a smaller open landing craft. The LCM's, Landing Craft Mechanized, were about 50 feet long and had three 225-horsepower diesel engines. They had a crew of three, and could carry 120 men or a medium tank or 30 tons of cargo. As we were loading one LCM, one of the crew looked up as I was watching. I recognized him right away! He said, "Hi Smitty! What the hell are you doing way out here?" His name was Martin O'Toole, from the Uphams Corner neighborhood in Boston, one of my classmates at Boston English High School. We shot the breeze for about 30 minutes. His boat was being loaded with the cases of K-rations we had stuffed in every nook and cranny below. He was assigned to one of the Attack Transports in the landing area. We were each grateful to see a familiar face, so far from home and in the danger of the war. I never saw him again; I hope he made it home.

The word was out that the Japanese Fleet had been alerted to attack the Assault Groups and the Fleet Transport Groups at Okinawa with all assets possible. Readers of the historical accounts will understand the Japanese were desperate to defeat the Allied forces, now so close to the Japanese homeland. The skies were filled with hundreds of kamikaze suicide planes. The battle raged on for days. We knew what was happening on our ship and around us, but most information for us enlisted was limited to what the Skipper told us.

President Franklin D. Roosevelt Dies April 12, 1945

The Skipper announced that the President had died of a stroke at Warm Springs, Georgia. Not much additional information was forthcoming, but all the crew I saw had a shocked look about them. The Captain ordered the flag flown at half-mast for 30 days in reverence to the President. We had no chaplain on our ship and the Skipper suggested that those so disposed extend their personal thoughts to honor his memory. It seemed a shame that with the war in Europe almost over and our hope to finish off Japan so close, that President Roosevelt would not have the opportunity to enjoy the victory. He was a true friend of the Naval Service and would be greatly missed. We all expressed the hope that our Vice President and now our new President Harry S. Truman would carry the ball successfully.

Tokyo Rose Radio Broadcast

The chief propagandist for the Japanese during the war was Tokyo Rose, a traitorous American who broadcast her thoughts on the President's death via world-wide radio. We enjoyed listening to her just for the latest American music on her programs. Many times she would hit the nail on the head when she referred to specific military forces and their location and she would attempt to cast doubt on the love and affection of the wives at home. When President Roosevelt's death was announced, she said, "We must express our deep regret over the death of President Roosevelt. The American tragedy is now raised at Okinawa with his death. You American soldiers and sailors must know by now that 70% of your Carriers and 73% of your Battleships have been sunk or damaged, causing 150,000 casualties. Not only your late President, but also anyone else would die in excess of worry to hear of such annihilative damage. The Japanese Special Forces will sink your vessels to the last Destroyer. You will see this in the near future."

Troops Lose a Well-known Supporter

On April 18, the news arrived that Ernie Pyle, "The GI's Buddy," and world famous reporter was shot and killed on Ie Shima Island. His death was compared to the losing of one's own family member. All who spread the word spoke his name with reverence and sadness. Years later, we would come to know that the soldiers of the 77th Infantry Division made a wooden coffin for him and buried him wearing his helmet. Later he was reburied at the Army cemetery on Okinawa and finally moved to the National Memorial Cemetery of the Pacific, Punchbowl Crater, located in Honolulu, Hawaii. The wooden cross on Shima was replaced by a permanent stone monument.

Convoy to Guam, Mariana Islands, April 29, 1945

The Captain received orders for our ship to form up with others for an amphibious ship convoy to Guam. Admiral Chester W. Nimitz had relocated the Supreme Headquarters from Pearl Harbor to Guam. We understood that it rivaled Pearl Harbor as a strategic supply and intelligence base. His whole staff was now domiciled there.

The *kamikaze* suicide attacks came every day. With the hundreds of armed ships in the assault forces, especially the amphibious ships, such as ours, we spent most of our time at anchor or station keeping. We had to wait to be unloaded and the availability of smaller landing craft to unload us. The beach area was full of supplies and it took time to move them so others could take their place and we heard that unloading reservations were given erroneously to ships that had departed. It took time to correct these problems. We were the closest to the beach and in the most congested area. Ships and Transports were everywhere. Destroyers and Destroyer Escorts protected the outer perimeter from the obvious Japanese submarine threat. The picket line further out to the north and the northwest was concentrated to intercept the incoming suicide planes. Some of the smaller landing ships with adequate anti-aircraft weapons were sent to picket line to help. The larger members of the fleet the Carriers, Battleships and Cruisers had an additional supply of Destroyers to assist them. The sound of the General Quarters alarm always gave us a sense of dread. We did what we were trained to do, but never did anyone forget the *kamikazes* were coming. Our ship was credited with shooting down one Japanese torpedo bomber.

When the word came down that we were on the way to Guam, an almost audible sigh of relief flowed through the ship.

We departed Okinawa for Guam and a probable reload; we were part of an amphibious ship convoy and had several Destroyer Escorts and a Destroyer for our Sonar and Radar screen. Several empty tankers, high in the water were on their way to Ulithi or Eniwetok for refills. The whole fleet was battling near Okinawa and they all had big thirsts for fuel oil and gasoline. We were alerted some days earlier that the Japanese Imperial Navy was concentrating submarine forces in the Okinawa area and several suicide torpedo boats were sunk trying to slip into the assault groups. We knew that the *kamikazes* were taking their toll. Every now and then we would see a Destroyer limping in, some with terrible damage; others never made it home.

Before we left for Guam, we were in an anchorage area awaiting orders to depart. A Destroyer came in slowly, under its own power. Some anchor buoys were in place on the periphery, but very few. The Destroyer was a sight; a *kamikaze* plane flying out on the anti-aircraft picket line had hit it. Everything was missing from the bow to just forward of the bridge. The only thing left of its main batteries was the turret with two 5-inch/38's in a turret on the afterdeck. All we could see was a sheared off forward area; the bulkheads above and barely above the water line were gone, the watertight doors that led forward remained and were visible. It was as if someone took a knife and separated the bow from the ship. The crew sent out a small boat and a line and hooked up to a ring on the buoy. We couldn't believe what had happened. The crew waved as we waved, but not a word was spoken by anyone. I don't remember its hull number; no one asked for a casualty figure. One thing that spurred all the ships into action to fight the daily dose of *kamikazes* was the sound of a General Quarters alarm from nearby ships. Usually orders came from the Task Force Commander's ship, but if someone got an early warning, all ships followed the alert. We had been on the edge for weeks on end and *kamikaze* attacks came out of the air several times a day. Everyone knew the way to their gun stations, even if blindfolded or in the pitch dark of night, it was automatic and a life and death matter.

The day after the damaged Destroyer's arrival, past the noon hour, our Skipper thought it might be a good idea to keep our crew on its toes. We were all groggy with lack of sleep from the air attacks and unloading our cargo. He pulled the General Quarters alarm handle and all hands ran like hell for their anti-aircraft weapon stations. The clanging from our General Quarters carried across the water to the Destroyer. The survivors on the Destroyer, or what was left of it, ran to their stations also. Their Captain had a bull horn and wanted to know where the planes were coming from. Our Captain used his loud hailer and said, "The alarm was just a drill." The Destroyer Captain yelled back, "You dumb son-of-a-bitch! What the hell is wrong with you?" Our crew could not have felt worse. If it had been possible to transfer off the ship, we would not have had a crew to get to Guam.

Losses on Both Sides in the Last Battle of the Pacific

The Battle of Okinawa would be declared over on July 2, 1945, 82 days after it commenced. Okinawa was transformed into an Allied air and naval base, for an assault on the Japanese homeland. The battle reset all records for most troops landing ashore, most supplies transported, most naval artillery fired, and most bombs dropped. Those records were accompanied by tremendous losses. Thirty-four Allied ships and vessels had been sunk, and 368 ships and craft were damaged. The Allied Fleet lost 763 aircraft. Over 4900 Sailors and 3443 Marines were killed or missing in action. There were 4824 Sailors and 16,017 Marines wounded; some died later of their wounds. Army casualties were 7613 killed or missing and 31,807 wounded or injured. Non-battle casualties numbered more than 26,000.

The Japanese concentrated all their land, sea, and air forces at the Battle of Okinawa. Historical records estimate over 107,000 Japanese were killed, and 10,755 captured or surrendered. There were estimates that probably half the Okinawa population, or 140,000 Japanese civilians, were killed.

Guam, Marianas Islands, May 6-June 11, 1945

After a short stop in Saipan, we arrived in one piece on an uneventful voyage to busy Guam Naval Base. As we came around a point of land, we saw dozens of small windmills, no more than four feet high, mounted over what looked like large commercial milk cans. We found out that they were wind-powered washing machines, devised by the military men to do their washing. The windmill was attached to a rod that was connected to a small crankshaft. The bottom of the rod had what looked like a small pie plate; it was a reflector from a jeep headlight. It moved up and down to agitate the water and wash the clothes. I was amazed at the ingenuity.

Our ship was now riding at anchor in Apra Harbor, and a big construction project was going on building a breakwater around the harbor. The Seabees unofficial motto was "The impossible we do right away, the miraculous takes a little time." They were building a breakwater around Apra Harbor. Empty concrete ships we had seen being towed by seagoing tugs to haul fuel oil products and other war material would be lined up, and the Seabees would slowly sink them. A road was built with rocks and dirt from the island, and the hulk was filled until it disappeared. The next one was done in turn until the harbor was completely protected from the weather and any Japanese submarine forces. We only saw the beginning of the project, but we got the idea. The Navy had established direct flights from Guam to San Francisco and a large postal installation was built by the Navy Seabees to expedite the military mail for personnel stationed in the Pacific.

My Surprise Journey Home

Sporadically for the last months, I was having terrible headaches. The pain was preceded by a zigzag display of lights; my vision was affected until the light display disappeared. As soon as the display quit, I would have nausea, vomiting or just a severe pain headache. When I recognized the symptoms starting, I took aspirin that I picked up at sick bay. It was the Navy's equivalent for aspirin, called APC's. It was a mixture of aspirin and caffeine, and was considered a remedy for anything. Although APC's gave me a stomach ache, which I countered with a candy bar or food, the headache pain subsided. I was always leery of anything that would call attention to my Amblyopia eye condition and I avoided any situation that would land me in front of a doctor.

After a day or two in Guam, several of the crew went to the newly erected Naval Hospital for overdue dental problems. I went along to have a molar filled or repaired. I made the mistake of mentioning my headaches to the dental staff and I was sent to an older doctor, who recognized my crossed-eye condition. Forget about headaches; there was real trouble ahead for me now. I was sent to an Ophthalmologist who blew the whistle on me. My eye condition was discovered and I was confined to the hospital!

Guam Naval Hospital, Base 18

The doctors had little time for ambulatory patients and may have felt that it was an imposition for me to take up their time. With the arrival of the seriously wounded from Okinawa, the medical facilities were overloaded. As soon as a patient was able to travel he was sent to Honolulu and then on to the U.S. mainland. The diagnosis of headaches and the suspected eye condition as well classified me as being ambulatory.

Quonset buildings were all over Guam, some large enough for aircraft. The ones I was sent to were at Base 18 Naval Hospital. Several of the hospital wards were H-shaped. The two legs of the H-shape were two buildings long and were joined in the middle by another Quonset hut, which was used as storage for the hospital. One small room was partially full of K-rations and some sinks and pantry items, and a coffeepot. Heads with several stalls and urinals were for the ambulatory men; the Nurses had separate restrooms in the same area. The pantry area was more like a military day room and had several small folding tables and folding chairs. These areas were always lighted to some degree even when it was lights out in the patient areas. The pantry area had the first flake ice machine I had ever seen; it was well used for the bedridden Navy corpsmen and Marines. My hospital billet was mostly for non-threatening medical cases, but the doctor in charge of this area was a thoracic surgeon. I only remember his last name was Montgomery. He was rarely in his office located in a closed off corner on the end of the building. Whenever I saw him he was either coming out of or going into a surgery, but he had just enough time to say hello.

After a few days in the hospital, one of the two Navy Nurses in my wing came by and told me I had an appointment with Dr. Montgomery the next morning. His office was just a few beds from where I was assigned. I entered and he introduced himself to me. I believe he was a Lieutenant Commander and had a pre-war practice in Philadelphia. He really looked beat. There were so many combat wounded coming through from Okinawa; the wounded were either going home for better care or they were dying. He asked me about my headaches and I tried to explain they had become so bad I mentioned them to the dentist. He gave me a physical and recommended that he start with a spinal tap to check the fluid. He would do the spinal tap at my bunk during the next day. He made no mention of my Lazy eye condition; I was really surprised. I always expected a couple of armed Shore Patrolmen to grab me and haul me off to the brig.

I had the spinal tap the next morning; it took about half an hour. I had a local anesthetic before they put the needle between the vertebrae and withdrew some fluid. He said that I had to lay flat for about eight hours after the tap, and if I raised my head I would have the worst headache one could imagine. I took his advice. One of the corpsmen Pharmacist Mates came with warm soup and a straw. I laid flat until that evening when they checked me out and allowed me to sit on the side of the bed. I had no after effects. Before the Nurse on my end of the medical ward went off duty, she gave me permission to raid the pantry K-ration locker for a meal. The Nurses were the only service women in the forward combat areas.

I was sleeping on my right side and awoke to noise near me. The bed next to me had been empty for a couple of days. Dr. Montgomery, along with another doctor and a couple of nurses were unwrapping a man in the bed. He was a Marine, just a kid, and unconscious. As they removed the bandages, underneath the dressings was a material like a rubber sheet covering more dressings. The doctors removed those dressings to expose a huge hole in the Marine's right chest, the size of a fist. The doctors conversed among themselves, reached in with instruments for a second or two, and rewrapped him with new dressings. One of the Nurses saw me wide-eyed and came over and whispered to me to turn over if it bothered me. I finally went back to sleep and when I awoke the next morning, the Marine was gone; he didn't make it through the night. He couldn't have been more than 19 years old.

The Nurse on the day tour asked me to run some errands for her. I did without hesitation; they were all working long hours and hardly had time for themselves. I would chase records and deliver records for them, fill ice buckets and do anything to be helpful; it made the time pass. Once as the day Nurse was going off duty, she asked me if I drank. I said yes. The next day and every day after, she came by my bunk and gave me a glass of lemonade with a good size shot of medical alcohol in it. To cover herself she always said in a stage voice, for all to hear, "Don't forget your medication, Smith."

In the evenings there was always a free movie in an open-air area with benches of split coconut logs and ice cold sodas for a nickel. As we walked to the theatre we had to pass between the Nurses' quarters; guys would grab their hearts and pretend they were about to faint when they saw the Nurses.

While I was at the hospital, we had three U.S.O. shows. They always had a comedian, several young lady dancers and a small musical group. No matter the size of the group, it was like being home and a view that many had almost forgotten. We had two major shows while I was there. The biggest was Bob Crosby and his orchestra; he was Bing Crosby's brother, and he was a great musician and musical innovator in his day. The Crosby show was a full orchestra and a stage production just like the ones at the New York Paramount or the Boston RKO theatres, but without the stage scenery. The music was sensational, playing all the hits of the time. The ladies in the show were the most beautiful we had ever seen. Even if the women had been bundled in fur coats, the guys would have fallen in love with them. Just to see someone from home was a treat.

We celebrated the end of the war in Europe on May 8, 1945, at the Base 18 hospital in Guam and thousands of miles from any formal celebration. The topic of conversation then was, "What are we going to do when we make it to the States?" We had never heard of such things as atomic bombs; we saw no hope of avoiding more deaths in making landings on the Japan mainland.

I had just one other meeting with Dr. Montgomery, but there was no diagnosis concerning the headaches. The hospital population was slowly being moved toward Hawaii; the ambulatory wounded stayed a week or two and moved out. One morning I woke and there was a young man in the next bed next to me. He was the latest Okinawa wounded to arrive. Shrapnel had severed his spinal cord and he was paralyzed from the waist down. He had a great sense of humor and never spoke of his future or complained about anything. His name was Raymond Olson; he was a farm boy from Hill City,

Minnesota. He taught me to play cribbage and he beat me every time. For the rest of my life, he would come into my thoughts and I wondered how he made out. Did he survive, did he get home?

I was able to take short trips around our area and started to familiarize myself with some of the units based on the island. I was hoping to see a boyhood chum named Leo Donovan who was a neighbor of ours in Boston. He was a few years older, had been in Boston College for two years, and gone through a Navy program to become an officer. I corresponded with him occasionally when I was in the South Pacific and looked for him wherever we landed. He was assigned to a Carrier Aircraft Supply Unit, CASU. The Fleet Post Office at Guam was unable to give me the information, and I never located him during the war or after.

The head nurse told me that I was on a list to be transferred to the Naval Hospital in Honolulu, but not the date. I wondered if I would be transported back home by LST. My Quartermaster friend Pat Healy, with Signalman friend Jim Madden, came by the hospital to visit. I told them I had no shred of hope of returning to the ship. They had no information on the next assignment for LST-759, but didn't think they would be staying long at Guam; they thought LST-759 would be taking more supplies back to Okinawa.

The ship's Executive Officer came by and told me he had put me in for 2nd Class Radarman. We spoke for a few minutes and he said goodbye. This was as final as he could say; I felt like my guts were ripped out. He was a fine officer and it was a real pleasure to have served with him. I wished him well. The invasion of the island of Japan was the next battle, and thousands or hundreds of thousands would die when it came to that. If the suicide *kamikaze* planes, suicide *baka* bombs, suicide *kaiten* human guided torpedoes, suicide swimmers, and suicide boats were any indication of the desperation of the Japanese, they were ready to fight to the last man. It was rumored that the Japanese were reinforcing the landing beaches on the island of Kyushu, and thousands of Japanese troops were being moved from Manchuria.

Dr. Montgomery came by one evening and gave me a brief examination. He said I was being sent to the Naval Hospital in Honolulu. He thought I might be there for a few weeks for evaluation and treatment if it was necessary. He told me I was being Air Medical evacuated and because of weight limitations for the long flight to Pearl Harbor, I was only allowed to wear my work uniform of dungarees and chambray shirt. I could hand carry one dress white uniform, a change of underwear, socks, the shoes I was wearing, and toilet articles. I would not be allowed to carry aboard my sea bag with all my other uniforms, winter and summer, and all my issued clothing, which by this time had all been replaced with tailored clothing. He said the bag would be shipped by other means and sooner or later would catch up with me. Well, it never happened. Later, I put in a claim for $200.00 and it was denied, with the explanation that leaving my sea bag behind was a voluntary action by me, and I would not be compensated for the loss. I remember seeing pictures in *"Life"* magazine of stacks of unclaimed Navy sea bags in warehouses in the Pacific area waiting for disposal. My bag was probably in a pile somewhere, my serial number stenciled on the outside, and a shipping tag wired to it. It was as if I was losing everything because of my Lazy eye.

RETURNING TO THE UNITED STATES

Farewell LST-759 and Base 18 Guam Naval Hospital

On June 10, 1945, a Navy bus came by at 0700 and picked me up with another sailor and a Marine; both had lost eyes or their vision was affected by their wounds. We were told that most of the evacuees were on litters; we were the few ambulatory. We arrived at the airport and were taken to a Navy-designated R5D Naval Air Transport Service plane, a four engine C-54 which was the Army designation; the manufacturer designated it Douglas DC-4 Skymaster. The wounded on the litters were carried aboard and their occupants were made comfortable, two were clearly sedated, with their wrists and feet secured to the litters and a sheet tied across the waist. Most of the other passengers were bandaged, blanketed and obviously sedated. We three ambulatory were loaded, and the two Navy Nurses, dressed in olive green coveralls, checked in food and beverages. Our names were checked off from a clipboard prior to the cabin being sealed.

The Navy flight crew of six came through and checked everything before the flight. One of the crew walked through the cabin with a canister that spewed a type of mist. The Nurses called it a Bug Bomb with DDT. The same thing was done in the under-floor compartment to eliminate the possibility of transporting any insects out of Guam. The atmosphere cleared after a while and we all began to breathe normally.

Our plane Commander was a Navy Lieutenant Senior Grade with an enormous mustache; his duty was to take off and land the plane. The other pilots had the flight deck for the airborne part of the trip. The Senior Nurse, whose last name was Redman, was a really beautiful woman, and even in an olive drab jumpsuit, it was difficult to keep our eyes off her. The pilots seemed to share our views. She ignored them as best she could; she had a tough job overseeing the evacuees in the passenger compartment, and never seemed to rest.

Fuel Stop on Kwajalein Island in the Marshall Islands

Our first stop to refuel was the island of Kwajalein in the Marshall Islands. It had been captured by the U.S. Army 7th Army Division after a four-day battle. Army casualties were 173 killed and 793 wounded. The island was approximately 1500 miles from Guam, and the time of flight was between five to six hours.

I stretched out on my litter and read or snoozed most of the time. There were just two seats on each side at the forward end for the nurses and crew. The crew compartment, through a door forward, had five berths for the crew on long overseas flights. I could see the entire island out the round side window as we made our landing approach. It looked just like the combat pictures I had seen; I never thought I would be in a position to be able to see this.

We were at Kwajalein just long enough for fuel and supplies. Ground crews swarmed all over the plane and we were on our way in a short time. As soon as the cabin was secured again, the same crewmember walked through with another fog-producing Bug Bomb. The Nurses had everything under control and nothing seemed to alter their duty schedule. This was my first real airplane ride and I knew that with each passing hour, I was getting closer to home. I realized that the war was over for me, but the fear of the outcome of my enlistment was tying my stomach in knots. I had fears that I would receive a Dishonorable Discharge not only for concealing the eye problem, but also for lying about my age in 1942. Years later I learned of organizations devoted to military members who enlisted under-age so those men would not be denied the benefits of the G.I. Bill.

U.S. Naval Hospital, Pearl Harbor

After a nine hour flight, on June 11, 1945, we arrived in Hawaii. It was daylight and a bus and Navy ambulances met the plane. They moved us to the U.S. Naval Hospital in Honolulu. Food and drink were available as we were split up and sent to different wards. I was given my own bed with clean white linen. The ward nurse came by after a while, took the basic military information and matched it with the manifest from the plane. She directed me to the ward galley that had a couple of tables and chairs and the typical bottomless Navy coffee pot. Several of the sailors in the ward came by and introduced themselves and wondered where we came from and the progress of the war around Okinawa. The only routine was up at 0700 and lights out at 2100. The cafeteria had breakfast at 0730, lunch at 1215 and dinner at 1615. The uniform of the day was dungarees and white dress uniform for shore liberty, if granted.

Most of the sailors in the ward were recovering from broken bones and most all were ambulatory. One was an Aviation Machinist Mate who was working on a plane's landing gear when a part broke and hit him in the face. It broke his jaw in two places and he had to have his teeth wired together as part of the recovery process. Another was a Navy Seabee who dove under a truck to get protection during a sniper attack; a bullet hit him in the center of his cheek and exited his other cheek. One cheek had a small hole, but on the other side it took most of his cheek and some of his teeth as the bullet went through. He was a long way from being recovered and would have to go through much plastic and dental surgery. This was a cross section of the ward of about 50 and I never found a sour puss in the whole lot. The Aviation Machinist was a real outgoing type of personality. Most all the sailors in the ward felt lucky to be alive and were air evacuees from all over the South Pacific. I was never asked why I was there. In my own mind I felt out of place. All I could think of was how my military career would end.

I can't recall the day of the week I arrived, but it seemed as if the staff was on a five-day schedule for ambulatory personnel. I was given a full physical exam after a couple of days and was scheduled for a comprehensive eye exam two days later. The Ophthalmologist who gave me the eye exam was very critical and asked me why hadn't I revealed the condition prior to it being discovered? I just told him of my wanting to get into the service when the war broke out. I spoke of my twin brother and his naval service; I didn't want to be left behind at home with the whole world in flames. I explained my training and service record showed my ability to do every technical job given to me and being awarded 4.0 grades in every position I was rated. He wanted to know how the eye condition was discovered. I related that the severe headaches I was suffering from were becoming more frequent and of longer duration, so I asked the dentist in Guam. The Honolulu doctor suggested my migraines could be congenital. I tried to explain that I didn't have any until I was in training at the Naval Base in Norfolk. I didn't tell him of the broken nose while I was there, although it was in my medical records.

He said he knew by his experience that the eye condition was present prior to my enlistment and that Amblyopia had no symptoms and was not the reason for the headaches. He left it at that. He said that if he had his way, he would see that I received a Dishonorable Discharge for a fraudulent enlistment. That was enough to scare the daylights out of me! I was 19 years old; I could list all my honorable service through the ranks, especially all the combat-related activities. The eye condition was never the cause of any accident or disaster during my enlistment. I did not know what he would do next. He concluded the examination in a surly manner; he looked at all the combat ribbons on my white dress uniform. Couldn't someone just say, "Hey kid, well done?" The Ophthalmologist was not going to approve my return to active duty; I was going to be classified as a medical evacuee.

The physical examinations were over and it seemed as if my personnel file had been dropped into a black hole. I was never assigned to any activity or a duty schedule. I was issued a liberty pass that gave me practically Free Gangway, a Navy term that allows you to come and go as you please. I was able to go on liberty at 1500 until 2400 and every weekend until 0700 on Monday mornings, if I so desired. I had to turn in my pass at the hospital ward desk and pick it up and sign out when I left. I had no funds other than 40 U.S. dollars I brought from Guam. I had no idea when I would have a payday.

During the day the hours dragged by. I finally located an athletic office in the hospital area and checked out a small rhythm bag and gloves and spent a couple of hours a day to pass the time. Across the road from my building were the mental wards for violent sailors and Marines, mostly combat related, I guess. Every man has his breaking point and I witnessed one the day of the landings on Okinawa, when the Marine was found hiding in the carpenter shop. Outside the mental ward I could hear crying now and then and wild and vulgar talk as some of the patients ranted. Armed Marines patrolled the chain link fence that surrounded the complex.

The food at the cafeteria for the ambulatory was very good. If I was going ashore I always stayed until dinnertime and caught a shuttle bus to a base movie or the Navy beer garden. I would wander the Ship's Service Store and I spotted a large gold star sapphire ring; I knew it was sure to land on my finger if I had a payday.

After about two weeks, an Ensign from the Finance Office came by with a list and cash for most of the sailors in the ward; I was included and given 150 dollars in cash. I caught a shuttle to the Navy beer garden off of Waikiki Beach called The Breakers. It always had Big Band music. I visited The Breakers several times while at the Naval Hospital. The Navy picked one of the most beautiful places on the island of Oahu. It was on Waikiki beach and almost in the shadow of Diamond Head.

Several of the sailors in the ward were being air-evacuated to the mainland, but they were mostly severe arm and leg injuries requiring further surgery and reconstruction. Several had profound hearing losses and a couple had each lost an eye. I hadn't seen a doctor in several weeks. I had to make a muster every morning but I never made a duty roster. Around the first week in July, the Navy Nurse came by and wanted to know where my belongings were. I told her that I was ordered to leave them on Guam for later surface trans-shipment. The only clothing I had been in my hand-carried ditty bag. She told me that I probably would never see my sea bag again and that it was not an unusual situation.

Goodbye, Pearl Harbor and Naval Hospital Honolulu

The evening of July 10, 1945, the Chief Master-at-Arms in charge of the security detail at the Hospital came by and told me to pack whatever I had and be ready to leave the Hospital at 0600 the next morning. The uniform for travel was white hat, clean chambray shirt and dungarees with black socks and GI shoes. He didn't tell me of the mode of travel or destination, just be at the ward entrance at 0600, and breakfast was at 0500 sharp. The only items to be taken were to be personal and hand-carried, same as before. He had a list on his clipboard and checked my name off. I assumed I would be shipping out on the "Magic Carpet" fleet, naval vessels in service to return American servicemen from the Pacific to the mainland.

I had a difficult time falling asleep that night. I figured that I was scheduled to take a slow boat to San Diego Naval Base and was in knots about the outcome of my enlistment. I had no information or contact with Coast Guard District Office officials. I assumed that they knew where I was and that my ultimate destination and disposition was in their hands. Being at the ward entrance at 0600 was the only alternative open to me.

Early Morning on July 11, 1945

I awoke at about 0430, after a restless night. I had the head almost to myself. I showered, shaved and headed to the mess hall for a cup of coffee. I grabbed a tray and had a good-bye breakfast of bacon, eggs and toast, with a glass of pineapple juice. I had my ditty bag with all my possessions along so I could linger at the coffee urn. I didn't recognize any of the sailors in the mess hall.

A Master-at-Arms came in and called for anyone who was leaving the hospital at 0600 to muster at the entrance. When I got to the entrance, a Navy bus was waiting and the driver called names from his list; my name was one of them. I boarded the bus with about a dozen others. There were plenty of seats; I grabbed one by myself, and in a few minutes we took off.

We arrived at what is now the Honolulu airport. I was shocked. I had no idea that I was being flown to the U.S. mainland! With so many ships headed to the mainland, it never entered my mind that Air Evacuation would be my mode of travel. We left the bus, went into a terminal and a Navy Flight Nurse dressed in dark green coveralls herded us together and called our names. We were headed for the U.S. Naval Hospital in Oakland, California, and the trip would take 13 or 14 hours flight time. In Oakland, we would be transported to the Oak Knoll Naval Hospital for further disposition.

The aircraft waiting for us was a four-engine Douglas C-54 Skymaster, Navy designation R-5D, like the one I had flown on from Guam. We boarded the plane after the medical personnel carried several patients on litters onto the airplane. The interior was set up the same, with canvas litters lining both sides of the aircraft. The door to the flight deck was open and it had about five or six bunks for the flight crew; it seemed as if the flight crew consisted of a Lieutenant Commander, two Lieutenants, and three enlisted men.

Provisions for the flight crew and the passengers were being loaded as we were shown the head to use and our canvas bunks. I was again in a middle tier and had access to a window. I could hear the doors to the cargo hold being secured and one of the crewmen came through with the preflight Bug Bomb, filling the whole compartment with fog. They had already Bug Bombed the cargo compartment.

The Flight Nurse walked over to each of us and made sure we were all secured to our litters by seat belt-like straps. The door was closed and the engines started one by one, the propellers powerfully shaking the plane with their vibrations. After a couple of minutes we began to taxi toward the main runway. The plane stopped and the pilots accelerated the engines. We taxied to the end of the runway and positioned for take-off. The engines roared at full throttle, shaking the plane and we began to move. We were traveling at high speed and all of a sudden the engines were shut down. We were about halfway down the runway; the plane turned off onto a taxi way and slowly returned to the area near the terminal. After we had come to a stop, the door opened to the outside and a couple of the flight officers exited the flight deck. It crossed my mind that I might not be leaving Hawaii, after all. A pilot came into the fuselage and said that one of the engines was acting up and it would take some time to fix it. He told us it was nothing to be concerned about and because of the long flight it would be prudent to check it out. I looked out my side window and saw several of the ground crew removing a section of cowling on the side of an engine. I had no idea what they were up to, although they did seem to be tinkering with the innards.

After about an hour the plane was again buttoned up and the Bug Bomb was used again. I have to say we were thoroughly debugged! The engines roared to life again and we headed to the main runway for take-off. This time the four engines roared at full throttle; we began to move down the runway and lifted off. The engines all had a steady and balanced sound. We were on our way; I still had an apprehensive feeling about my military career. I lay back on the canvas bed and slept as best I could, as we climbed to cruising altitude. The engines were throttled back for cruising and a steady hum replaced the roar.

One of the Flight Nurses passed out old paperback books and a few Honolulu newspapers. After a couple of hours, a Nurse came by and asked us if a big ham sandwich and some cold milk would hit the spot. I think all the evacuees still had their appetites. She opened up one of the large thermal containers and distributed the food. There wasn't much conversation among the patients; I think we were all thinking about the next chapter in our lives. Most of the passengers were deep within their thoughts, especially ones who had rehabilitation time and required additional surgery. We had heard that the San Francisco hospital was the plastic surgery center for terrible disfiguring injuries. I had seen some horrific burn injuries at the Pearl Harbor Naval Hospital; it didn't seem as if corrective plastic surgery was possible.

After about six or seven hours, the aircraft commander came back and spoke to the two Flight Nurses and they came and told us that the engine repaired at Pearl Harbor had to be shut down and that there was nothing to worry about. The other three engines were operating without any problem. We would continue on to Oakland, because we were past the halfway point. The flight crew didn't seem worried, and treated it as if this was a normal procedure! There was nothing between us and Oakland except the vast Pacific Ocean.

I started to wish I was on a large, slow LST sailing back to the mainland.

Thankfully, our flight continued without any further mechanical glitches. The Flight Nurses passed out more sandwiches, cold drinks and hot coffee, and while most of us snoozed, they worked on paperwork and medical duties. Night came and the only sense of travel was the sound of the remaining three engines. The view out the window was just darkness. There hadn't been much to see during the day, just a flat expanse of bluish gray. The Flight Nurses dimmed the interior lighting; all seemed to be quietly sleeping or alone with their thoughts. All the injured men knew the war was over for them and they were on their way home.

Mainland USA

Early the next morning as the sun peeked above the eastern horizon, we could see the tops of the California mountain ranges poking through the clouds. The cloud layer obscured the rest of the land and the sea. The plane commander came back to our area and requested four ambulatory men to come forward to provide additional weight on landing to compensate for the shut-down engine. He said the plane nose wheel needed more weight at the front. We were to land at the Alameda Naval Air Station in Oakland, California in about thirty minutes.

The four of us went forward to the flight deck and sat in jump seats and buckled up. The two pilots and a flight engineer had on headphones and started their landing routines and checklist. This was my first experience witnessing an instrument landing, or any landing for that matter. There was no chitchat between the pilots. We entered the cloud layer and all I saw was gray through the windshield. I had a familiar dry mouth that usually happened when I was in active battle. The pilot and the co-pilot were talking to a ground controller and their attention was riveted to their instruments. It seemed like forever that we flew through the clouds. All of a sudden we were on final approach and the runway was in sight a few miles ahead. It was an amazing experience for me, and the crew wasn't the least nervous or concerned. We landed and taxied to a terminal where I saw several Navy ambulances and a couple of buses waiting for us. It had been a long time ago that I had left the United States by way of New Orleans. I had traveled thousands of miles in and around the South Pacific, and I couldn't believe I was back in my country, safely home. The date was July 13, 1945. That date July 13, would become even more special, because that is the birthday of Lorraine Brodeur, who would become my beloved wife.

Oakland, California

I didn't have the slightest idea of how long I would be here and it was time to play it by ear. Navy hospital corpsmen came aboard the plane soon after we pulled into the terminal. All the ambulatory sailors were asked to get their ditty bags, disembark from the plane, and gather close to the two Navy buses nearby for further orders. The stairway was removed and a forklift type apparatus lifted two litters at a time to the ground. Hospital corpsmen carried each person on a litter into the Navy ambulances. It was easy to see that the crew doing the work knew their business; the plane was unloaded in a matter of a few minutes.

The ambulances left the area as soon as the litters were secured. A Navy Chief Pharmacist mate checked off our names as we boarded the bus and said it would be a twenty-minute ride to the Oak Knoll Naval Hospital. We would have the opportunity to eat at the hospital cafeteria as soon as we were checked in. Not much was spoken on the way to Oak Knoll. We heard that most of the wounded able to be transported or air evacuated came this way from Base 18 Hospital in Guam after a short stay in the Honolulu Naval Hospital for evaluation.

Oak Knoll Naval Medical Center

Oakland Naval Hospital was known to all who were patients and staff as Oak Knoll. In 1942, the Navy built a cluster of redwood barracks to use as an emergency hospital. The number of patients eventually outgrew the original facility, prompting the Navy to build a larger medical facility. The hospital was on a wooded hill at the east end of the city. It offered a spectacular view of San Francisco and the bay.

The hospital's main duty was to care for men wounded during World War II. During the height of the war, from 1942 through 1945, the hospital treated 8000 daily inpatients. This Navy facility was closed on April 1, 1996. At the closing of the facility, the hospital's last commander, Captain David Snyder, said of Oakland Naval Hospital property, "But remember that God smiles on it because it has been consecrated for all time by the dedication and sweat, and in many cases the tears and the very life's blood, of . . . men and women at arms who have served here, suffered here, lived here and sometimes died here." The Navy officially turned over the property to the city a few months later.

Oakland and San Francisco

All the arrivals on my air-evacuation flight from Pearl Harbor were assigned to medical wards and were escorted to them by staff Pharmacists Mates. Those needing immediate medical attention were taken to emergency medical areas. I was registered and assigned my billet. I was to report to the duty nurse for further directions the following morning at 0800. Those of us who were ambulatory went to the hospital cafeteria and grabbed trays and went down the chow line. It seemed as if it was open 24-hours a day with the comings and goings of Navy and Marine Corps patients. We all received specific times for meals and we were expected to adhere to them unless notified by our ward duty officers. The food reminded us all of what we had been missing in the South Pacific, but mostly the abundance reminded us that we had finally arrived home.

The next morning we all went our different ways to various medical specialties; I went to neurology and ophthalmology. The staff had examined my medical records; I really wasn't examined physically or given any specific information. I was thanked for being on time and directed to return to the ward and carried some papers in a folder to the duty nurse. She read a report and said I had no duty assignments and suggested I go to a recreation area to pass the time until lunch.

The nurse explained that the ambulatory patients were steadily being sent to other Navy rehabilitation facilities around the country. I was told that every day I must check a bulletin board at the main registration desk; several days before being transferred, the ambulatory patient's name would appear on a list with the time and specifics of the trip to the rehabilitation facilities. The bulletin board was the hub of Oak Knoll and patients combed the posted lists with the hope of going home or getting closer to home.

We had liberty every day, starting a 1300 to 0700 the following day. We picked up our liberty cards at the main desk prior to leaving the hospital and turned them in when we returned. Most of the time, I stayed for the noon and evening meal before heading into Oakland. I went to a uniform shop and ordered a set of tailor made, custom-fitted Dress Blues. The shop was running full blast and the measuring didn't take long and they would be ready to wear in two days. The cost was $37.00 dollars and was heavy-weight blue serge with rayon lining on the back of the cuffs and the inside of the jumper. I bought a set of Undress Blues for casual wear on the base when dungarees weren't allowed. The uniform shop was doing high volume business with the patients from the hospital; the fine material and the quality workmanship kept the shop working three shifts six days a week.

There was always entertainment for the troops at Oakland Naval Hospital. Volunteers by the hundreds provided live music almost every evening. It was as if everyone in the Bay area wanted to express thanks to all the returning veteran patients. Motion picture films were first run and no charge. During my stay, one of the films shown was *"Sun Valley Serenade,"* starring John Payne, Sonja Heine and the Glenn Miller orchestra. The movie story was set in Sun Valley, Idaho. The beautiful scenery made it unforgettable to me.

I buddied up with a Marine Gunnery Sergeant who had an eye injury and lost most his hearing during the battle of Iwo Jima. He was from Medford, Massachusetts. Usually we would hitchhike to the Lower Peninsula towns of San Mateo, San Carlos, Menlo Park, Burlingame and the college area of Palo Alto and Stanford University. On our first trip, we passed by a fire station in the town of San Mateo. One of the firemen was sitting outside, leaning against the wall in an old round back chair. He was wearing dark blue trousers, light blue shirt with suspenders and a dark blue hat with a Maltese cross emblem. He noticed our campaign ribbons and wanted to know where we were stationed. We told him we were patients at Oak Knoll Naval Hospital. He wanted to know where we intended to stay overnight. We told him we had no plans, but wanted to see the area before we shipped to a convalescent hospital. The fireman stood up from the chair and invited us into the station house. We walked into a room outfitted with twenty or thirty double-decker bunks, all made up with fresh sheets, pillows and blankets. The fireman told us we were welcome to stay overnight. We signed a guest book, thanked him for his generosity, and returned later that night to sleep. The trip back to Oak Knoll Naval Medical center was simple; all a serviceman had to do was to walk along the highway toward Oakland and a driver would stop and offer a ride. The people of the area all knew where we were headed and, thanks to their kindness, the Gunnery Sergeant and I never missed keeping our liberty curfew.

Decision Time at Oak Knoll

I went to the bulletin board one day and saw my name; I was on the list of about one hundred. The posting announced there was a choice of two convalescent hospital facilities; one facility was Yosemite National Park in eastern California and the other was Sun Valley Resort in central Idaho. I remembered seeing the film *Sun Valley Serenade* in the recreation room. I signed up for Sun Valley before anyone beat me to it!

Several of the patients that I had gotten to know made plans for a farewell visit to San Francisco. Many had been given orders that sent them closer to their homes and hospitals if they needed further care. We made the grand tour of the watering holes and the famous hotels of the day, splitting the taxicab bill six ways. The tour was expensive for a sailor's wages and my wallet was running dry. We were all a bit woozy, but it gave us a taste of San Francisco. The famous Fairmont Hotel and the Mark Hopkins were the high points for me. Little did I know that a few years after I was in San Francisco, my future brother-in-law, John Brodeur, would be passing through here on shore leave as a Navy seaman aboard the USS Hornet CVA-12, to visit our young family in Kingman, Arizona.

Goodbye, Oak Knoll Naval Hospital

On July 25, 1945, the servicemen slated for the Sun Valley Naval Convalescent Hospital in Idaho were informed by the Master-at-Arms that breakfast the next day was at 0600 and all ambulatory patients would muster at the lobby desk, with their personal gear, no later than 0730 for transportation to the Oakland railway depot.

Overnight it was difficult to sleep with the many thoughts that passed through my mind. I had no idea what was ahead. The only

Oak Knoll doctor I had met with read my medical record and stated it was apparent that I didn't need any medication. He said if I had any problems I was to see the nurse on our ward. Everyone in my ward was ambulatory and they all felt that they were on their way home. The hospital beds were needed and there was a continuous outflow of patients to other facilities.

After breakfast I went back to the ward and said my goodbyes to everyone I had gotten to know. We exchanged the usual "look me up if you get to Boston or wherever" and we took off for the lobby with our personal gear. This was not the time to miss the bus.

Sun Valley, Idaho, Here We Come

It was quite a sight when we arrived at the lobby. All the servicemen had on their best Class A uniforms, and the ribbons on their chests made it look as if this was to be a full dress parade. We filed out to the buses as our names were called and I tried to get a window seat for the last views of the Oakland side of the bay. We arrived at the railway depot and saw the train bound for Sun Valley, Ketchum, Idaho. All of the Pullman cars had large red crosses with white backgrounds on placards placed in some windows on both sides of each car to indicate it was a Hospital train. We boarded the Pullman sleeping cars. Some of the lower sleepers were made up and occupied by patients with casts and other types of injuries; the uppers would be made up in the evening for the ambulatory men. The lower berths not made up seated four passengers opposite each other and had a table available for their use. We had two dining cars in the middle of the train. Commissioned Officers had a couple of sleeping cars all to themselves and the rest were for enlisted men of all rates. Navy medical personnel walked through the cars to be available if any help was needed.

Train Trip to Idaho

On leaving the California coast, we passed into some of the most beautiful mountain country I had ever seen. There was an occasional small country town, with six or seven cabins, a General Store, and usually a one pump gas station. Each seemed to have a railroad siding with cattle loading pen and a small train depot close to the tracks. As we climbed higher in elevation, the roofs on the buildings appeared steeper to handle the winter weather.

The locomotives that pulled the train were oil-fired steam locomotives; as we climbed the mountain grades, the train sometimes slowed to a crawl. The Pullman sleeping cars were air conditioned by loading ice into bins on either ends of the cars from hatches on top of the cars. The icing was done at major section points, where train crews were exchanged and the whole train was serviced. Some of patients opened the windows to enjoy the cool mountain air, until the smoke from the locomotives became a problem. Our meals in the train's dining car were first class; the food was as good as that served in a fine restaurant. After mealtimes a full coffee urn was available 24-hours of the day. None of the patients we talked to were familiar with the Sun Valley Resort but, as in any naval experience, the scuttlebutt was a foot deep before we arrived.

The next morning, July 27, 1945, after an early wake-up call and breakfast, we pulled into a mountain town named Shoshone; it seemed to be on the edge of a prairie. The town was laid out like a western movie with all the buildings on one side of the street along the railroad tracks. While we were stopped, the train was checked, fueled and watered. We were now on the final leg of the trip. The train conductor said the end of track was about 60 miles, a short distance from the resort. We were to be met with buses from the Naval Convalescent Hospital.

Sun Valley, Idaho, and the Sawtooth Mountains

A few hours later, we arrived at the end of the track. A string of gray military buses were lined up at the train terminal to receive us. Our sea bags had been transported in a baggage car and were off-loaded onto a Navy truck. We would get them back when we checked into our hospital rooms. We had no idea what the resort looked like or how the accommodations would be set up.

It was only about a 15-minute ride from the depot to the small town of Ketchum, Idaho. A sign outside the town said the population was 1,010 and we were at 6,000 feet in elevation. The main buildings had log exteriors and roofs that extended over raised wooden sidewalks. Older commercial buildings were red brick with ornate facades. The town was mainly in the forest and surrounded on three sides by gently sloping mountains. The bus driver told us that the saying around town was, "the sailors and Marines went to Sun Valley and the girls came to Ketchum."

Sun Valley Lodge and Sun Valley Challenger Inn

Our buses followed a narrow, two-lane road through the trees to the northeast, out of Ketchum. We passed through meadows in a valley and arrived at Sun Valley Lodge; it seemed just a short walk from Ketchum. Our first view was a huge central multi-storied redwood building with two four-story wings on each end. The two wings formed a V-shape at either end of the central building. The Lodge sat in a flat valley, with mountains rising up behind and chair lifts up the slopes for the ski season.

To one side of the Lodge was a round heated swimming pool, surrounded by high glass walls framed by redwood timbers. In the cold mountain weather, the steam from the water rose from the pool's surface. The main hospital for medical or emergency treatment was in Sun Valley Lodge, and officers were billeted here.

As our buses passed the Lodge, we saw there were other buildings behind it. They looked like small two-story pastel Swiss chalets all joined together forming a U-shaped layout with a large, shallow pond at the center of the U-shape. There was parking space in front of the center building. This was the Challenger Inn. Along one side was the dining room and through the building windows we could see some of the military personnel domiciled here.

My Home Away From Home

All Navy, Marine and Coast Guard personnel not requiring constant medical care would be billeted in the Challenger Inn. We exited the buses and assembled in the courtyard between the buildings. A Navy Chief Hospital Corpsman told us of the regulations posted and the location of the sick bay staffed by a Navy Nurse Officer and a Pharmacist Mate. Sick bay would be open 24-hours a day for any emergency, and a regular morning sick call was scheduled for each day.

I was assigned to a room with three others; we each had a single bunk. Our carpeted room included full size bath with tub and shower. A housekeeper supplied linen; it was our responsibility to maintain a clean ship. The Chief came in and introduced a Chief Bos'n who was the Master at Arms for the Inn. He told us we had to attend 0700 muster each day except Saturday and Sunday.

Weekend liberty was granted from 1200 Friday until 0700 the following Monday morning. During the week, liberty was from 1500 to 0700, Monday through Thursday. Many of the patients' wives and girlfriends had arrived to be near the hospital, and some had taken jobs in the Ketchum. There was a variety of entertainment to lift the morale of the wounded. The Lodge had first run movies, and the U.S.O. brought in bands, vocalists and big name performers. Bing Crosby, a major star at that time, performed at Sun Valley for the troops.

The one regulation strictly enforced was an absolute ban on alcohol; no alcohol of any description was allowed on the property. Anyone wanting a beer took the short walk to the bars in Ketchum. We had one gate and a Marine guard thoroughly inspected everyone who entered. No one I knew risked losing liberty privileges for trying to bring booze aboard. Hopping the fence didn't work very well; the fields were muddy and not worth the effort. Liquor was rationed at the State of Idaho liquor store and we were each issued a liquor ration card. The State store checked-off each purchase with a pencil mark on the ration card. The ambulatory patients soon realized that the pencil mark could be gently erased. The only ration requirement to buy hard liquor was the shopper also had to buy a bottle of a liqueur. Wine was available once every week, but liquor was available once every two weeks.

A Sailor's Paradise, Beyond Our Dreams

We hadn't been at the resort very long before we all became acquainted with the mandatory behavior regulations. They weren't complicated, but serious violators would be put on the next bus out to who knew where.

A Navy First Class cook was in charge of the dining room. The cook in charge told us that the lodge had permanent Navy personnel on all mess details except the serving lines. He also told us that if anyone wanted to volunteer to work the serving lines at mealtime, it would be appreciated; they usually had enough volunteers to cover every day.

When the four of us returned to our room, we talked about joining the serving line detail. The four of us, and four from another room, went to the cook in charge. He was happy we came to see him. He said we had to be in the galley 15 minutes prior to meals during the week and that one of us would be issued a key to the dining room and the galley. We would have free access to the galley 24-hours a day! The permanent personnel would do the entire cleanup after the meals, and we would have to do any after-hours cleanup ourselves.

The cook took us on a tour of the huge commercial kitchen facility, the bakery, butcher shop, the refrigerated spaces, and the large walk-in freezer. Our attention was drawn to the large, new 35-gallon galvanized cans in the freezer. Each one contained individual cuts of meat and signs on the cans identified the particular cuts. Visions of a sailor's dream, steak and eggs, floated in front of us all.

The first evening of the volunteer galley duty, several of us went back to the kitchen after the staff quit for the day and before the butchers and the bakers arrived for the night shift. We each took a large pie plate, went into the freezer and found the best steaks available. We added a huge slice of butter and a couple of fresh eggs on top of it all. We put our loaded plates into the rotary oven and fired it up. We all waited until the steaks were as done as we wanted them; we couldn't believe our good fortune. We didn't overplay our hand, and we always cleaned and washed anything we used.

Buses were available to take the patients to the ski lift that went to the top of Bald Mountain, part of the Sawtooth Mountain range. The mountain was called the best single ski mountain in the U.S. We took the lift up to the top many times; a Park Ranger signed souvenir cards for each of us. Guided horseback camping trips could be reserved into the interior mountains, but I really didn't know how to ride a horse well enough to be at ease and camping was not my cup of tea.

Because of my Lazy eye, I kept a low profile. My greatest fear still was being kicked out of the service if someone up above gave my file any thought. I continued to have headaches, but I would go the sickbay for APC's. The young Navy Nurse in charge was named Betty Santieu, and she was from Chicago. With the men in our wing, she was busy all the time. After a few days of taking the aspirins, my headaches would subside and be forgotten, until the next round.

We had a library with donated books and many of the national daily newspapers. News of the war in the Pacific was always available and talked about. Everyone in the lodge wanted to know about the B-29 raids on the Japanese home islands. We all hoped that Japan would surrender without our invading. After what we had seen, we knew thousand upon thousands of Americans would die taking the Japan main island. Many of the Navy patients in the lodge were survivors of ships sunk or savagely damaged by the *kamikazes*. Marines were survivors of the Island Hopping campaigns, many from Iwo Jima and Okinawa. The strange thing was never once did I hear any war stories from my buddies convalescing at Sun Valley; it was just too fresh in everyone's mind. If an injury was apparent and you asked about it, a time and place would be the only answer and that was it.

Twin Falls, Idaho

The nearest large town was Twin Falls, and most weekends I hitchhiked to there. Most of the time, I got a ride all the way to Twin Falls. If the ride was shorter, it was just a matter of minutes before another car came along. Several times I got as far as the railroad town of Shoshone, which was about 50 miles or about half way.

Once, it was getting late in the day and I was worried about being stranded in Shoshone. I went into one of the bars and two men at the bar asked me where I was going; I told them Sun Valley Lodge. They told me they were on their way home to Hailey, which was south of Ketchum. They were pretty drunk and wanted me to drive them home. I was happy to oblige. I neglected to tell them that I really didn't know how to drive! My only experience behind the wheel was on Pavuvu in the Russell Islands northwest of

Guadalcanal, when I taught myself by driving a jeep up and down the beach one night before it was loaded onto our LST.

The two went outside and got into a good-looking Chevrolet coupe that was fueled and ready to go. They gave me the keys and fell asleep! It only took a few minutes to learn to handle the car on the road; the traffic was very light, with gasoline still being rationed. I guess I drove at about 30 miles an hour. They both woke up a couple of times and saw we were doing well. Hailey, Idaho, was only a couple of miles south of Ketchum, Idaho. As we approached Hailey, the two fellows were really snoring up a storm. Instead of stopping, I continued through town to Ketchum, pulled onto the road to the Hospital, slowly got the car turned around facing back to Hailey, and safely parked off the shoulder. Slowly and silently I exited the vehicle, softly closed the door and ran like hell up the road to get back before curfew. I knew that the two snoozing guys would be better able to drive the couple of miles home to Hailey when they woke up.

V-J Day, Japan Surrenders

The radio news on September 2, 1945, was all about Japan's unconditional surrender soon after the second atomic bomb was dropped on Nagasaki. Most of us gathered in front of the outdoor movie theatre. The staff had piped the radio broadcasts into the outside public address system. We listened as the reports of the celebrations went from coast to coast. The announcers would say, "We now take you to New York, Chicago, and Los Angeles." All the major cities across the nation were a mass of cheering and shouting. The sounds of the celebrations and the descriptions made us feel left out.

Four of us decided to take a few days off and head for the largest city near Sun Valley. We checked an atlas and found Ogden, Utah, the closest, on a direct route from Sun Valley. We left the Hospital grounds, walked to Ketchum and started to hitchhike to Ogden. We didn't have to wait long; a pickup stopped and the four of us hopped into the back. The farmer took us non-stop to Twin Falls, Idaho, where we caught another ride to Burley, Idaho. The highway to Utah was busy and a large flatbed truck, piled high with hay stopped for the four of us. The driver and his helper said they were going to Brigham City, Utah, and it would be a short trip on the same road to get to Ogden. We arrived in Ogden in the afternoon and headed for a place to stay. The local hotel had no vacancies. We walked around town and found a country bar with an open-air pavilion for dancing; it was the center of all the servicemen's activities and the party had already started.

Many Army veterans, all amputees, some multiple amputees, confined to wheel chairs, greeted us when we told them we had come all the way from the Naval Convalescent Hospital at Sun Valley, Idaho. The amputees were from the Bushnell Army Hospital in Brigham City, Utah; it was devoted to amputees from all theatres. Girls sat on their laps and the guys wheeled them around the dance floor. They were having a heck of a time and we partied on into the night.

I went back to the hotel and grabbed a few winks in a remote part of the lobby. Several other servicemen did the same thing and the hotel management kindly looked the other way. In the morning, I washed up in the hotel men's room and then walked down the sidewalk to a coffee shop for breakfast. The other three sailors from Sun Valley had the same idea and came straggling into the same coffee shop I had found. We all talked about the return trip to Sun Valley, wondering about the repercussions of the unauthorized leave. It was a long weekend that would have been called a three-day leave, or a "72."

It took about six separate, dusty rides to get back to Sun Valley. We arrived after dark, thinking we would land in the brig. Avoiding the guarded gate, we hopped the three-rail fence, crossed the fields and the four of us made it to our room in Challenger Inn without being discovered. We made muster in the parking lot the following morning at 0700. We expected to be challenged when our names were called, but nothing happened when we yelled, "Present." During our absence, when our names were called, someone had answered in our place! As we went to the dining room for breakfast, several sailors asked about our trip. The four of us went back to our room and slept the whole day through. It was the only time I ever left Challenger Inn like this; I guess everyone at the facility was celebrating and the confusion helped cover our absence.

American Red Cross Assistance

Every other week the representatives of the American Red Cross organization set up a table in the dining room at the Inn. They had Navy Medical Staff available with the medical records of the patients being transferred. They were there to assist patients in filing disability claims to be submitted to the Veterans Administration upon being discharged. Some servicemen thought they would file sometime later in future years, but they may have regretted their decision. In 1973, many medical and military records would be lost in a fire at the National Personnel Records Center (NPRC) in St. Louis, Missouri. The fire would destroy approximately 18 million Official Military Personnel Files (OMPF). The only way to file a claim after the fire would entail contacting witnesses and or ship mates who were aware and familiar with their problems at the time it happened, an almost impossible task.

The Honorable Leverett Saltonstall from Massachusetts

The Medical department must have set my file aside; no one checked on my medical condition or made any demands on me. I had only received a quick physical examination when I arrived and again a few weeks later. I could not complain about the food,

housing, and outdoor activities for us to occupy our days. How
was I going to go home and receive an Honorable Discharge? I
was 19 years old and a combat veteran with almost four years of
service. My roommates were talking about the GI Bill, a fully paid,
four years of college, including a small stipend paid each month,
$65.00 without a disability and $90.00 with a rated disability. As
the wounded were being transferred closer to their homes, several
of the galley volunteers that I associated with headed to hospitals
nearer to home for military discharge. I had no information as to
when I would be able to leave.

I wrote a letter to U.S. Senator, the Honorable Leverett Saltonstall
from Massachusetts, and requested his help in getting home. The
letter wasn't really a complaint about anything; I just explained to
him my military service would not continue because of the limited
sight in my left eye. I wrote of my combat service on the USS
Ramsden and USS LST-759. I told him I hoped he could expedite
my return home. I mailed the letter the next day. At the time I did
not know that Senator Saltonstall was the Chairman of the Naval
Affairs Committee. Within two weeks, Senator Saltonstall's staff
answered my letter and promised to check into my discharge. In
about one more week, the medical office requested that I attend
the next Red Cross session in the dining room to complete the
paperwork for the Veterans Administration. I knew I was on my
way home to my family in Boston!

October 1, 1945

Winter was arriving in Sun Valley; the snowfall was creeping
down the mountains. On October 1, 1945, my travel orders came
through! I was being sent to the Coast Guard Barracks outside of
Seattle, Washington, prior to being sent in a group to Boston for
processing and separation. I knew the war was over for me and felt
that I had upheld the honor of the U.S. Coast Guard and every ship
and station I served on. The Coast Guard Barracks at Paine Field,

Washington, were the beginning of the end of my service in World War II.

Departing Sun Valley, Naval Convalescent Hospital

The morning of October 2, 1945, I boarded a bus that took me from Idaho to Seattle, Washington. As I departed I was awash with the memories of the great people who expressed their appreciation every day to the returning veterans, even if it was just a smile and a "Hi Sailor." I thought about all the wounded and how they would get on with their lives. By December 1945, four months after the war ended, Sun Valley was decommissioned as a Navy hospital and reopened as a ski resort.

Seattle and Paine Field, Washington

I arrived in Seattle early in the afternoon along with other personnel on their way to Paine Field for transit assignments. We were met by a Chief Bos'n who directed us to the usual gray Navy bus; sea bags were loaded for those who had them, and we departed as soon as Chief Bos'n determined that no others were waiting inside the bus depot.

The Paine Field Receiving Station consisted of a group of doublewide military barracks and was primarily for troops in transit. We were told it usually took a week or ten days before transportation schedules were assigned. I learned the following day that as the senior rated man, I would be in-charge of a group of four sailors; three would be going as far as Chicago, one would stay with me to Boston after an overnight stay in Chicago. All of the sailors were medically disabled in various degrees and not able to stay in the military; most had the necessary combat and had gained the required points to be discharged for non-medical reasons.

The Coast Guard was giving us the red carpet treatment at Paine Field. The food was great and we had free gangway each day from 1200 hours until 0700 the following day. Local transportation was free to men in uniform and it was easy to get around. I was paid in cash, and had enough to explore the downtown a bit. I tasted the local beers and visited the local U.S.O.'s. My objective was to get home in one piece.

Our departure orders with the names of each group were posted on the bulletin boards in the mess hall and the main lobby. My group was posted and the four sailors were unknown to me. I would be given their orders, records, food, and transportation tickets at 0700 on Saturday, October 13, prior to departure.

The Train to Chicago

All the personnel leaving were awakened at 0500. Dress Blues would be the uniform of the day. Breakfast was to be served at 0600. Sea bags were to be in the lobby area no later than 0700. Departure for the Seattle train depot would at 0730. I was traveling light, because my original sea bag never arrived from Guam; I only had a minimum of uniforms. Most of the servicemen were sitting around the lobby as soon as breakfast was over, all with smiles on their faces. They were going home.

When we arrived at the depot, our names were called and checked off; my group was escorted to a numbered Pullman car. We boarded and were stunned when we saw our accommodations. Our car and the rest of the train consisted of First Class compartments, with upper and lower beds and separate restroom facilities. I couldn't believe the royal treatment the military was giving us. After we boarded, our Coast Guard Officers and Enlisted escorts shook our hands and wished us well on our final journey home; they gave me all the paperwork for the trip and departed. We had about 30 minutes before our train was due to leave, and a few headed to the shopping areas in the terminal for travel supplies. I had meal tickets for each leg of the trip and gave them to the Dining Car Steward. I gave the transportation orders to the Head Conductor.

I hadn't had any previous contact with any of the sailors placed in my charge. The only thing I knew was that I had a large packet containing their medical and service records, which was to be turned over to whoever was taking them to their final destination, after we arrived in Chicago. I introduced myself to my group before we were given our sleeping compartments. Three of the sailors were traveling to other destinations after Chicago. The one sailor going to Boston for Separation and Discharge was to stay with me.

As soon as the train departed, we were all sitting in our separate lounging compartment and the Boston sailor pulled out a pint of whiskey and started to drink it straight. It wasn't long before he was bad-mouthing the service, the train and anything else that came to his mind. He was a big man, in his late twenties or more, and spoke of being a professional football player. He also spoke of his family's political connections where he lived. I remember that his name was Mack. He had a roughed up face like someone who had boxed.

He told me he wanted me to open the individual record envelopes contained in the larger package. He wanted to remove anything adverse before we arrived in Boston. I told him in no uncertain terms that I wouldn't do such a thing and I had no intention of even looking at my own. He asked me several times and my answer was the same. The more he drank the mouthier he became. I told him that if he didn't straighten out I would turn him in to the Conductor of the train or Shore Patrol at my first opportunity. That seemed to quiet him down. Mack never got to the staggering stage and nodded off. There was no bar car on the train and no liquor was served in the dining car, so Mack must have bought his booze before we left the station in Seattle and stashed it in his ditty bag.

One section of our car was a chair car, with just enough seats for the people with the compartments. All in this car were military, mostly enlisted men, but we had some who were members of the Army Air Force. One in particular was a Major with Command Pilot Wings. He was probably in his early thirties and had several rows of ribbons with stars clusters and oak leaves on his uniform jacket. He was very pleasant and we made small talk, now and then.

One time I came into the chair section, and Mack was arguing with the Major. The only thing I heard was Mack saying, "I can buy and sell you," in a threatening tone. The Major stood up to his full height and told Mack to shut-up and sit down, which he did, mumbling until he nodded off again. I went to the Major and apologized. He said, "Don't worry kid, I can handle that bum."

While Mack was in the diner that evening for dinner, I opened the package of records and read his. He was being sent to Boston for Separation and a Medical Discharge for Chronic Abuse of Alcohol. None of the other sailors in the group were any trouble and were happy to be on their way home. Mack must have eventually run out of booze and remained half-civil for the rest of the trip to Chicago.

I spent most of the daylight hours watching the scenery as we were leaving Washington State; it seemed as if there were miles and miles of commercial flower fields, each with long rows of the same vibrant color, separated by more rows of another beautiful color. Whenever the train did stop for service or crew changes, there were no shops close by and Mack didn't have the opportunity to hop off the train to buy any liquor.

A Major Mistake of Judgment

We arrived in Chicago at LaSalle Street Terminal on October 14, 1945. The LaSalle Street Station was a multi-storied red brick building. The main lobby had barred windows along one side for ticket sales. There were dozens of long rows of high backed wooden benches in the passenger waiting area. In the center section of the huge room was an information desk, and newspaper stands and food counters sold their goods to travelers. A huge four-sided clock hung down from the rafters.

The three sailors in our group who were going to other areas were given their packages. Mack and I had to catch the train to Boston at 0700 the next morning. Mack was ready to tie one on. General Quarters alarms should have been going off in my head! He told me he knew his way around Chicago and would see me at the train in the morning. I gave him my home phone number and our address in Boston. I also told him that if he missed the train to get the next available train and call me when he arrived; I said I would meet him, and we would go into the Boston Receiving Station together. I would go in no later than the next morning. This was one of the worst decisions I was to make in my previous 19 years; this failure to use good judgment raised the possibility of a Summary Court Martial for me!

I turned the records and the transportation orders over to the Office of the Commander of the Shore Patrol for safekeeping, to be released to me the next morning, prior to departure. I was given a receipt.

Never having been in Chicago before, I went to the Aragon and Trianon Ballrooms, with the Big Band music of the day. I returned to the LaSalle Street Station where the Navy had a sleeping facility for us and bedded down for the night. I was really nervous thinking about the next day's final leg of the trip to Boston, with or without Mack.

October 15, 1945

I got a wakeup call at 0600 the next morning and dressed for my last military overnight trip. I spent the next hour checking to see if Mack had shown up. I went to the Shore Patrol Office and told the officer in charge my name and rank and who I was missing. I gave him Mack's train and meal tickets, keeping his Service and Medical Records with me as I boarded the train. The train pulled out at its scheduled time and I was on my way, without Mack. I had no idea what the end of the line in Boston had in store for me. The whole car was First Class, like the one from Seattle, and was all military, all from various military hospitals. I had the separate sleeping compartment to myself for the overnighter.

Boston 1945, Where the Journey Began in 1942

When I awoke early the next morning, a jumble of thoughts ran through my head. Our arrival was scheduled for 0800 and I left a wakeup call with the Porter for 0630. We approached the South Station Terminal and I saw the huge South Postal Annex attached to the terminal complex. All the mail for the New England states arrived and was dispatched by train and highway vehicles in those days. Even Air Mail had to be distributed within this huge mail center, after arriving from Boston's Logan International Airport.

My plan was to call my mother and hope she was home, I had told her of trip home, but had not known the details to tell her. I knew I was on thin ice when it came to Mack's time of arrival. Last time I talked to him in Chicago, he was to get the next available train and then call me when he arrived. I would meet him and we would present ourselves together at the Separation Center.

Familiar Territory

I said my goodbyes to everyone I had gotten to know on the train and headed for the subway system. My heart was racing at the expectation of seeing my family for the first time. The subway sped on to the end of the line in Dorchester; the surroundings were all familiar. The subway plunged below ground level after the Fields Corner Station before arriving a few minutes later at Ashmont Station and its network of buses and streetcars. I left the subway train and walked to the track that had the Talbot Avenue car waiting to leave, several passengers were seated and it was just a moment when we departed. I couldn't believe I was finally home. The main streets were all granite cobblestones, and as the homes, apartment houses and the businesses passed by, nothing much seemed changed. I was headed to the part of Boston we lived in, the town of Dorchester.

We passed the huge yellow brick buildings of Dorchester High School for Girls; the alma mater of my mother and Lorraine, my future sweetheart. We arrived at the main intersection of my boyhood neighborhood, Washington Street and Talbot Avenue, with its Codman Square business district and its white steeple colonial-styled Presbyterian Church set in huge trees and beautiful manicured lawns.

I felt a little weak in the knees when I realized this was it. After all the travel and all the wartime activities, I was home! I was so happy to see everyone, it all seems a blur. I spent the evening at home recounting my travels.

I had hoped and hoped that I would get a telephone call sometime during the day to meet Mack and check in at the Separation Center at the address on Commercial Street in Boston, but the day turned into evening without a call. With no call forthcoming, I set the alarm for 0600. With dread weighing me down like an LCT on my back, I was on my way before 0700 via streetcar and subway to the Separation Center.

The U.S. Coast Guard Separation Center

When I arrived at the Separation Center, I presented my identification to the front desk and was told to wait. In just a short time two sailors with Shore Patrol armbands asked for my identification; they almost bodily carried me to the Commanding Officer's Office. Standing by the door was Mack! He had a sheepish grin on his face and he said he was sorry to have screwed up. The bum had ignored my words to him in Chicago. When he arrived at the Chicago LaSalle Street Station, he had missed the train. He had gone to the Shore Patrol Headquarters, retrieved his ticket and the food chits I had left for him, and caught the next train to Boston. He arrived a few hours after me and he went directly to the Center while I was reuniting with my family, waiting for his phone call! Instead of calling my house to pair up and report together, he reported alone, without me. Now I was in real hot water!

The Commanding Officer called me into his office and read the riot act to me. He said that I had taken an unauthorized delay enroute. The gist of his scathing message was that my being the senior rated man with Mack in my custody, I was derelict in my duty to report in immediately after I arrived, with or without Mack. Since he missed the train, he would have been absent without leave and subject to disciplinary action when he arrived in Boston. The Commanding Officer put the question to me, "What would have happened if he was injured or worse and no one knew of his dilemma?" He told me that what I had done was certainly a court martial offense. I really began to sweat. Here I was, 19 years old, staring at an enormous penalty. I was a fool for relaxing the rules for Mack; I placed all I had worked so hard for in jeopardy. Making matters worse, Mack would be discharged the next morning and given a train ticket to his home.

The Commanding Officer told me to return later in the day; he would make a decision on my punishment. Mack was still standing in the corridor, looking contrite. I told him I never wanted to see his face again, but probably something more unpublishable. He turned and walked away.

When I returned to the Commander's office that afternoon, standing by the desk was a Chief Bos'n I had met in Provincetown, many years before. He recognized my name and me. He said, "I knew I'd meet you again before the war was over." He was the Chief in Charge of the station. He was to supervise any punishment issued by the Commanding Officer. I thought at that moment, the war was over, but not for me.

The Commander told me he took into account all he had read in my service record, all the ships and stations I had served on and the proficiency reports along the way. Out of respect for my service record, he was making our meeting an off-the-record Captain's Mast with no punishment recorded. He told me it was in his prerogative to delay my discharge for 30 days, but he reduced it to three days. I would be required to do any manual labor in the station that the Chief Bos'n deemed suitable. Chief Bos'n said I was to clean the heads in the morning, prior to being discharged. Even though it wasn't a really bad job, cleaning bathrooms was a heck of a way to leave the service. But, it was better to clean toilets than to have four years of service flushed down them!

My Final Day, October 24, 1945

I was notified by the Commander's Office that I was to attend a mandatory pre-discharge meeting for everyone being processed that day. About ten of us were required to sit at separate tables in a large room, with our Service and Medical records. We were told to read them thoroughly and, if any additions or corrections were necessary, a Medical officer and a Yeoman at his typewriter, in the front of the room, would make the changes and initial them. We were required to be there for one hour continuously with no early dismissal, and no chit-chat between the participants was allowed. This was the last opportunity to make any changes and after this session, the records were to be considered closed and final. We had to sign a register that this procedure was followed.

Later we received our final cash payout, and Honorable Discharge Button, nicknamed the Ruptured Duck. Our prepared Honorable Discharge papers were presented by the Commanding Officer. He told us that the U.S. Coast Guard was proud of us and our service to our country. He announced that the Coast Guard had a Reserve Program if we were interested. We were told to remember to take advantage of the GI Bill. The Commanding Officer shook our hands and we were dismissed.

Even though my service ended on a slightly sour note, by my own doing, I look back and thank my crew mates and all who had confidence in me during those years. I met so many brave, good people. I feel fortunate that my twin brother, Gerry, and I survived. Gerry would remain in the military for many more years, compiling a distinguished service record. I had under-age enlisted at 16 years old and was a combat veteran before 20 years old. This Happy Hooligan was going to return home and start a new chapter in life, as were the other World War II veterans.

Turning the Page on a New Chapter

The Boston Rapid Transit Subway system and the connecting buses and street cars gave me the final trip home, the same way it started, when I was on my way to the U.S. Customs House to have the enlistment oath administered in 1942.

With so many servicemen coming home, jobs and housing were in short supply, especially in New England. We had to share the load as most families came together to live in whatever space they could find. The first thing I did was to register at the Draft Board. I had never registered for the draft, having already been in the service before reaching draft age! I received a classification of "1C-Discharged" and a book of ration stamps. Civilian life had its complications also.

I returned to wearing my eyeglasses, after taking them off in 1942. My life would change drastically a year later when, while walking down the sidewalk, I would meet the woman of my dreams, my beloved future wife, Lorraine Brodeur. We would be married on September 11, 1948, and move to Arizona. At times I deeply regretted moving away from family and friends in Boston, especially because Lorraine was so far away from her parents, Leo and Simone Brodeur, and her brothers and sister, Robert, John and Eileen. We would raise our three daughters, Patricia, Elizabeth and Catherine, among other World War II veterans who were drawn to Arizona's opportunities, but I would never forget the bravery I witnessed while I served in the "Hooligan Navy," the U.S. Coast Guard. *Semper Paratus.*

AFTERWORD

Frank's brother, Gerald, remained in the U.S. Navy for 23 years. He married Janet Mae Hart on February 18, 1967. They welcomed daughters Julia and Mary Catherine, and made their home in Connecticut, then Maryland. Catherine Cullen Smith and daughter, Barbara Marie Smith, moved to Arizona, near Anne Smith Panarello, her husband, Guy, and their children, Donna, Diane, Jay and Joanne. Barbara would marry Harold Saad in 1955, giving birth to Brion, Michael and Joseph, before Harold died in 1961. Daughter Kerry would be born after Barbara remarried to Laurence Ockenfels. Barbara is now married to Ernest Ludwig. Catherine Cullen Smith, the family historian, attended the baptisms and weddings of many grandchildren and great-grandchildren, passing in 1997, at the age of 94. She is interred next to her husband, Frank Smith, Sr., at Saint Francis Cemetery, Phoenix.

Frank and Lorraine moved to Arizona, near the Kingman Army Airfield soon after they were married in 1948. Work resumed on the construction of Davis Dam, located near Kingman on the Colorado River. Frank, along with hundreds of war veterans found jobs in Kingman. He became active in the American Legion wartime veterans service organization. The U.S. Post Office was expanding service in the city, and Frank became Kingman's first city carrier. In the 1950's, Frank and Lorraine welcomed their three daughters, Patricia, Elizabeth and Catherine in Kingman's Mohave County Hospital. Lorraine worked a few years as a bookkeeper, and gradually adjusted to desert life. The family relocated to Scottsdale, Arizona in 1967. Frank remained with the U.S. Post Office in various positions, retiring after 35 years. He eventually received a CT scan that revealed broken bones in his face from the 1943 Norfolk incident; they were thought to be the cause of his headaches. Over the years, the surviving USS Ramsden crewmembers held reunions organized by crewman Ed Toczylowski, and Frank attended many. Frank and Lorraine sailed to post-war visits of Panama Canal and Pearl Harbor. During their 59 years of marriage, they celebrated the births of three children, seven grandchildren and three great-grandchildren. Lorraine fell ill in February 2008, eventually passing on August 7, 2008, just a few weeks before their 60th wedding anniversary. Frank passed on September 12, 2010, just one day after their wedding anniversary. After all the years living in Arizona, they never lost their Boston accents. They are interred in the same gravesite at National Memorial Cemetery of Arizona, Cave Creek, for veterans of military service. The family established the Frank and Lorraine Smith Memorial Scholarship Fund for needy children at Our Lady of Perpetual Help Catholic elementary school, Scottsdale, Arizona.

ACKNOWLEDGEMENTS

This story was published after the death of our parents, Frank A. Smith, Jr. and Lorraine R. Brodeur Smith. We three daughters, Patricia A. Smith, Elizabeth A. Doerning and Catherine M. Ethington, promised that Dad's efforts would be shared with family and friends. Thanks to the United States Army Records Management, United States Coast Guard Archives, and the United States Navy, Naval History & Heritage Command for providing accurate documentation.